HIGHER HISTORY

Britain and Scotland

1850s–1979

Sydney Wood

Hodder & Stoughton

A MEMBER OF THE HODDER HEADLINE GROUP

Contents

Introduction

The content of the book

Between 1850 and 1979 life for British people in general, and Scottish people in particular, changed dramatically. This book deals with some of the most important of these changes, changes that still affect all our lives today.

- Firstly there has been a transformation in politics. In 1850 few men and no women had the right to vote to choose members of parliament. For those able to take part, voting took place quite openly, not in secret, making bribery of voters quite a common event. By 1979 all adult men and women were able to vote in secret, and highly organised political parties fought for their support using all the weaponry of modern mass media.

- Secondly there has been a transformation in government. Mid-nineteenth century governments did not like to interfere in the daily lives of ordinary people, had just a small number of officials to help run government, and a very small amount of tax money to spend. By 1979 governments controlled daily life in ways that would have amazed Victorians, using huge tax revenues and great numbers of civil servants.

- Thirdly there has been a transformation in the way that the very poor and other people in need are cared for. In the 1850s very little was done for the elderly, the sick, the injured, children in need and those unable to find work. Only the most desperately needy received any help. By 1979 Britain had a welfare system that tried to care for all in need.

- Finally, life for people in Scotland changed greatly. In 1850 Scotland did not have the separate administration that it had gained by 1979. Few mid-nineteenth century Scots demanded a Scottish parliament: in 1979, so strong was this demand, that a referendum was held about setting up a Scottish parliament; the majority of those Scots who actually voted supported the idea.

Daily life changed too, as Scotland became a country where most people lived in towns and cities, were better educated and could go to mass-entertainment like football or the cinema.

Through studying the material in this book you will build up an understanding of these changes and of why they came about.

Occasionally the views of people of the time and of modern historians are included. All this material should not just be seen as a collection of separate parts, but as developing an appreciation of certain important ideas, i.e.:

- *Ideology*: the ideas of politicians and of other people wanting to change Britain in general and Scotland in particular.

- *Identity*: the views of people on what sort of country they wanted, what sort of social group they belonged to, whether people saw themselves as British, Scottish, or both.

- *Authority*: the growth of the power of government and the ways in which governments used their power, especially in terms of helping the needy.

The activities in the book

Different sorts of activities are included:

- At the beginning of chapters there are 'Tasks'. These will help you to focus on the reasons for studying that chapter and help you gather and record material.

- At the end of chapters and the sections in which chapters are grouped, there are essays. These will enable you to use the knowledge you have built up and thus develop the essay writing skills that are so vital for success in passing Higher History.

- At certain points there are source-based questions. These will help further develop this skill and will be especially useful for those taking the Intermediate 2 examination.

- At the end of the book there are suggestions for titles suited to the Higher Extended Essay and the Intermediate 2 Extended Response, and notes offering advice on essay writing skills.

By working through this book you will be engaging in the skills needed to study history. Both Higher and Intermediate 2 examinations test these skills. (They are also skills that are invaluable to students in higher education and equally important in many areas of employment!). They include:

- Using knowledge that is relevant.

- Using knowledge to show an accurate understanding of an aspect of the past.

- Being able to place a past event or issue or development in context.

- Being able to properly explain a past event or issue or development.

- Being able to justify your views by referring to the evidence on which they are based.

- Being able to clearly organise and structure, your knowledge and ideas.

- Being able to reach a soundly based conclusion for any development, event, or issue you are considering.

In addition, for the Intermediate 2 examination:

- Evaluating sources to take account of their origin, or purpose or context.

- Evaluating sources to take account of their content.

- Comparing two sources.

The best way to develop such skills is to:

- Study conscientiously.

- Make clear and well organised notes.

- Ask about anything you don't understand.

- Plan any task you are asked to undertake.

- Work on planning with someone else.

- Write clear and relevant answers, considering the topic or question at all times.

- Read through your answers, checking them to see if they cover the points listed above.

For reference – the Higher History and Intermediate Courses

The material in this book provides coverage of the Higher History, Later Modern course 'Britain 1850s to 1979'. The prescribed course consists of:

Britain 1850s–1979

A study of political and popular attempts to influence the development of democracy and attempts to resolve conflicts arising from economic, political and social pressures in Britain in the period 1850s–1979, illustrating the themes of ideology, identity and authority.

Democracy and the British People: the growth of democracy, including the major changes, which widened the franchise and extended democracy 1867–1928; the reasons for these changes and their effects on the political identity of Britain.

Political and popular attempts to influence the development of democracy, exemplified by:

◆ The growth of the labour movement from 1890s to 1922.

◆ The movements for women's suffrage up to 1928.

Government and people: socio-economic problems in the period and the changing role of central government in addressing them exemplified by:

◆ The Liberal Government 1906–1914 and the problem of poverty.

◆ The impact of the Great Depression and the response of the National Government to the problems of the period 1931–1939.

◆ The post-war Labour Government 1945–1951 and the establishing of the welfare state.

The changing identity of Scotland in the UK as identified by **either** *Changing Scottish Society 1880s–1939*: the impact of urbanisation on Scotland with reference to:

◆ Leisure/popular culture.

◆ Religion.

◆ Education.

Or *The Rise of Political Nationalism* with reference to:

◆ Changing attitudes to the union 1880s–1939.

◆ Issues of devolution and independence circa 1930–1979.

This book also covers the following topic at Intermediate levels:

From the cradle to the grave? Social welfare in Britain 1890s–1951

A study of the changing role of central government in tackling the problem of poverty; considering the themes of ideas and rights and the development of new relationships between the people of Britain and their government.

The problem of poverty at the turn of the century: belief in self-help; the voluntary system; the surveys of Booth and Rowntree; changing attitudes towards poverty and its causes. The Liberal reforms 1906–1914: groups at risk – the young, the old, the sick, the unemployed; reforms to help these groups – the 'Children's Charter', the old age pensions, health and unemployment insurance, labour exchanges; assessment of the success of the reforms.

The Labour government 1945–1951: effects of wartime experiences on attitudes to poverty, especially the impact of bombing, rationing and evacuation, the 'Five Giants'; the National Insurance and National Assistance; the National Health Service; housing reform; the idea of a Welfare State; assessment of the government's achievement.

Considerable parts of the following topic at Intermediate levels are also provided:

Campaigning for change: social change in Scotland 1900s–1919

A study of social change in Scotland, considering the themes of rights, economy and community.

The changing role of women; campaigns for women's suffrage; public and government response to WSPU militancy; impact of the First World War on the campaign and the status of women; votes for women; attitudes to women's social and domestic role in the inter-war years.

Changing patterns of employment: the effects of the First World War on industry – the decline of 'old' and the growth of 'new' industries; Red Clydeside, post-war disillusionment and mass unemployment; the Second World War and the impact of conscription and the changing role of women in the workplace; the continued decline of the heavy industries; North Sea oil; the growth of the service industries; assessment of the effects of changing employment patterns.

Changes in Scottish popular culture; the growth of entertainment – the music hall, the cinema, newspapers and the radio to 1939; changing leisure and sporting activities to 1939; education from the 1920s–1940.

> **ACTIVITIES**

1 Make a copy of the syllabus that you have to cover.

2 List the activities that make up the historical skills that your work on this topic should show.

Boys from the Claygate Meccano Club with some of their inventions, 1920. Technology mattered, even as a toy.

TIME LINE *of Key Events*

1867 The Second Reform Act; The Conservative National Union is set up

1870 Education Act (England)

1872 The secret ballot is introduced. Education (Scotland) Act

1877 The National Liberal Federation is set up

1881 The Social Democratic Federation is established

1883 The Corrupt Practices Act

1884 The Third Reform Act; The Fabian Society is established

1886 Liberal Unionists split away

1893 The Independent Labour Party is founded

1899 Beginning of Boer War

1900 The Labour Representation Committee is established

1901 Taff Vale decision

1903 Liberal-Labour electoral pact; Founding of Women's Social and Political Union

1906 Liberal victory in general election

1908 Old-age pensions introduced

1909 The Lloyd George budget; The Osborne judgement

1910 The first Labour Exchanges open

1911 The Parliament Act; Introduction of limited health and unemployment insurance

1914 Outbreak of the Great War

1915 Asquith's coalition government

1916 Lloyd George replaces Asquith and leads new coalition

1918 The Fourth Reform Act – adult males and some women get the vote; Labour Party Constitution; 'Coupon' election won by Lloyd George

1922 Fall of Lloyd George's coalition

1923 Liberals reunited

1924 First Labour Government under Ramsay MacDonald

1926 The General Strike

1928 Universal suffrage – women get the vote on terms equal to men

1931 Formation of the National Government led by Ramsay MacDonald

1935 Baldwin becomes Prime Minister

1937 Chamberlain becomes Prime Minister

1939 Outbreak of the Second World War

1940 Churchill forms coalition

1942 The Beveridge Report

1945 Labour electoral victory

1946 National Health Service Act passed; Insurance Reform

1975 Thatcher becomes Conservative leader; EEC referendum

1979 March, devolution referendum; May, Conservative election victory; June, European elections

SECTION A

A Developing Democracy

Introduction

The material in this section covers the period from the middle of the nineteenth century up to the point when all adult men and women over the age of 21 finally obtained the right to vote in parliamentary elections. What happened in those years transformed the British political system and created the basis for modern British politics. In just over 60 years the right to vote moved from being the preserve of a small number of better-off men to being the right of all adults.

Such a change deserves to be seen as a revolution and had all sorts of consequences for how Britain was governed and for political life in general.

As a result of studying the material in this section you should have an understanding of:

◆ The main changes in who had the right to vote (the franchise or suffrage).

◆ The reasons for these changes.

◆ The results of these changes for the political identity of Britain.

◆ The particular circumstances and events involved in winning the right to vote for women.

◆ The growth of the Labour movement, a development that had very significant political consequences.

It is important to have a full understanding of all the issues involved in this section on the development of democracy, for it can provide essay titles in the examination, e.g.:

◆ What actions contributed most to the extension of the franchise between 1860 and 1928?

◆ How accurate is it to describe Britain in 1914 as a democratic country?

◆ *'Although the suffragettes gained more news headlines, the suffragists actually contributed more to the gaining of votes for women.'* Do you agree?

◆ Account of the emergence of a sizeable Labour Party by 1922.

◆ To what extent did the widening of the franchise change British politics between 1850 and 1928?

It is worth thinking about the issues raised by these titles before you study this section. What evidence might you need to gather in order to be able to answer each of them? Once you have worked through the whole of this section, return to these essay titles and consider how confident you feel about answering them.

Chapter One
The Political System in the 1850s

An understanding of the mid-nineteenth century political system is the first essential stage in mastering the issue of the development of democracy. As a result of studying material in this chapter you should have an understanding of:

◆ The political system of the 1850s.

◆ Different views on this system.

◆ Reasons for this system.

The mid-nineteenth century system was itself the result of recent reform. In 1832, after a lengthy struggle, the right to vote in elections was altered, increasing the number of voters to about 653 000. Yet 20 million people lived in Britain at the time. The reform left the vast majority of men and all women without the vote, for voting was seen as the right of a small number of well-to-do people. Moreover the voters recorded their choice of candidate at election time in a quite open fashion rather than in secret. This meant that voters might be bribed or bullied by the wealthy and ambitious.

TASK

Note down relevant points under two headings:

◆ What can be said to justify this political system of the time?

◆ What criticisms can be made of it?

To consider:

◆ Which group had the strongest reasons for resisting change?

◆ Which group(s) had the strongest arguments for getting the vote?

The British political system

Power in Britain was divided between the monarch, the House of Lords and the House of Commons. To remain in office for the seven year period between elections (in practice usually for a shorter time) any government needed, above all, to have the broad support of the majority of MPs. Many important politicians were to be found in the House of Lords, whose members were there either because they had inherited their titles or because they were bishops. The Lords still enjoyed considerable power, being able to block measures passed by the Commons.

Nor was the monarch a mere figurehead. Victoria had considerable influence in choosing a Prime Minister but, as time passed and political parties became more organised this influence shrank. Victoria did not find it easy to adjust to this situation and was very prone to interfere, especially if she disliked her current Prime Minister. Her poor relationship with Gladstone led her to show his letters to the leader of the opposition.

The House of Commons was made up of unpaid MPs who were overwhelmingly drawn from the wealthy sections of society. Many of them avoided having to fight an opponent at election time by making deals. Elections that did take place were marked by corruption and by intimidation, for the relatively small all-male electorate recorded their choice of candidate openly, not secretly. British politics, then, was dominated by wealth and class. It excluded women and working class men.

Who had the vote?

1 There was two quite separate types of constituencies:

Boroughs. A number of places were designated parliamentary boroughs. The vote here belonged to:

- Men who owned property with a £10 annual value (when assessed for rates), who had paid their rates and taxes, and had lived in the property for at least a year.
- Male lodgers and tenants of properties (where the landlord was not in residence) with a £10 annual value, who had paid their rates and taxes, and had lived there for at least a year.

Counties. The vote here belonged to:

- Owners of property worth at least £2 for the payment of rates (the 'forty shilling free-holders').
- People with various kinds of leases on property not their own, including 'copy-holders' of land worth at least £10, holders of leases of at least twenty years on land worth £50, and holders of sixty-year leases on land worth £10.
- Tenants of land worth £50 a year.

In addition, people who for different reasons had possessed the right to vote before 1832 usually retained this right.

2 All voters had to be male adults over 21 years of age. The 1832 Act clearly stated this. Up till then there had been a handful of female voters.

3 Men who were peers, or men who worked for the customs and excise or for the post office, policemen, paupers, lunatics and aliens were not allowed to vote. (It was thought the people in government jobs would not vote independently.)

4 It was not easy to become a voter even if a man was technically qualified, for a complicated system of registration had to be followed.

5 Voting took place openly, not in secret.

6 Voting did not take place on one day throughout the country, but was spread over two or three weeks to allow the police to cope.

This system gave the vote to about one out of every seven adult males living in the United Kingdom. By the early 1860s around 1.43 million could vote out of a total population of 30 million.

This system did not give equal representation to the different parts of the United Kingdom. Poverty in Ireland meant that only around one in twenty adult males was able to vote whereas the average in England was one in five. There were grumbles from Scotland that an allocation of 53 seats in Parliament was insufficient. Twenty-three of these MPs sat for Scottish burghs and thirty for the counties.

The dominance of the wealthy

The parliamentary system of the 1850s was not democratic. It was not meant to be. Democracies were regarded as being at the mercy of ignorant people unfit to possess power. It favoured the wealthy in a number of ways. Until 1868 there was a requirement that no man could become an MP for a county unless he had a landed estate worth at least £610. In boroughs the required property had to be worth at least £300. Fighting an election (especially in boroughs) often cost between £400 and £1000 in official expenses, and to this had to be added unofficial expenses. Since voting openly was defended as manly and the secret ballot scorned as furtive, candidates could observe how the relatively small number of voters exercised their franchise. All sorts of inducements could, and were, offered to the voters. Votes were sometimes openly sold, perhaps for as much as £15. In 1865 the 1408 voters of Beverley managed to have £14 000 spent on them. In 1870 a Royal Commission reported on the constituency of Bridgewater.

'It is always three fourths, at least, of the actual constituency who are said to be hopelessly addicted to the taking of bribes. Rank and station appear to make no difference . . . It is the chronic disease of the place.'

Buying drinks for voters could lead to uproarious election scenes. Marches and counter-marches, demonstrations and fights were features of borough elections. Non-voters happily joined in the excitement, which including pelting candidates with vegetables, refuse and dung. County elections were less likely to be so troubled with upheaval. The distribution of seats to boroughs still heavily favoured the land-owning classes. Around half of the MPs of the 1850s were near relatives of peers, clear evidence of the justice of the claims of Lord Grey, Prime Minister in 1832:

'I am indeed convinced that the more the bill of 1832 is considered the less it will be found to prejudice the real interests of the aristocracy.'

Since landowners provided work, help in times of hardship, and a focus for social life, it is not surprising that rural voters chose their nominees. The House of Lords consisted of bishops and peers who had inherited their titles. It was able, if really determined, to completely block laws (other than financial ones) passed by the House of Commons.

Different views on the political system

The system of the 1850s was designed to bind the middle classes to the upper classes. Britain's leaders were well aware of the violent revolutions that had occurred in France after 1789, and again in 1830. They were determined to avoid similar revolutions in their own country, and this was most clearly put by Thomas Babington Macaulay, MP and historian:

The principle is . . . to admit the middle classes to a large . . . share of the representation without any violent shock to the institutions of our country. There are countries in which the condition of the labouring classes is such that they may safely be entrusted with the right of electing members of the legislature . . . if employment were always plentiful, wages always high, food always cheap, if a large family were considered not as an incumbrance but as a blessing the principal objections to universal suffrage would be removed. But, unhappily, the lower orders are occasionally in a state of great distress . . . distress makes even wise men irritable, unreasonable, and credulous, eager for immediate relief, heedless of remote consequences, it blunts their judgement, it inflames their passions, it makes them prone to believe those who flatter them. I oppose universal suffrage because I think it would produce a destructive revolution. I support this measure because I am sure that it is our best security against a revolution . . . we must admit those whom it may be safe to admit . . . We say that is it not by mere numbers, but by property and intelligence that the nation ought to be governed.

Parliamentary Debates

Some upper working class voters existed in places like London and Bristol where high property values brought them into the system. In total they may have amounted to a quarter of all the voters, but they were to be found in a limited number of places, not evenly spread. There were bitter complaints from would-be democrats, such as this writer in *The Poor Man's Guardian* of 1832. He complained about the wealthy political leaders:

They knew that the old system could not last, and desiring to establish another like it as possible, and also to keep their places, they framed the BILL, in the hope of drawing to the feudal aristocrats and yeomanry of counties, large reinforcement of the middle class. The Bill was, in effect, an invitation to the shopocrats of the enfranchised towns to join the Whigocrats of the country, and make common cause with them keeping down the people, and thereby to quell the rising spirit of democracy in England.

Quoted in D G Wright, *Democracy and Reform*

Protest boiled up into a major campaign, with a Charter of six major reforms. The wealthy closed ranks against petitions requesting that the vote should be given to all men and should be exercised in secret, that MPs should be paid and freed from needing property, and that parliaments should be elected anew every year by electoral districts reformed to be equal in population.

Lord Cockburn, a leader of Scottish society, voiced fears for the future. He saw the desire for a wider franchise as being about taking property from the better off. He said:

Extension of the franchise is the phrase, but division of property is the object; and in the manufacturing population of which about half is always hungry and the passions of this hunger always excited by political delusion, it is not easy to see how wealth and sense are to keep their feet.

After the final big Charter effort of 1848, demand for reform faded and would-be reformers despaired. One of them, Richard Cobden, complained:

We are a servile, aristocracy-loving lord-ridden people . . . we have the labour of Hercules in hand to abate the power of the aristocracy and their allies – the snobs of the towns.

In vain the Whig, Lord John Russell put forward new reform bills in 1852, 1854 and 1860. His leader, Lord Palmerston, was not interested, nor was there great popular pressure for change. Experience after 1832 helped to reduce fears of the consequences of slowly widening the franchise. Walter Bagehot, a leading contemporary expert on the constitution of these times, wrote:

The mass of the £10 householders did not really form their own opinions . . . they were in fact guided in their judgement by the better educated classes, they preferred representatives from those classes . . . they were influenced by rank and wealth . . . they liked to have one of their 'betters' to represent them; if he was rich they respected him much, if he was a lord they liked him the better. The issue put before these elections was which of two rich people would you choose?

. . . There is much that may be said against the Reform Act of 1832, but on the whole it has been successful. It is common-place to speak of the legislative improvement of the last 25 years . . . Scarcely less important is the improvement which the Reform Bill has introduced into the general tone of our administration. Nor is this all. So much agreement is . . . surprising as the nation is now less homogeneous in its social structure than it once was. The growth of manufacturers and trade had created a new world in the north of England . . . It is impossible not to ascribe this agreement to the habit of national discussion, which the Reform Act has fostered.

Two defects may be discussed. Parliament certainly has an undue bias towards the views of the landed interest (and) too little weight is at present given to the growing parts of the country, too much to the stationary.

Essays on Parliamentary Reform, 1896

British society in the mid-nineteenth century

The historian FML Thompson suggests that the 1832 Reform Act, which created the political system of the 1850s, was a response to economic upheaval that was altering Britain's identity. He wrote:

The First Reform Act was an attempt to adapt political institutions to the alteration in the balance of social forces brought about by this transformation (of the British economy).

The Rise of Respectable Society

It is easy for people living in a modern democratic society to condemn the political system of the mid-nineteenth century. But British society has changed greatly in the past 150 years. Moreover in the 1850s, it was common in most countries to find politics controlled by small numbers of wealthy people. In some countries, such as Russia, power was held by just one person. It is important, therefore, to consider what British society was like in the 1850s. Were the adult people of Britain ready for each of them to exercise the vote?

Around half the 20 million people in mid-nineteenth century Britain lived in the countryside. Agriculture prospered, employing large numbers. Wealthy aristocratic landowners watched over enormous estates from the comfort of their elaborate country houses. In parliament such men wielded great power in the House of Lords; over their tenants and villagers they exercised enormous influence, providing employment and even insisting upon attendance at church.

According to one historian:

The average man of the mid-nineteenth century was much more likely to accept without question his inherited social rank and to defer to his 'betters' than his descendant would be a century later. A deeply rooted respect for rank and strong feeling of the obligations of authority were the basis for much of the social behaviour of the mid-nineteenth century.

J Roebuck, *The Making of Modern English Society*, 1973

A rural scene, 1857. Little traffic troubled people's lives.

Agricultural production was expanding and there seemed little to fear from foreign competition. Prosperous tenants and owner-occupier farmers were able to rebuild their homes, providing their families with sizeable properties in which to live in comfort. But prosperity had yet to reach the farm labourer. Whether housed in the farm buildings or in a cramped and squalid cottage, the labourer endured endless toil, low wages, and a diet monotonous in its dependence on bread, porridge, potatoes, cabbage, milk and occasional pieces of bacon.

The wealth of the landed aristocracy was often swelled by factors other than farming production. Britain had experienced a century of economic change and population growth. Some landowners found their land contained coal or

Mending the roads, 1857.

iron; others sold or rented land to shipyards and railway companies. Yet further profit might be derived from land required by house building. By 1850 the population of urban Britain equalled that of rural Britain. This represented a revolution marked by the coming of steam power and factories. Mines and quarries transformed the appearance of the country. Towns and cities like Manchester, Leeds and Glasgow expanded rapidly, giving far more emphasis to the north of Britain than it had ever had in an earlier rural age. The new industrial age brought a crowding together of people in cramped town dwellings. It brought dirt and smoke that meant that dark drab clothes were the only sensible forms of clothing for ordinary people. Dreadful diseases like cholera and typhus flourished in the filth of middens and in polluted water. In 1858 the Thames stank so foully that parliament had to abandon its sitting.

Trongate, Glasgow, in the 1860s. Urban pressures are evident.

Yet the achievements of textile factories, engineering works and other developing centres of activity were such that Britain could truly claim to be the workshop of the world. In 1851 these achievements were celebrated in a Great Exhibition held in a glass construction so vast that mature trees were enclosed by its walls and roof. It is a sign of the times that the well-to-do went to the exhibition on Tuesdays when admission was a guinea. It is also a sign of the times that six million other people were able to go to the exhibition on the ordinary shilling days: the dawning age of the railway made possible travel unheard of 20 years earlier.

By the 1860s Britain produced half the world's coal, over half the iron and steel and nearly half the cotton goods.

Ordinary people lived very vulnerable lives. The dangers of disease and the weariness of long working days (including Saturdays) troubled their existence; and sudden trade slumps, illness or accident, could plunge them into poverty. Around 15 or 16 babies out of every 100 born never reached the age of one. Those that did survive were not required to attend school, and, if they did, they experienced a very limited and repetitive education. Skilled workers and an expanding middle class struggled to establish for themselves a life of comfort and respectability. Church congregations were larger than those of modern times. But this was also an age when prostitution flourished, for many women were desperate to survive without being compelled to enter a workhouse or poorhouse. No state welfare system existed to support those in distress. Bleak institutions awaited the desperately poor, where they were housed in dormitories, controlled by strict rules, and deprived of freedom. The dawning age of the machine and the factory threatened the livelihoods of those who had sustained their existence by skilled handwork. In 1850 there were still 50 000 handloom cotton

Workers at a South Wales ironworks, 1857.

By the 1850s not having to work had become a badge of female respectability. As one wealthy lady wrote:

A lady, to be such, must be a mere lady and nothing else. One must not work for profit or engage in any occupation that money can command ... ladies, dismissed from the dairy, the store room, the poultry yard, the kitchen garden, have hardly yet found themselves a sphere equally useful and important in the pursuits of trade and art to which to apply their too abundant leisure ... Life is too often divested of any real and important purpose.

Diary of Margaret Grey, 1853, in T May, *An Economic and Social History of Britain*, 1987

British society in the 1850s was in a state of rapid change and development. Its unsettled condition can be seen in political affairs too, for the efforts of the Chartists to spread the vote so widely as to create a democratic state were only a year or two in the past.

weavers. Half those involved in producing woollen cloth worked at home or in small workshops. Tailoring and shoemaking too were still largely small-scale operations. Such people viewed the spread of the steam-powered factory with alarm.

Whatever the kind of employment involved, women were likely to be more poorly paid than men. Married women had no control of their possessions or their children – these were the property of their husbands. Divorce required an Act of Parliament. Many women found a kind of security by joining the vast numbers who earned their living as domestic servants.

> **ACTIVITIES**

1 Work in pairs to plan an essay on either:
   a) 'In 1850 Britain was a dangerously divided society.' Do you agree?
   or
   b) 'The political system of the 1850s suited its times.' Is this an acceptable view?

2 To what extent are the sources by Macaulay and by Lord Cockburn in agreement about the politics of the time?

Chapter Two

Towards Democracy, Before 1914

Between 1867 and the outbreak of the First World War several major changes were made to Britain's political system. As a result of these changes the vote was extended to embrace about two thirds of the adult male population and the act of voting was carried out in secret. The material in this chapter covers these changes and considers some of their causes. As a result of studying this chapter you should have a sound understanding of:

◆ The detail of the reforms of parliamentary voting that took place.

◆ The reasons why these reforms took place.

TASK

Which British citizens deserved to have political rights?

How might a journalist of 1913 have looked back over the previous 50 years to consider and write about this issue? Work through this chapter, making notes, in order to show your readers:

◆ The main changes that took place.

◆ The reasons for them.

◆ Who gained the vote?

◆ Who still did not have the vote?
◆ Whether more could and should have been done, and would still need to be done.

An Outline Calendar of Nineteenth Century Franchise Reforms

In 1858

◆ The property qualification for MPs was abolished.

In 1867

◆ Most men who lived in the larger towns and the cities, except the very poor, got the vote.

◆ Several larger places gained MPs at the expense of smaller places.

◆ Scotland got seven more MPs.

In 1872

◆ The secret ballot was introduced.

In 1883

◆ The Corrupt and Illegal Practices Act limited election expenses.

In 1884

◆ A standard franchise giving the vote to male house owners, tenants of at least a year's standing and better-off lodgers was introduced.

◆ The old county/borough division of constituencies was abolished.

In 1885

◆ A redistribution of seats took place, giving more to the growing towns and cities.

◆ Scottish MPs increased to 72.

Was a changing economy a major cause of reform?

According to a modern historian:

Parliamentary reform was largely a reflection of changes in the economic and social structure of the country.

D G Wright, *Democracy and Reform*, 1970

In the late nineteenth century a Wolverhampton businessman put forward the same view when he said:

. . . 50 years ago we were not in that need of Representatives which we are at present as we then manufactured nearly exclusively for home consumption. But the face of affairs is now changed; we now manufacture for the whole world and if we have not members to promote and extend our commerce, the era of our commercial greatness is at an end.

Quoted in FML Thompson, *The Rise of Respectable Society*

What were the economic changes that so altered the identity of British society as to persuade the politicians of the time to increase the number of voters?

The population increased

In 1871, 31.8 million people lived in the United Kingdom. By 1911 this had increased to 45.3 million. Numbers in towns and cities grew especially and by 1911, 80 per cent of people lived in them. Towns and cities in the Midlands and North grew especially rapidly.

Railways created a more United Kingdom

A mere 7360 kilometres of railway track in 1848 had become 28 800 by 1914. There were few places of any size without a railway station. Better signalling, better coaches (the standard coach with corridor and lavatories appeared in 1882), lower fares and improved locomotives created a network that tied together the different parts of Britain as never before.

The Forth Bridge, north of Edinburgh under construction in 1887.

The combination of railways and urban growth had all sorts of consequences. New towns grew up. Railways allowed the wealthier to move further away from city centres, and to travel into work from suburbs. House builders exploited stations near cities, putting up properties and advertising them as offering country life close to city amenities. The Great Eastern Railway led other companies into providing cut-price travel for working people. By 1900 thousands of commuters to London spilled out of trains daily. Moreover the Underground system had grown from its small beginnings in 1863, when it only linked Paddington to Farringdon Street. The transformation of an area by a railway, and the implementation of the 1883 Cheap Trains Act (requiring the running of workmen's trains), were personally felt by the Great Eastern Railway's manager. In 1884 he grumbled that Stamford Hill had been altered beyond recognition:

That used to be a very nice district indeed, occupied by good families, with houses of from £150 to £250 a year, with coach houses and stables, a garden and a few acres of land. But very soon after this obligation was put upon the Great Eastern to run workmen's trains, speculative builders went down into the neighbourhood and, as a consequence, each good house was one after another pulled down and the district is given up entirely to the working man. I lived down there myself and I waited until most of my neighbours had gone: and then at last, I was obliged to go.

Royal Commission on the Housing of the Working Class, 1884

The railways moved goods as well as people. In 1860, 90 million tonnes travelled by train; by 1900 the figure had risen to 425 million. National newspapers reached large areas and arrived regularly. Even clocks and watches told exactly the same time, from Wick to Plymouth:

Workmen at the Great Eastern Railway's Liverpool Street Station, 1884.

local variations could not be accepted by railway timetables. In 1889 an Act of Parliament standardised time throughout Britain.

Industrial production increased

The rapid growth of population in areas other than Southern England reflected the kinds of industries that flourished. Coal, textiles, iron and steel, and engineering provided employment for much of the population. The numbers working in textiles remained steady at around 1.3 million, but the labour force in coal mining increased from 200 000 to a million by 1911. Together these occupations provided about half the economy's output in 1907, and furnished employment for a quarter of the working population. The size of the typical industrial unit grew during the nineteenth century; the typical worker of the 1900s worked in larger premises for a more remote employer. Many working in small-scale workshops and at home could not compete. The late nineteenth and early twentieth centuries were a time of increasing mechanisation. Skilled craftsmen watched with alarm as enterprising manufacturers copied American products, installing machines such as automatic, high-speed cutting tools, or turret lathes that could handle complex shaping operations. Such machinery allowed employers to use semi-skilled rather than skilled labour, and to pay lower wages as a result.

Britain's traditional industries provided the backbone of her export drive. In 1870 Britain still contributed almost a third of the world's manufacturing output. But by 1913 dangerous rivals – notably the USA and Germany – had emerged, and Britain's share of world manufacturing had sunk to 14 per cent.

Britain's rivals seemed readier to invest in new equipment and to deploy a more skilled labour force. Their enterprise showed in their ability to develop new industries for making motor vehicles, chemical products and electrical goods. By the 1900s worried observers in Britain noted not only that Britain lagged behind in these 'new' industries, but also that the older industries were looking increasingly dated. But, for the moment, with British coal and cotton and Clydeside shipping all in great demand across the world, such anxieties were voiced by the few.

Agriculture ran into difficulties

In 1850 around 20 per cent of Britain's labour force worked in farming; by Edwardian times under 9 per cent were similarly employed. Behind these figures lay a dramatic downturn for the farming industry which saw a 63 per cent shrinkage of the area devoted to wheat-growing, land falling into disuse, and farmers ruined. Foreign competition lay behind this disaster. Railways opened up continents, whilst steamships and clippers moved vast quantities of food across the oceans. Wheat from the American prairies and meat from Argentina and Australasia undercut the prices of home-produced foods. In 1867–1871 the average price of wheat had been 56s. a quarter hundredweight; by 1894–1898 it had fallen to 27s. 3d. In 1880 a British ship docked in London with forty tonnes of Australian beef and mutton on board. The development of refrigeration menaced the British meat producer, just as the vast area of the American prairies threatened the cereal grower. Oats and barley fell less sharply in price, and enterprising farmers turned increasingly to producing milk, eggs, fresh fruit and vegetables. The governments of the time resolutely resisted any calls for the taxing of foreign foods. Their commitment to free trade went beyond wishing to see cheap food reach the town dweller – it had become a matter of belief. All these changes, coupled with the increased mechanisation of farming and the low wages paid to farm workers, added up to a sharp shrinkage in the significance in British society of the 'landed interest'. Even aristocratic landowners became increasingly ready to see their sons and daughters marry the children of rich businessmen and American millionaires.

White-collar workers increased in number

About 1.3 million people were recorded by the 1901 census as members of professional and public services. Postmen and policemen, civil servants and teachers were but some in this expanding area of employment. From 1870 entry to the civil service was by examination instead of by influence as previously. The whole area of clean respectable 'white collar' work grew: it included clerks, typists, draughtsmen, accountants and shop workers. Such work provided jobs for an increasing number of women and was often marked by a strong desire for a decent law-abiding existence that helped make society in 1900 seem more settled than it had been in 1850. Riots and machine-breaking as ways of protesting about a changing economy were rare now, as machines and factories had become part of an accepted way of life. Instead workers began to get organised in trade unions, and professional people in societies (such as the Institute of Chartered Accountants of 1880).

A better life emerged for many

The lifestyles of the wealthy in Edwardian times show the riches created by economic growth. Vast country houses and spacious town houses provided the setting for balls and banquets. A calendar of social events like Ascot and Henley, shooting, and visiting fashionable foreign resorts like Cannes and Biarritz completed a lifestyle amazing in its opulence. Vast armies of butlers, footmen, grooms, gardeners, cooks and housemaids toiled endlessly to ensure that their employers endured as little inconvenience as possible. In 1896 Lord Roseberry's income was such that he thought nothing of spending enough money to feed an ordinary family of four for a year, on out-of-season strawberries for one course of one meal. Behind the very rich came growing numbers of well-to-do middle class families living in large properties and employing many servants – indeed the ability to pay for a servant was one of the signs of social success. A family with an income of £800 a year would commonly expect to afford a cook and housemaid, and even on £200 a year a family could hire a servant girl.

A well-to-do Edwardian family meal.

Skilled and white-collar workers enjoyed a standard of living that probably rose in the late nineteenth century. One estimate suggests that real wages went up at least 10 per cent between 1889 and 1900, though they may then have started to fall back. Such workers were more likely to have a little leisure. Half-day working on Saturdays became widespread. Bank holidays arrived in 1871. Working hours were slightly reduced, sometimes helped by legislation, as in the case of shop workers. The leisure growth can be seen in the expansion of day trips and holidays and the consequent growth of seaside centres. In 1873, 850 000 people visited Blackpool; in 1931 the figure was four million. Spectator sports flourished as people had time and money to attend them. The rules of association football were set out in 1863, and the first cup final in England took place in 1872. The 1883 victory in this event of the working men of Bolton Olympic over an Old Etonian side was a further sign of changing times.

Holiday makers enjoy themselves on the beach of late Victorian Scarborough.

The population's health was improving. A death rate of 22.9 for males and 21.2 for females per 1000 people by 1838–1842 had fallen to 15.0 and 13.1 per 1000 by 1914. In the 1830s only 60 per cent of children survived to the age of 5; in the 1890s the figure was 80 per cent. In part this may have been because of improved cleanliness: water supplies were provided in urban areas and the soap industry expanded after the abolition of a tax on soap in 1853. Certainly many people ate far better in the 1900s than in the 1850s. Tea consumption increased fourfold from the 1850s to the 1900s, and the average consumption of potatoes, eggs and meat went up. After 1870 ordinary people began to eat fruit, initially as jam. By the 1900s fish and chip shops had spread from their humble beginnings in 1870 in John Rouse's mobile cooking range in Oldham; cheap foreign food helped the town dweller by lowering food bills; and railways brought in fresh produce to the towns. By 1900 large-scale producers of food like Cadbury and Huntley & Palmer were turning out great quantities of mass-produced items and convenience foods in cans (machine-made from 1868); even cornflakes from America were available. The family that could afford them had a greater range of food items to choose from than ever before and a greater range of shops in which to buy them. Multiple branches of firms like Boots and Lipton's spread across Britain, and large department stores opened, selling a great variety of items. The Co-operative Society was especially successful in Scotland and northern England, providing a 'dividend' (a payment to shoppers from the Co-op's profits) for the working people who shopped at its many branches. Medical science had improved, hospitals had expanded, and a properly trained nursing profession had been established. For those who felt ill, and could afford treatment, care had greatly improved. Mass-produced clothing helped lower the cost of being properly clad. The falling size of families may have helped people to live more comfortably, since there were fewer mouths to feed. In part this may have been because of the increasing age of women at the time of marriage (over 26 in 1902) and because of the numbers who remained unmarried. It may also have been due to the spread of methods of birth control, though the rubber condom despite being available from 1870s, was not widely purchased before the Great War.

Certainly the population of the 1900s was better educated and better informed than the population of the 1850s. Education from the age of five to the age of twelve was now a requirement and beyond twelve an increasing possibility. In 1855 *The Daily Telegraph* appeared, Britain's first national penny newspaper. In 1880 the publication of *Titbits* marked the opening of a campaign to provide mass-circulation papers and magazines. *Titbits* contained illustrations, undemanding stories, and scraps of information. In 1896 Alfred Harmsworth published *The Daily Mail*, and in three years was enjoying the profits of sales of well over half a million papers a day. With the repeal of the paper duty in 1861 and the development of high-speed presses, cheap book production became possible. The railways which took newspapers to every part of the kingdom were the focus of the sales of cheap books too. By the late nineteenth century station bookstalls of firms like W H Smith were stocked not only with fiction but also with works like Cassel's *Popular Education* that sold at a penny an issue and encouraged an interest in history and in languages.

The *Illustrated London News* printing press, 1857, high speed machinery that changed the availability of news.

By 1900 a lifestyle had emerged in many parts of urban Britain that, the historian E J Hobsbawm noted,

came to be thought of as age-old and unchanging because it ceased in fact to change very much until . . . the affluent 1950s, . . . it was neither a very good life nor a very rich life but it was probably the first kind of life since the Industrial Revolution which provided a firm lodging for the British working class within industrial society.

E J Hobsbawm, *Industry and Empire*, 1968

This life of factory work, watching football matches, visiting music halls, and a sense of loyalty to and community with fellow workers may have become a myth. At the time it impressed some observers as an enormous achievement. In 1898 one such commentator wrote:

During the last 25 or 30 years the wealth of Great Britain has increased in an extraordinary degree. The increase in the amount of property assessable to the income tax from 1855 to 1885 (is) about 100%. 50 years ago one third of the working masses of the United Kingdom were agricultural labourers: at present less than one eighth of the whole number are so employed. Money wages of all classes of labour have advanced 100%; the purchasing power of the British people in respect of necessities and luxuries of life has therefore been progressively increasing.

D A Wells, *Recent Economic Change*, 1899

Why did reforms of parliament and voting take place in 1867?

By the mid-1860s pressure for reform was building up once more. The journalist Henry Mayhew noticed the keen interest in politics taken by skilled workers in London:

In passing from the skilled operative of the west-end to the unskilled workmen of the eastern quarter of London, the moral and intellectual change is so great, that it seems as if we were in a new land, and among another race. The artisans are almost to a man red-hot politicians. They are sufficiently educated and thoughtful to have a sense of their importance in the State. . . . The political character and sentiments of the working classes appear to me to be a distinctive feature of the age, and they are a necessary consequence of the dawning intelligence of the mass.

The unskilled labourers are a different class of people. As yet they are as unpolitical as footmen, and instead of entertaining violent democratic opinions, they appear to have no political opinions whatever; or, if they do possess any, they rather lean towards the maintenance of 'things as they are', rather than towards the ascendancy of the working people . . .

Henry Mayhew, *London Labour and the Labour Poor*, 1861–1862

It may be that the American Civil War encouraged renewed discussion of political rights. Certainly Gladstone was impressed by the steady support given by Lancashire cotton workers to the anti-slavery North, even though they suffered from the way war interrupted raw cotton supplies from the South. In 1864 a Reform League was born out of a group who originally gathered to organise a welcome for the Italian republican democrat, Garibaldi. The same year saw the establishment (in old Manchester headquarters of the Anti-Corn Law League) of the National Reform Union. It campaigned for the secret ballot, a more equal distribution of seats, votes for all ratepayers, and for a general election at least every three years. The veteran campaigner John Bright emerged once more to rally large public meetings, especially in the north. Within the Liberal Party, radicals saw reform of parliament as the necessary prelude to further changes, such as reform of the army, the civil service and the church. Some party leaders were persuaded that it was necessary to bind the skilled working class to the ruling establishment lest, in frustration at exclusion, they should organise hostile activities (such as an increasingly effective trade union system). The generally peaceful behaviour of skilled workers, their interest in politics and their educational achievements were noted by Gladstone in 1866:

There never was a period in which religious influences were more active . . . It is hardly an exaggeration to say that . . . the civilising and training powers of education have for all practical purposes been . . . brought into existence as far as the mass of the people is concerned. As regards the press, . . . for the humble sum of a penny, or even less, newspapers are circulated by the million . . . carrying home to all classes of our fellow countrymen, accounts of public affairs, enabling them to feel a new interest in the transaction of those affairs by measures relating to labour, to police and to sanitary arrangements, Parliament has been labouring . . . to raise the level of the working community . . . we instituted for them Post Office savings banks, . . . and what has been the result? . . . there are now 650 000 depositors in those saving banks . . . Parliament has been striving to make the working class progressively fitter and fitter for the franchise; and can anything be more unwise, not to say more senseless, than to persevere from year to year in this plan, and then blindly refuse to recognise its logical upshot – namely, the increased fitness of the working class for political power.

Quoted in D G Wright, *Democracy and Reform*

The death of Palmerston in 1865 cleared the way for reformers to lead the Liberals. Lord John Russell became Prime Minister, and Gladstone became the Chancellor of the Exchequer.

Nor were the Conservatives necessarily opposed to reform. Their leaders, Lord Derby and Benjamin Disraeli, feared that total opposition to all reform might exclude their party from power for very many years. They also entertained hopes that working class voters might prove to be on their side rather than on that of the Liberals. In 1865 the constituencies where working class voters formed a majority returned nine Conservative and five Liberals. Nor could they ignore the way that the over-representation of southern England had become more of a glaring abuse than ever. By 1865 a fifth of the electorate in England and Wales was returning half the MPs in the House of Commons.

Carrying out reform

Having decided to work towards reform, Russell (Prime Minister in 1865) was pushed into prompt action by his dependence on the votes of the radical wing of the party. The discussion as to who should now get the vote was conducted on the assumption that it should go to those sufficiently educated and with a large enough stake in society to act responsibly. Not even John Bright demanded the vote for all men. And few MPs were enthusiastic about John Stuart Mill's suggestion that women too should gain the vote.

Gladstone, who took over management of the measure, eventually settled upon £7 as the property valuation for rating purposes above which all male adult householders would gain the vote. Yet his bill to implement this was defeated, and the government was forced to resign.

Gladstone pitched the franchise at this level believing the upper working class to be Liberal, and fearing that the lower working class might prove to be Tory. His radical supporters were not pleased. But far more serious was the attitude of the wealthy remnant of the old Whig party that still formed a wing of the party. In Robert Lowe they found an outstandingly gifted speaker who tore apart Gladstone's arguments. Lowe predicted the consequences of awarding the franchise to the working class:

The first stage ... will be an increase of corruption, intimidation, and disorder, of all the evils that happen usually in elections ... The second will be that the working men of England, finding themselves in a ... majority ... , will awake to a full sense of their power. They will say, 'We can do better for ourselves ... Let us set up shop for ourselves.'

... Where is the line that can be drawn? ... those who flatter and fawn upon the people are generally very inferior to the people, the objects of their flattery ... We see in America, where the people have undisputed power, that they do not send honest, hard-working men to represent them in Congress, but traffickers in office, bankrupts, men who have lost their character and been driven from every respectable way of life and who take up politics as a last resource ... Now, Sir, democracy has yet another tendency ... It is singularly prone to the concentration of power. Under it, individual men are small, and the Government is great ... and ... absolutely tramples down and equalises everything except itself. And democracy ... looks with the utmost hostility on all institutions not of immediate popular origin, which intervene between the people and the sovereign power ...

. . . with our own rash and inconsiderate hands, we are about to pluck down upon our heads the venerable temple of our liberty and our glory. History may tell of other acts as signally disastrous, but none more wanton, none more disgraceful.

Hansard, 3rd ser., clxxxii, 1866

With Russell increasingly unwell, Gladstone was unable to cope with the crisis. Lowe gathered around him a sizeable group of rebels nicknamed 'Adullamites' (from the Old Testament story about David being chased into the cave of Adullam). Disraeli pounced upon the opportunity, skilfully exploiting the split. Together the Conservatives and 'Adullamites' brought down the government.

THE DERBY, 1867. DIZZY WINS WITH "REFORM BILL."

A Cartoonist's view of Disraeli's gamble with electoral reform.

Lord Derby led the Conservative government that now took office. He had already come to the conclusion that his party must attempt to introduce parliamentary reform. The scale and frequency of pro-reform demonstrations (including one in Hyde Park that erupted into violence) added urgency to his efforts. Once he had been persuaded that Derby was right, Disraeli displayed wit, tactical skill, and great mastery of detail in piloting Conservative proposals through the Commons. He cheerfully accepted a whole range of amendments that gave the vote to more people than he had originally intended, provided that those amendments did not come from Gladstone. The Conservatives watched gleefully as Disraeli ridiculed and outmanoeuvred Gladstone. Gladstone's furious opposition even helped rally the doubtful to Disraeli's cause. Three Conservatives – Peel, Cranborne and Carnarvon – did resign from the government, but they remained an isolated small faction. And Disraeli had the satisfaction of winning radical Liberal support since his bill was more democratic than Gladstone's. Radicals flatly refused to help Gladstone insert a £5 property clause into borough franchises.

A BAD EXAMPLE.

DR. PUNCH. "WHAT'S ALL THIS? YOU, THE TWO HEAD BOYS OF THE SCHOOL, THROWING MUD! *YOU OUGHT TO BE ASHAMED OF YOURSELVES!*"

Punch's **view of the political battle between Gladstone and Disraeli.**

The consequence of the amendments was to treble the number of people to whom it had been originally proposed to give the vote. The reforms left the counties little changed and set up a boundary commission (to sort out the constituencies) which was dominated by Conservatives. The extension of the vote to lodgers probably added, initially, only about 12 000 new voters. Derby called his party's reform 'a leap in the dark', but it was nevertheless a cautious leap confined by the belief that the vote had to be earned; it was still not seen as the automatic right of all citizens.

Its effect in Glasgow, for example, was to increase the number of skilled workers who could vote from 4130 to 16 590 and of semi-skilled voters from 1670 to 8130. Business and white-collar workers who could vote rose to 12 090 from 8600. Nearly 6000 unskilled workers also gained the vote.

The question of corruption

Since voting continued to be conducted openly, bribery, corruption and intimidation remained common at elections. In 1872 Gladstone's

The Reform Act of 1867

1. In boroughs all male householders satisfying a one-year residence qualification could vote.

2. In boroughs all male lodgers living in rooms with an annual value of at least £10 (for rating purposes) could vote, provided that they had lived there for at least one year.

3. In counties all men owning property with an annual value of £5 could vote.

4. In counties all men renting property with an annual value of £12 could vote. (In Scotland the property value had to be £14.)

5. 35 boroughs with populations of under 10 000 lost one of their two MPs; 17 boroughs lost their MPs altogether and were merged into their counties.

6. Counties gained 25 extra MPs.

7. London University gained an MP.

8. The large cities of Manchester, Liverpool, Leeds and Birmingham each gained a third MP. Voters here had two votes each.

9. Scottish constituencies were increased in number from 53 to 60 (despite demands for 68).

10. 13 seats were awarded to new boroughs.

11. Two boroughs, Salford and Methyr Tydfil, received a second MP.

This reform increased the numbers of voters by about 1 120 000, the bulk of them (around three quarters) being in the boroughs. The electorate in Leeds, for example, rose from 7217 to 30 010 and in Glasgow from 18 000 to 47 000. Yet southern England (excluding London) was still over-represented. Wiltshire and Dorset, for instance, with a rural population of 450 000, returned 25 MPs, three more than the West Riding of Yorkshire where two million people lived.

Liberal government attacked the problem by bringing in the secret ballot (where each voter cast his vote in secret). Even so the proposal was attacked. One Conservative MP, Colonel Barttelot, argued:

This Bill indirectly cast a great slur upon the working class of the community by insinuating that they were unable to protect themselves in giving their votes, but he was prepared to contend that the working classes were as independent and able to protect themselves as any class of people in the country. The small shopkeepers were not nearly so able to protect themselves, but the Government during the time that this class had power never introduced any Ballot Bill . . .

Quoted in M Willis, *Gladstone and Disraeli: Principles and Policies*, 1989

Working men voting in 1874 – corruption still existed despite the secret ballot.

Even this reform was insufficient. In small boroughs and counties especially, agents of the wealthy were able to observe those going to vote and guess the result since ballot boxes were separately opened to count the votes. A Royal Commission reporting on the conduct of the 1880 election in Macclesfield noted:

. . . it seems doubtful whether a contested election has ever been fought in Macclesfield on really pure princi-

ples, the corruption of the late election was far more widespread, and far more open than had been the case at any previous Parliamentary election, at all event, of recent years, though the bribes were, in most cases, trifling in amount . . . of those who were proved before them to have received bribes . . . a large number of them were persons who would not have accepted money from the opposite side, but who thought that if money was going amongst their friends they were as much entitled to have some as anyone else, and therefore accepted their day's wages, or a few shillings wherewith to treat themselves before or after polling.

Quoted in M Willis, *Gladstone and Disraeli: Principles and Policies*, 1989

Where voters were very numerous the secret ballot certainly made a difference. In London, the Chief Commissioner of Police reported:

Since the passing of the Ballot Act we have never had the slightest trouble at any election that has taken place in London, and the places that used to be the worst are now the best . . . (In 1868) the Tower Hamlets election was carried on in a general state of riot; we had to have 400 or 500 police on the ground to keep the peace.

Quoted in M Willis, *Gladstone and Disraeli: Principles and Policies*, 1989

In 1883 the Corrupt and Illegal Practices Act introduced fines and prison sentences for those who exceeded a set list of election expenses and engaged in activities like hiring carriages. Wealthy people began supplying these free to those who were going to the polling stations to vote for them. The increase in the numbers of voters made bribery more difficult, though influence lingered on in smaller towns which were dominated by one or two employers. (In Norwich, for example, J J Colman, the mustard manufacturer, was regularly backed by the local community.) However, elections certainly become more orderly.

Though property qualifications for MPs vanished in 1858, attempting to enter Parliament remained very expensive. Agents' salaries could run to £100 or more a year and permissible expenses might rise to more than £800. Spending between elections continued too. In 1895 the novelist Rider Haggard fought Norfolk East and wrote:

From the moment a candidate appears in the field he is fair game and every man's hand is in his pocket. Demands for 'your patronage and support' fall on him thick as leaves. I was even pestered to supply voters with wooden legs! Why should an election cost, as this one did, over £2000?

The Days of My Life, 1926

The Third Reform Act, 1884–1885

By the 1880s it was widely agreed that male inhabitants in counties ought to have the same political rights as those in boroughs. A Bill was introduced in 1884 by Gladstone, who declared:

Is there any doubt that the peasantry of the country are capable citizens, qualified for enfranchisement, qualified to make good use of their power as voters?

Lord Salisbury, the Conservative leader, agreed with the justice of the argument. Parliamentary reform, therefore, was not just the cause of radicals like Joseph Chamberlain, although in fact Chamberlain saw it as just one of a cluster of measures that included land reform and the provision of free elementary education.

The details of the reform were set out in two separate acts. The first of those, in 1884, changed the voting system. The second (the Redistribution Act of 1885) took account of the growth of population in the more northerly parts of Britain and increased the number of MPs here, at the expense of southern England.

The Main Changes, 1884–1885

1. The old county/borough division was abolished; very small boroughs of under 15 000 people lost their MPs; and those from 15 000 to 50 000 people kept one MP. A basic principle of trying to create constituencies of around 50 000 people was adopted.

2. The 1867 franchise applied in all places; so adult males who were house owners, or tenants who had lived in a house for at least a year, and lodgers who had lived at least a year in rooms valued at £10 a year for rating purposes, all had the vote.

3. Plural voting (i.e. voting for more than one person) was permitted. University graduates had a second vote for their university MPs; borough freeholders could also vote in the counties except in four places; and those who owned property in several different constituencies could vote in each of those constituencies. By 1911 plural voting counted for 7 per cent of the votes. One man had 23 votes. Even the radical Chamberlain had six.

4. A redistribution of 142 seats took place, cutting the old dominance of southern England and increasing Scottish representation to 72.

5. Voting was still spread over three weeks, enabling men to stand in more than one place. For example, in 1900 Keir Hardie stood in both Preston and Merthyr.

The vote was still denied to women. Also excluded were sons living at home, people on poor relief, servants living with their employers, and servicemen living in barracks. Since working class people moved home frequently (one estimate reckoned that 30 per cent moved every year), it was often difficult for them to meet the residence qualification. In Glasgow just 52 per cent of males were entitled to vote in 1900.

THE CONTENDING SWAINS.

This cartoon shows the two political parties seeking the support of rural voters.

Lodgers had to go through a complex system of registration, which required annual renewal in the presence of an appointed lawyer, and this of course involved time off work. So the reform was by no means complete.

The reform increased the tendency of voters of a particular social group to dominate constituencies. There were suburban seats that Conservatives controlled, and working class seats were eyed hopefully by candidates from the emerging Socialist and Labour parties. Joseph Chamberlain pointed out the implications of a parliament,

... elected by 5 millions of men, of whom three fifths belong to the labouring population. It is a revolution which has been peacefully and silently accomplished. The centre of power has been shifted.

Pressure for the vote for all men was ineffective prior to the Great War as those still denied the vote did not form a coherent group capable of effective organisation. The unskilled labouring man was still regarded with suspicion. Many politicians felt that such a voter would be swayed by short-term emotional appeals, and was so dominated by the need to earn a living as to be incapable of informed political decisions. Bills attacking plural voting were rejected by the House of Lords.

In 1885 the UK electorate was 5.7 million; by 1911 it was 7.9 million, but it did not include a single woman, and by 1911 this had become a major issue.

➤ ACTIVITIES

1 Do you agree that *'Parliamentary reform was largely a reflection of changes in the economic and social structure of the country?'*

2 *'We must admit those whom it may be safe to admit.'* (Macaulay)

   Was this the principle that governed parliamentary reform in this period?

3 Why did Disraeli succeed in reforming parliament in 1867 whilst Gladstone failed?

4 Use Robert Lowe's views (Page 24) and your own knowledge to explain who opposed parliamentary reform in 1867. (Explaining as historical developments and events.)

5 To what extent do Henry Mayhew's views (Page 23) support Gladstone's (Pages 23–24) on the question of workers' readiness to receive franchise? (Comparison of sources.)

Chapter Three

The Issue of Women's Suffrage and the Coming of Universal Suffrage

In 1867 John Stuart Mill suggested to Parliament that women should be given the vote. He got little support. But, over the next 50 years, this issue grew in importance to become one of the main questions of the day. When women finally got the vote, in 1918, it was not on terms that were equal with men's. Not until 1928 were women to achieve this goal.

The First World War of 1914–1918 helped women to win the vote. It also helped the awarding of the vote to all men regardless of the property they owned. Thus 1918 and 1928 are key dates in British history for they mark the final arrival of a democratic system of voting.

From studying this chapter you should develop your understanding of:

◆ The question of women's rights in the period.

◆ The campaign for women's suffrage.

◆ Different approaches to that campaign.

◆ Why women finally obtained the vote.

◆ The coming of universal adult suffrage and the reasons for this.

TASK

Account for the coming of universal suffrage, 1900–1928.

You have been asked to write the above essay. Work through this chapter, looking back over the previous chapter too and make notes on the following:

✦ Why there was hostility to women's suffrage.

✦ The ways in which campaigns for suffrage were fought; the degree of their success or failure.

✦ The effect of the First World War.

✦ The nature of the 1918 reform.

✦ The reasons for further reform in 1928.

✦ An overview judgement on what really brought success.

The changing role of women in society

The legal situation

The struggle to win votes for women was just one of a number of battles that were fought to improve the place of women in society. When Victoria became queen, society officially took the view expressed in the late eighteenth century by the eminent lawyer William Blackstone:

By marriage the very being or legal existence of women is suspended, or at least it is incorporated and consolidated into that of the husband under whose protection and cover she performs everything.

A society that denied women legal status equal to that of men, offered them inferior education, and gave them wage rates well below those of their male counterparts was not likely to regard women as worthy of the franchise. In 1854 Barbara Leigh Smith Bodichon's book *A Brief Summary in Plain Language of the Most Important Laws Concerning Women* noted:

A man and wife are one person in law: the wife loses all her rights as a single woman and her existence is entirely absorbed in that of her husband. A woman's body belongs to her husband and he can enforce his right. What was her personal property before marriage such as money, jewels, clothes, etc. becomes absolutely her husband's. Money earned by a married woman belongs absolutely to her husband. The legal custody of the children belongs to the father . . . the father may take them from her and dispose of them as he thinks fit. A married woman cannot enter into contracts except as the agent of her husband, that is, her word alone is not binding in law.

Quoted in J H Murray, *Strong Minded Women*, 1984

In fact, in 1839 women did win rights to the custody of their children under the age of seven, provided that the Lord Chancellor agreed; and a husband did need his wife's consent to dispose of her freehold land. Nevertheless, this was a situation bitterly resented by a growing number of wealthy intelligent women who had plenty of time to focus on the injustices of their position. The Victorian age evolved an attitude to women which regarded their proper role – if material circumstances allowed – as one of near idleness. The period has left us the furious recollections of women like Florence Nightingale, who were frustrated by a life devoted to supervising servants, socialising, and practising hobbies like music and needlework. The philosopher John Stuart Mill took as his second wife Harriet Taylor. She helped to persuade him of the justice of votes for women, stating:

When we ask why the existence of one half of the species should be merely ancillary to that of the other, why each

woman should be a mere appendage to a man, allowed to have no interests of her own that there may be nothing to compete in her mind with his interests and his pleasure, the only reason which can be given is, that men like it. It is agreeable to them that men should live for their own sake, women for the sake of men.

Quoted in J H Murray, *Strong Minded Women*, 1984

Education

Education was an area of life where such women battled for change. The Education Act of 1870 (1872 in Scotland) created a system of elementary education for girls as well as boys. But most leading campaigners for women's rights were equally concerned with the fee-paying and higher education sectors to which their family wealth gave them access.

The education issue was of special importance to women who had to earn their own living. In the 1860s nearly a quarter of all adult females were either spinsters or widows. Since two thirds of this figure were spinsters, the importance of being qualified for (and having access to) a range of worthwhile careers was a matter of major importance to the women concerned. (In 1913 63 per cent of subscribing supporters of the Pankhurst suffragettes were spinsters.) So there was pressure for an education similar to that provided for boys. In 1853 Cheltenham Ladies College was founded. It offered its pupils subjects like Latin, Greek and Mathematics as well as the traditional literary and artistic accomplishments. During the century the number of such schools increased. Emily Davies (who in 1869 founded what eventually became Girton College, Cambridge) wondered:

Is the improved education which it is hoped is about to be brought within reach of women to be identical with that of men? Only women can understand the weight of discouragement produced by being perpetually told that as women nothing much is ever to be expected of them, that whatever they do they must not interest themselves, except in a second-hand and shallow way, in the pursuits of men. Every effort to improve the education of women which assumes that they may study the same subjects as their brothers does something towards lifting them out of the state of listless despair of themselves into which so many fall.

Quoted in J H Murray, *Strong Minded Women*, 1894

Science at Cheltenham Ladies College.

At the same time, there were women who argued in just the opposite way. In 1868 Sarah Sewell, an opponent of women's rights declared:

The education of girls need not to be of the same extended classical and commercial character as that of boys: they want more an education of the heart and feelings and especially of firm, fixed moral principles. The profoundly educated women rarely make good wives or mothers, women who have stored their minds with Latin and Greek seldom have much knowledge of pies and puddings nor do they enjoy the hard and interesting work of attending to the wants of little children.

Quoted in J H Murray, *Strong Minded Women*, 1984

But slowly access to higher education was prised open. In 1878 London University abandoned a 12 year experiment of offering women separate awards and opened up all its degrees equally to men and to women. Two years afterwards, Victoria University, the forerunner of both Manchester and Liverpool Universities, did the same, and in 1895 Durham University followed suit. The work of Elizabeth Garrett Anderson and Sophia Jex Blake led to the establishment of the London School of Medicine where women could train as doctors. It is significant that Emily Davies and Elizabeth Garrett Anderson were also responsible in 1866 for taking to parliament the first petition for women's suffrage. Gradually more careers opened up to a suitably trained women. In 1860 the Nightingale School of Nursing at St Thomas's Hospital began the work of making nursing a proper career. The extension of education opened up teaching as a career for women, as long as they remained unmarried. Women found employment in the post office, the civil service, and in private businesses, yet still they could not elect or be elected as MPs.

It might be thought that the presence of a queen on the throne helped their cause. Not so. Victoria wrote:

The Queen is most anxious to enlist everyone who can speak or write, to join in checking this mad wicked folly for 'Women's Rights' with all its attendant horrors on which her poor feeble sex is bent, forgetting every sense of womanly feeling and propriety. It is subject which makes the Queen so furious that she cannot contain herself.

However, even royal hostility could not prevent legal reforms to improve women's circumstances.

Changes in the Law in Victorian Times

1. 1857 Matrimonial Causes Act. Divorce could now be obtained through the law courts instead of by a private Act of Parliament. The Act's main purpose was to ease divorce for men. For them, the proof of a wife's adultery was sufficient, but women had to prove more than adultery – an offence such as bigamy, incest, cruelty or desertion was required too. Nevertheless it did give women increased control of their property, especially where judicial separation or desertion was involved.

2. 1869 Municipal Franchise Act. Single female ratepayers could vote in local elections. (Married women got the same right in 1894.)

3. 1870–1894. Women obtained the right to vote for, and stand for election to, organisations like School Boards (1870–1872), Poor Law Guardians (1875), County Councils (1888–1889), Parish and District Councils (1894).

4. 1870 Married Women's Property Act. This Act was a rather ineffective attempt to increase women's rights over their property, income and legacies.

5. 1875. The age of children over whom women could claim custody was raised from seven to sixteen.

6. 1882 Second Married Women's Property Act. This gave married women the same rights over their own property as were already possessed by unmarried women.

7. 1886 Married Women's (maintenance in case of desertion) Act. Women could sue for desertion without first having to go to the workhouse.

8. 1886 Repeal of the Contagious Diseases Act. This had allowed the forcible examination and imprisonment of any woman in an army garrison town or naval port who was thought to be a prostitute.

9. 1886 The Guardianship of Infants Act. In deciding the custody of children, their welfare was now to be the most important factor.

Pressure for women's suffrage

When parliamentary reform was being debated in 1867, John Stuart Mill proposed an amendment that would have given the vote to women on the same terms as men. It was rejected by 194 votes to 73. It marked the beginning of a long campaign that eventually became quite violent, but had still not met with success by 1914. Some men (and women) were opposed to it in principle, arguing that physically and intellectually women were not suited to the rough and tumble of politics. There were even female reformers like Octavia Hill and (for a while) Beatrice Webb who did not favour votes for women. Some male politicians feared the long-term implications of such a reform. William Randall Cremer, MP, said:

He had always contended that if once they opened the door and enfranchised ever so small a number of females, they could not possibly close it and that it ulti-

mately meant adult suffrage. The government of the country would therefore be handed over to a majority who would not be men, but women. Women are creatures of impulse and emotion and did not decide questions on the ground of reason as men did.

House of Commons Debates, Vol 155

Some politicians supported the woman's cause. In the Labour Party there were several, especially Keir Hardie. There were a number in the Liberal Party, notably Sir Edward Grey. The Conservative Party was by no means wholly hostile, A J Balfour for example, privately expressed his sympathy. Yet the cause of women's suffrage was enmeshed in other considerations that always seemed to prevent action. The Liberals feared that giving women the vote on the property qualification basis would create Conservative voters. The Conservatives wished to see a more general reform which would cut the number of Irish MPs upon whom the Liberals depended in the last few years before the Great War. The Labour Party buried the issue in a general demand for adult suffrage. Some MPs pointed to reforms already carried out and argued that the existing system was well able to respond to women's interests; and many argued there were more urgent issues that had to receive priority. Nor was there an overwhelming and united pressure for reform from women. Some opposed it; some concentrated on other issues (like housing and health reforms, or working conditions); and most ordinary women were so overwhelmed by the daily battle for existence that they had no time and energy left for the cause. Moreover those who did support the cause were divided, and argued about tactics at a crucial period in the campaign.

The suffragist movement

In 1867 the London National Society for Women's Suffrage was set up. It grew out of a committee that had organised petitions to try to get parliament to include votes for women in the 1867 Act. Similar groups were set up in other cities and in 1872 they combined to form the National Society for Women's Suffrage. Initially their leader was Lydia Becker, later it was Millicent Fawcett. By 1897, after various upheavals, the movement became the National Union of Women's Suffrage Societies (NUWSS).

A poster advocating women's right to vote.

This movement hoped to succeed through peaceful activities. They held meetings, produced pamphlets, drew up petitions, and tried to win MPs' support. In 1867 John Stuart Mill got the support of 72 other MPs in trying to change the Reform Act and various other MPs proved ready to argue the case – but without success. Till 1914 the suffragists accepted that, since not all men could vote, neither should all women. Yet giving women the vote on terms equal to men meant allowing the franchise to just over a million female householders or property occupiers paying rates. Married women were excluded. The historian Martin Pugh suggests:

Suffragists would probably have done better to have made common cause with all unenfranchised men and women from the start and thereby they might have extended their appeal

Votes for Women in Britain 1867–1928, Historical Association, 1994

Although the movement struggled to remain above party politics and thus attract backing from as many MPs as possible, it suffered division and arguments between Conservative and the more numerous Liberal members. Even Millicent Fawcett appeared on Conservative Party platforms, pushed in this direction by her opposition to Gladstone's Home Rule for Ireland policy.

Many Liberals and Labour men and some Conservatives backed the suffragette cause. They were able, after 1893, to draw on the experience of New Zealand where giving all women the vote met an enthusiastic and peaceful response: several New Zealand politicians came to Britain to speak for the suffragist cause. Women had also demonstrated their interest and competence in government through the local government bodies for which they could vote and on which they could serve. Mainstream party organisations relied increasingly on women to raise funds, speak at meetings and try to win over voters. Even votes in parliament (especially after the Liberal triumph of 1906) showed a steady swing of support for women's suffrage. The militant suffragette activities brought the cause even more publicity and led to an increase in membership of the suffragist movement. By 1914 there were over 50 000 people in 500 societies affiliated to the NUWSS and increasingly they worked for the party keenest on their cause – the Labour Party.

The suffragette movement

The leader of this movement was Mrs Emmeline Pankhurst. She complained:

Our leaders in the Liberal Party had advised women to prove their fitness for parliamentary franchise by serving in municipal office ... A large number of women had availed themselves of this advice and were serving on Boards of Guardians, on School Boards and in other capacities.

When I came into office I found that the laws in our district were being very harshly administered. The old board had been made up of the kind of men who are known as rate savers.

They were guardians not of the poor but of the rates. Old folks I found sitting on benches. They had no privacy, no possessions, and not even a locker ... It does gratify me when I look back and remember what we were able to do for the children.

The trouble is the law cannot do all the work, even for children. We shall have to have new laws and it soon became apparent to me that we can never hope to get them until women have the vote ... I thought I had been a suffragist before I became a Poor Law Guardian, but now I began to think about the vote in women's hands not only as a right but as a desperate necessity.

My Own Story, 1914

Mrs Pankhurst was to return repeatedly to this view – that the issue of 'votes for women' was not only right in itself, but the necessary means to other urgently needed reforms. In an appearance in a law court she argued:

We believe that if we get the vote it will mean better conditions for our unfortunate sisters. We know what the condition of the woman worker is. Her condition is very bad. Many women pass through this court who I believe would not come before you if they were able to live normally and honestly. The average earnings of women who earn their living are only 7s. 7d a week ...

We have been driven to the conclusion that only through legislation can any improvement be effected and that the legislation can never be effected until we have the same power as men have to bring pressure to bear upon our representatives and upon Governments to give us the necessary legislation.

It was the failure of other approaches that led Mrs Pankhurst to action, as she explained in her memoirs:

It was on October 10 1903 that I invited a number of women to my house for purposes of organisation. We voted to call our society the Women's Social and Political Union (WSPU). We resolved to limit our membership exclusively to women, to keep ourselves absolutely free from any party affiliation and to be satisfied with nothing but action ...

The old suffragist ... clung to a hope that a private member's bill would sometime obtain consideration. Every year the association sent deputations to meet so-called friendly members. The ladies made their speeches and the members made theirs and renewed their assurances that they believed in women's suffrage and would vote for it when they had the opportunity to do so. Then the deputation, a trifle sad, took its departure and the members resumed the real business of life, which was support of their parties' policies.

Emmeline Pankhurst and her daughters Christabel and Sylvia were members of the Independent Labour Party in Manchester. The WSPU was born out of their frustration at male reluctance to make their cause a priority.

The Daily Mail dubbed her followers 'suffragettes'. They adopted tactics that were more aggressive than those of other groups: they interrupted political meetings with banner-waving and heckling; they organised rallies, marches and petitions; they set up a newspaper, and won a great deal of publicity. Failure to win success pushed the movement into illegal actions that led to suffragettes being imprisoned. Some of them went on hunger strike and were forcibly

fed. This forcible feeding attracted such bad publicity that the Liberal Government's 'Cat and Mouse Act' was passed to permit temporary release and arbitrary rearrest. From 1909 the WSPU's methods became more violent. Windows were smashed, properties set on fire, acid poured in letter boxes, golf courses and flower beds wrecked. In 1914 Mary Richardson tried to slash an important painting, Velasquez's *Venus*, but her activity was nothing in comparison to the tragedy of the previous year: during the Derby horse race of 1913 Emily Wilding Davidson rushed on to the course, attempting to seize the bridle of the king's horse, Anmer. The frightened animal fell, injuring her fatally.

A pro-suffragette demonstration in London, 1906.

By now the suffragettes knew that women in New Zealand and in South Australia had received the vote. Yet all efforts in Britain failed. The increasing violence alarmed Conservatives especially. In 1912 the Labour MP George Lansbury resigned to fight his Bow and Bromley constituency again, specifically on the issue of female suffrage. His reward was to be soundly beaten by an anti-suffrage Conservative.

Cartoon showing the Dundee suffragettes on the warpath.

Fragments of the WSPU split off through differences with Mrs Pankhurst and her daughter Christabel about the issue of violence and the leadership style of the Pankhursts. From 1910 the membership lists of the WSPU began to shrink.

The home life of a suffragette and her husband – by a hostile author.

In 1913 Asquith's Liberal Government proposed giving the vote to female householders and to the wives of householders. But the bill was wrecked by a strange alliance of Conservatives with Irish Nationalists determined to see Home Rule safely in place before there was any further reform of the franchise. This curious combination of enemies sprang from Irish fear that reform would drastically cut their Westminster representation: the average electorate in an Irish seat was by 1914, about half that of one in England. (Ireland's population had been falling, while England's and Scotland's had been expanding.) Asquith had been pushed into this proposal rather reluctantly by more enthusiastic colleagues who also pointed out that skilled fund-raisers and organisers from the NUWSS were now rallying to Labour to help it fight anti-suffrage Liberals. Asquith now dropped the measure and within a year the Great War had swept it aside.

Did the Pankhursts' tactics help the cause of votes for women? The historian Martin Pugh argues:

The Pankhursts proved a highly divisive force within the women's movements . . . they inflicted a catalogue of splits among militant forces . . . There are no grounds for the view that the WSPU shifted public opinion in its favour, rather the reverse.

M Pugh, *Women's Suffrage in Britain*, 1980

However, the film maker Midge Mackenzie, who has produced a book on this issue, believes:

Prior to 1914 it was the militant vanguard, the WSPU, that revitalised the question of votes for women with its tactics of political confrontations and the immense publicity that ensued.

M Mackenzie, *Shoulder to Shoulder*, 1980

The outbreak of war led Mrs Pankhurst to set aside her campaign in the interests of winning the war.

The impact of the First World War

This dreadful conflict involved the country in a huge human effort. So many men were needed for military service that, in 1916, conscription for all 18 to 41 year olds was introduced. Only those in essential work were excused.

Between 1914 and 1918 over five million served in the war, nearly three quarters of a million were killed and a million seriously wounded.

Many who lived through these years detected a change in people's behaviour and attitudes. In working class Salford, Robert Roberts observed:

The First World War cracked the form of English lower class life and began an erosion of its socio-economic layers that has continued to this day. In our community, well before the war was over, we began to see basic alterations in certain habits and customs. Similar changes were taking place in every industrial corner of the land. 'Things,' people repeatedly told one another, 'will never be the same again.' Daily newspapers, magazines, periodicals, comics and, as people grew richer, even books made their appearance in homes almost bare of print before the war. Communications from husbands and sons, official forms, and later, ration books all made hitherto unknown demands upon the unlettered.

The Classic Slum

The war had a particularly noticeable impact on the place of women in British society. Their services were needed in a whole range of occupations to replace the men who had volunteered for, or been conscripted into the armed forces. To many women who had hitherto been badly paid domestic servants, factory work brought better pay and more free time. Wartime work demonstrated women's ability to undertake employment from which they had hitherto been excluded. It emphasised the crucial importance of their contribution to the economy at a time of crisis.

A woman working in a munitions factory during the First World War.

Without their female recruits the munitions industry, for example, would not have been able to cope. Munitions work may have been dangerous, but its weekly wage of £2 for women was better than the average pre-war wage for women of 11s. 7d. By 1918 nearly a million women worked in munitions and engineering. The number of women working in transport services arose from 18 000 to 117 000, and in clerical jobs from 33 000 to 102 000. *The Daily Mail* noted shorthand typists' wages rose in a year from £1 to £1 15s. 0d. and added:

The wartime business girl is to be seen any night dining out alone or with a friend in the moderate-priced restaurants in London. Formerly she would never have had her evening meal in town unless in the company of a man friend. But now with money and without men she is more and more beginning to dine out.

Quoted in A Marwick, *The Deluge*, 1965

Robert Roberts noticed now the war changed women's attitudes:

It undoubtedly snapped strings that had bound them in so many ways to the Victorian age. Wives in the shop no longer talked about 'my boss', or 'my master'.

Master had gone to war and Missis ruled the household, or he worked close to her in a factory, turning out shell cases on a lathe and earning little more than she did herself. Housewives left their homes and immediate neighbourhood more frequently, and with money in their purses went foraging for goods even into the city shops, each trip being an exercise in self-education. She discovered her own rights. The events in 1914–1918, then, did not start, but they accelerated significantly, a movement already well developed, one which would go some way to release that other general social undermass of the time – the working-class women of Britain.

R Roberts, *The Classic Slum*

Historians may differ in detail, but in general they are agreed about the importance of the Great War. To Martin Pugh:

The experience and response of the mass of people during the First World War were of major importance in shaping the modern pattern of British politics.

The Making of Modern British Politics

G E Mingay writes:

World War I marked the end of the old Britain, the beginning of the new. Life was never quite the same again.

The Transformation of Britain, 1986

With the outbreak of war suffragettes and suffragists alike ceased campaigning. Mrs Pankhurst turned her magazine *The Suffragette* into the vigorously pro-war *Britannia*. She devoted her formidable energies to supporting the drive to recruit soldiers. Her daughter Christabel declared to an American audience in 1914:

You must not suppose that because the suffragettes fight the British Government for the sake of the vote . . . that on that account the suffragettes are not patriotic. Why should we fight for British citizenship if we do not most highly prize it? . . . We want to see the strength is more and more going to be used for the good of the whole world. Our country has made mistakes in the past . . .

But we are going to do better in the future – above all when British women co-operate with the men in the important work of Government.

Quoted in M Mackenzie, *Shoulder to Shoulder*

Sylvia Pankhurst pursued social work in the East End of London and adopted an increasingly anti-war viewpoint. So too did Emmiline Pethick Lawrence. Her campaigns in the USA helped to create the Women's Peace Movement and led to the holding of a Women's Peace Conference in the Hague. Members of suffragist groups tended to be rather more critical of the war than followers of the Women's Social and Political Union.

The coming of universal adult suffrage

Because electoral reform (including votes for some women) emerged at the end of 1918, it is easy to assume that the war did much to bring it about. The historian Arthur Marwick suggests that in this, as in other matters:

It is difficult to see how women could have achieved so much in anything like a similar time span without the unique circumstances arising from the war.

Ed. H Winkler, *Twentieth Century Britain*, 1976

His fellow historian, Martin Pugh, is more cautious, commenting that 'careful study tends to show how little change resulted from the war, not how much'. He does note that the eventual decision of 1918 for giving women the vote was:

the vote of the suffragist majority elected in 1910 but for whom the Party considerations that had proved an obstacle before, now ceased to apply.

Women's Suffrage in Britain, 1980

However, he also observes:

By 1918 the press had already begun to lose its enthusiasm for women workers who were now urged to surrender their jobs for returning soldiers

Votes for Women in Britain

There were grumbles. The suffragist leader Millicent Fawcett noted of the 'householder' clause for women:

There was some outcry against this on the part of ardent suffragists as being derogatory to the independence of women . . . I felt, on the contrary, it marked an

Representation of the People's Act, 1918

1. The vote was given to all adult males aged 21 or over who satisfied a 6 month residence qualification. Peers, prisoners and the insane were excluded, but those receiving poor relief were no longer disqualified.

2. Women aged 30 or over could vote, provided that they were householders, or wives of householders, or university graduates.

3. Voting was to take place on one day only, and was not to be spread over several weeks.

4. Electoral administration was reformed. Candidates had to deposit £150, which they lost if they polled under an eighth of the votes cast. Party agents no longer decided who was on the register; this task went to local government officials who annually made up lists of voters. Returning officers' expenses and election costs were to be met from public funds, and not by candidates.

5. Servicemen of 19 and over were permitted to vote in the immediate post-war election. By 209 votes to 171, the Commons decided to disqualify for five years all those who had been conscientious objectors.

6. Certain people continued to have more than one vote, but the number of votes anyone could possess was now limited to two. Those entitled to two votes were either university graduates who could vote in one of the twelve university seats, or owners of business premises. University electors could vote by post, but business electors had to vote in person. Between 1922 and 1945 the Conservatives owed about nine seats to university electors, and between seven and eleven seats to business electors.

7. Constituencies were reorganised so that each was as near 70 000 votes as was reasonably possible. Ten double-member borough seats were allowed to survive, but otherwise the old borough/county division disappeared.

8. As a result of suffragist pressure, voting by women in local government elections was put on the same footing as in parliamentary elections. This widened the franchise in local elections, for up till now the only women who had been able to vote were those who were householders in their own right.

important advance that it recognised in practical political form a universally accepted and most valuable social fact namely the partnership of the wife and mother in the home. We did object to the absurdly high age.

M Fawcett, *The Women's Victories and After*, 1920

The main effect was to give the vote to married women, but to deny the vote to many women war workers.

Debates were also marked by public confessions of changes of mind by some who had once opposed female suffrage. Herbert Asquith was the most prominent of such people:

How could we have carried on the War without (women)? Short of actually bearing arms in the field, there is hardly a service which has contributed to the maintenance of our cause in which women have not been at least as active and as efficient as men. But what ... moves me still more ... is the problem of reconstruction when this War is over. The questions which will then necessarily arise in regard to women's labour and the women's activities in the new ordering of things are questions which I feel it impossible to withhold from women the power and right of making their voice directly heard.

House of Commons Debates, 1917 Vol. 92

The bill passed comfortably through the Commons. In the House of Lords it faced the hostility of the Leader, Lord Curzon, although he publicly recognised that resistance was pointless. The Lords passed the bill by 134 to 71 votes. 8.4 million women now gained the right to vote – women who were regarded, by the men who had carried out the reform, as being stable and mature family women who were likely to be influenced by their husbands. In any case they were outnumbered by the thirteen million male voters. The total (male) electorate in the last pre-war election had been a mere seven million!

A separate Parliamentary Qualification Act allowed women aged 21 and over to stand for election to parliament.

The Great War ended on 11 November 1918. Just over a month later a general election provided a good test of the new electoral system. The results removed the fears of those apprehensive of the consequences of enfranchising women and working class men. The victorious wartime coalition won a massive majority. No separate women's party emerged in parliament, despite the efforts of Christabel Pankhurst to fight this cause in the constituency of Smethwick. One woman managed to become elected: Constance Gore Booth, Countess Markiewicz, won the St Patrick division of Dublin. But since she was a fervent Irish Republican, she did not recognise Westminster's authority in Ireland, and refused to take up her seat. The first woman actually to attend the Commons as an MP was an American who had never fought the female suffrage cause. Lady Nancy Astor, captured the constituency of Plymouth when her husband moved from the seat to take up a peerage in the Lords. She found the House ill-organised to receive her – indeed the only women's lavatory was a half-kilometre walk from the debating chamber! In 1921 she was joined by Margaret Wintringham, a Liberal who fought Louth when her husband, the previous MP died. In the 1922 election 33 women stood as candidates and in 1923 Scotland's first woman MP entered Parliament.

During these years it was possible for a woman who was not entitled to vote in elections to become an MP, for the rules governing the circumstances of those who could stand for election differed from those determining who could be an elector. The Labour MP Ellen Wilkinson told the Commons:

When I was first elected to this House I happened to live in furnished rooms and having neither a husband nor furniture I was not eligible for a vote ... independ-

ent wage-earning women should be represented in this House where so much of our legislation directly concerns them.

House of Commons Debates

The post-war electoral scene led politicians to conclude that there was nothing to fear from giving women the vote on the same terms as men. Soon each party had its women's branch and annual women's conferences. The Conservative Stanley Baldwin promised to tackle this issue during the successful electoral campaign in 1924. He honoured his pledge in 1928, and received support from all parties – though hostility from two of his own party, Churchill and Birkenhead. The reform added to the register about 3.5 million women aged between 21 and 30 and 1.8 million hitherto unenfranchised women over 30 years old.

Young female voters going to the polls for the first time in 1929.

In the general election of 1929 women formed 52.7 per cent of the electorate, though they provided only 69 of the candidates, and the Labour Government which emerged from this episode contained the country's first woman cabinet minister. Margaret Bondfield, Minister of Labour, began work as a shop assistant at the age of 14 and, through trade union activities, rose in the Labour movement.

In the opinion of the historian A J P Taylor, the successful campaign for adult suffrage had very modest political consequences:

In the long run more women voters probably benefited the Conservatives and more voters altogether probably injured the Liberals who were the least suited to become a mass party.

English History 1914–45, 1965

The WSPU disbanded. The National Union of Women's Suffrage Societies turned itself into the National Union of Societies for Equal Citizenship, and launched campaigns to improve women's rights in law, in employment, and in social conditions. The historian Martin Pugh regarded their efforts with a critical eye when he wrote:

The bulk of the movement had been too socially conservative to embrace the feminist objectives which remained to be taken up by a later generation of women for whom the franchise campaign was a distant memory.

M Pugh, *Women's Suffrage in Britain*

Many who had fought for women's suffrage saw it not only as a right in itself but also as a means of achieving a major improvement in women's rights and opportunities. The times when the franchise was finally won were also times when other successes were achieved. The doors to a number of hitherto closed occupations were prised open. The 1919 Sex Disqualification Removal Act provided women with the opportunity to enter professions like law and accountancy. 1921 saw the qualification of the first woman barrister, Helena Normanton. In 1920 Oxford University agreed to award full degrees to women. (Cambridge did not carry out the same reform until 1947.) In 1921 the government gave way to pressure to let women sit examinations for entry to all grades of the civil services; and in 1925 three women won admission to the highest (administrative) grade.

Women were to be found playing an increasing part in public affairs. In 1919 they became liable for jury service. By 1923 there were about 4000 women magistrates, mayors, councillors and poor law guardians.

Reforms in 1926 and 1935 allowed married and single women to hold and dispose of property on the same terms as men. The 1923 Matrimonial Causes Act made grounds for divorce the same for women as for men, and a further act in 1937 added cruelty, desertion, or the insanity of one's partner as reasons justifying divorce. In 1925 wives were granted guardianship rights over their children on terms equal to those of their husbands. In the event of a split, the courts were to decide who had custody. Social reforms like widow's pensions (1925) of 10s. a week, the development of clinics for pregnant women, and easier access to birth control brought some improvement to women's lives.

Nevertheless the mood of the inter-war years was unsympathetic to providing full equality for women. The advertising and the magazines that boomed in these years stressed women's roles as wives and mothers. The increasingly numerous branches of the Women's Institute (from its beginning in 1915 in Anglesey) placed most emphasis on women's domestic activities. Women's pay was markedly lower than men's and not till 1942 did the TUC pledge itself to fight to achieve equal pay. In the words of the historian, John Stevenson:

Many of the high hopes of the early feminist pioneers for full equality had not been achieved ... A measure of equality and an element of independence had been obtained, but only within a culture and economy which remained male-dominated in all important features.

J Stevenson, *British Society 1914–45*, 1984

SHADE OF OLD MILITANT : " So this is what I fought for ! "

A cartoonist's view in 1929 on how women's lives had changed after receiving the vote.

> ► **ACTIVITIES**
>
> 1 Work in pairs to develop the case for either:
>   **a)** The suffragist approach to winning the vote for women.
>   **b)** The suffragette approach.
>
> 2 Attempt the essay in the Task at the start of this chapter.
>
> 3 Use Mrs Pankhurst's views on the franchise for women as a means to other changes (Page 35) and your own knowledge, to explain why women wanted the vote. (Explain historical developments and events.)

Chapter Four

The growth of the Labour movement 1890–1922

The pressure for a much wider franchise came at a time when economic change had turned Britain into a country where large numbers of people were employed in workshops, shipyards, mines and factories. In the late nineteenth and early twentieth centuries the pressure for better working and living conditions became bound up with demands for a more democratic society in which workers would have a political movement to fight for their needs. By 1924 this 'labour movement' had achieved the remarkable success of a Labour Government led by people from very humble origins. The material in this section deals with the growth of this labour movement.

From your study of this chapter you should have a sound understanding of:

◆ The development of the Labour movement.

◆ The different sorts of organisations involved in this development.

◆ The emergence of the Labour Party.

◆ The reasons for its growth.

TASK

How might a veteran Labour Party member have explained the rise of the party to new young members?

Work through the chapter noting down points to explain:

◆ The importance of trade unions.

◆ Why Labour and Socialist societies grew up.

◆ Why an organised Labour Party was created.

◆ What policies and beliefs the Labour Party stood for.

◆ Why the Labour Party was able to grow, up to 1922.

Organised labour in the late nineteenth century

Workers tried to deal with the problems that they faced by organising themselves in a number of ways.

Friendly societies

By the 1870s four million people were members of Friendly Societies. Some were small in size, collecting in money from their members that was then paid out in times of crisis such as illness, unemployment, or to meet burial costs. Some

Societies were huge; in 1886 for example, there were over 667 000 members of the Foresters. These organisations usually held regular meetings – most commonly using public houses as their meeting places.

The co-operative movement

From small beginnings in Rochdale in 1844, the Co-operative Movement had grown to have 300 000 members and 72 branches by 1872. Each branch consisted of a shop selling goods (especially food and clothes) that produced profits which were then shared out among members in an annual dividend. By 1890 the movement had established a Co-operative Wholesale Society running biscuit and clothing factories and fruit farms. The Society held annual congresses (from 1869) and had a special section for women (from 1833).

Trade unions

Trade unions had a history that went back well before 1890. Early unions were usually small, made up of the members of a particular craft. They tried to protect their members' jobs and improve working conditions as well as supporting members in difficult times, very much as Friendly Societies were also doing.

Unions of mid-Victorian times had little to do with politics. Their limited aims were summarised in 1867 by one of their number:

The South Yorkshire Miners Association has many objects. First, to raise from time to time by contribution among the members, funds for the purpose of mutual support. Secondly, striving to obtain better legislation for the efficient management of mines. Thirdly, compensation for accidents. Fourthly, to assist all members when unjustly dealt with by their employers. Fifthly, a weekly allowance to members when injured following their employment. Sixthly, a grant at the death of any member caused by accident while following their employment. Seventhly, to shorten the hours of labour. The benefits of our local lodges are, a weekly allowance to members when sick, and allowance at the death of any member (or) member's wife.

H Browne, *The rise of British Trade Unions*, 1979

These benefits came from subscriptions that only well-paid skilled workers like engineers and carpenters could afford. Attempts to form unions among the less skilled were more difficult to sustain.

Nevertheless, the unions that did exist were alarmed by the bad publicity they were getting and concerned about changes in the law that might threaten them, so delegates from them came together in 1868 to form the Trades Union Congress. The TUC's Parliamentary Committee watched over their political interests. The TUC's secretary from 1875 to 1890, Henry Broadhurst, sat in parliament as an MP – but as a Liberal.

New unionism

Events in the late nineteenth century, however, began to change the character of unions. The growth of foreign competition led employers in Britain to try to cut their costs by reducing wages and increasing hours of work.

New unions emerged which sought mass membership (rather than a membership of limited numbers of skilled workers), and which behaved aggressively in their battles to establish themselves. In 1888, for example, Will Thorne helped to develop a union for gas workers. In 1889–1890 this union held strikes in the provinces that succeeded in reducing the length of shifts. Unskilled workers in building trades and on the railways began to organise. The Seaman's and Fireman's Union swelled to 65 000.

A Trade Union demonstration in Manchester to support farm labourers.

The matchmakers demonstration in London against working conditions, 1888.

Older unions changed too. Some of them merged to form more powerful bodies like the National Miners Association, organised by a Scot, Alexander MacDonald, and the National Union of Railwaymen (1913) formed from three separate unions. This whole development was encouraged by two successful strikes. In 1888 workers in Bryant and May's match factory won a battle against the dangerous, disgusting and ill-paid circumstances in which they toiled; in the following year Ben Tillett and Tom Mann led a lengthy strike for better pay in the London docks. From mid-August to mid-September 1889 dock workers went on strike for pay to be raised to sixpence an hour, for a minimum contract in a day of four hours (dockers were casual workers) and for overtime at eight pence an hour. The strike's success owed much to wider support (from as far away as Australia) which brought in money, and to the relief centres set up by the Lord Mayor where dockers could get meals.

The spread of socialism among the unions

The attitude of employers (some of whom were Liberals) encouraged trade unionists to think of supporting socialism. In addition, trade unionists eager to enter politics found that, even at a local level, the Liberal Party preferred to choose wealthier candidates. This encouraged such men to think of the need for a separate party. The changing mood of the times can be seen in the start of May Day celebrations in 1890 in London, when people marched along singing the new socialist song, 'The Red Flag'.

Counter-attacks by employers

Employers mounted successful counter-attacks. By 1894 Tillett's union had been ousted from the docks. Employers also increasingly used non-union labour, helped by the setting up of an organisation to supply them, for in 1893 William Collinson, an anti-union ex-bus driver, formed the National Free Labour Association. Moreover, employers began to group themselves. In 1894 the Federation of Engineering Employers was set up, and in 1898 a parliamentary committee was formed to protect employers' interests.

Government and the law

An unsympathetic government and legal system seemed to be in control. The Conservatives tended to support the employers. The Liberals, badly beaten in 1895, seemed divided, and were concerned with imperial and church matters. In 1896 the attitude of the legal system was shown in the case of Lyons vs. Wilkins: through it union rights to picket were severely restricted.

All these factors led the TUC to vote in favour of a resolution put forward by a delegate from the Amalgamated Society of Railway Servants.

TUC Resolution of 1899

That this congress having regard to its decisions in former years and with a view in securing a better representation of the interest of Labour in the House of Commons hereby instructs the Parliamentary Committee to invite co-operation on lines mutually agreed upon in convening a Special Congress of representatives from such of the above-named organisations as may be willing to take part to devise ways and means for securing the return of an increased number of Labour members to the next Parliament.

H Pelling, *The Origins of the Labour Party*

The man who proposed this resolution was not only a trade unionist, he also belonged to the Independent Labour Party, one of a number of political organisations that emerged in the late nineteenth century to fight for workers' interests by political action. Events were pushing together many trade unionists and those eager to develop a special political party for workers.

Why did labour and socialist parties emerge?

There are a number of possible reasons why organisations like the Independent Labour Party grew up in the late nineteenth century.

The spread of the franchise

By 1885 far more men could vote than 20 years earlier, and voting now took place in secret. Many working men, therefore, were encouraged to take an interest in politics. Some even hoped to become MPs, for in 1868 the rule requiring MPs to be considerable property owners had been swept away.

Social and economic conditions

Changing social and economic conditions in the late nineteenth century seemed favourable to the rise of socialism. Working people had more time for politics and there was a greater likelihood of their being able to read the numerous newspapers and magazines of the time. These publications included some, like Robert Blatchford's *Clarion*, that favoured reforms which would benefit the lives of ordinary people. In addition, it was easier to travel to meetings. It did not cost so much to travel by the electric trams of the 1890s and some skilled workers of the 1900s might even aspire to the ownership of a bicycle. As travel became easier and Britain's urban population grew, so the wealthier moved out to the suburbs. This left considerable areas – about 95 corresponded to parliamentary constituencies – which were dominated by working class housing. Amid this housing stood libraries where books were freely available, schools where education was provided, mechanics institutes where education was encouraged, and chapels where workers could develop public-speaking skills. Later Labour leaders like Philip Snowden were warm in praise of their chapel training.

The spread of socialist thinking

Writers spread socialist thinking through a number of popular books. For example, though the American Harry George would not have called himself a socialist, he argued for large-scale land reform in *Progress and Poverty* (1883). He maintained:

Everywhere you find distress and destitution in the midst of wealth, you will find that the land is monopolised; that instead of being treated as the common property of the whole people it is treated as the private property of individuals.

Over 100 000 copies of George's book sold in Britain in the 1880s. The author made a triumphant tour too.

The poet, designer and artist William Morris also argued for the transformation of society. He became a socialist when he despaired of the Liberal middle class ever really committing themselves to reform, saying:

as to real social changes, they will not allow them if they can help it. I can see no use in people having political freedom unless they use it as an instrument of leading reasonable lives; no good in education if, when they are educated, people have only slavish work to do. This release from slavery, it is clear, cannot come to people so long as they are subjected to the bare subsistence wages that are a necessity for competitive commerce.

In a very popular work entitled *Merrie England*, Robert Blatchford described how life would be improved if only society were reorganised:

I would set men to work to grow wheat and fruit and rear cattle and poultry for our own use. Then I would develop the fisheries and construct great fish breeding lakes. Then I would restrict our mines, finances, chem-ical works and factories to a number actually needed for the supply of our own people. Then I would stop the smoke nuisance by developing water power and electricity. In order to achieve these ends I would make all the land, mills, mines, factories, works, shops, ships and railways the property of the people. I would have towns rebuilt with wide streets and detached houses, with gardens and fountains. I would have public parks, public theatres. I would have all our children fed and clothed and educated at the cost of the State. I would have the people become their own artists, actors, musicians, solicitors and police.

The enormously popular novels of Charles Dickens encouraged people to think about social conditions. In addition investigators like Charles Booth, William Booth and Seebhom Rowntree wrote different kinds of works, carefully conducting interviews and compiling facts and figures which showed the poverty and misery of many lives.

Karl Marx, the greatest socialist thinker of all, spent the last thirty years of his life living in London, although he was German. He died in 1883. His major work *Das Kapital* was not translated into English until 1887 and remained largely unread even by most social reformers of the time.

Skilled workers were more likely than unskilled ones to read reformers' works. On the railways, for example, it was reckoned that the train drivers were far more radically minded than the porters (perhaps the latter were affected by their partial dependence on tips from wealthy passengers).

Socialist and labour societies

During the last 20 years of the nineteenth century a number of influential organisations emerged that favoured a drastic overhaul of society and government.

The Social Democratic Federation (1881)

This was one of the most socialist-minded of these groups. Yet, curiously, it was led by a respectably dressed top-hatted wealthy ex-Etonian, H M Hyndman. Hyndman was one of the few political figures of the time who had actually read *Das Kapital* (in 1881 he worked through a French translation). He had little time for trade unions, and his forceful and dominant personality drove away some of his early recruits, including William Morris, and Karl Marx's daughter Eleanor. The SDF developed branches across Britain, but its main power base lay in London among skilled workers. By the 1890s its membership may well have been around 2500. Its efforts in parliamentary elections met with complete failure, but in local council elections it did better.

Sidney and Beatrice Webb.

A 1907 rally of the Social Democratic Federation. The crowd includes Robert Tressell, author of a popular book *The Ragged-Trousered Philanthropist.*

The Fabian Society (1884)

The Fabian Society shared Hyndman's suspicion of trade unions, but otherwise had little in common with the SDF. It adopted the name of the Roman general Fabius who won a war by avoiding open battle and by slowly wearing down enemy strength. The society aimed to spread its socialist ideas gradually through discussions, lectures and publications. It produced a huge array of pamphlets (which even included worthy topics like 'Allotments and How to Get Them'). Its members included the playwright Bernard Shaw, the sociologist Graham Wallas and Sidney Webb and his formidable (and wealthy) wife Beatrice. The Webbs were influential members of investigating committees. Sidney Webb came to believe strongly in the work of councils and of government as a means of spreading socialism by slow reform. He wrote:

Important changes can only be (1) democratic and thus acceptable to a majority of the people and prepared for in the minds of all, (2) gradual, thus causing no dislocation, (3) not regarded as immoral by the mass of the people and (4) in this country at any rate, constitutional and peaceful.

The Independent Labour Party (1893)

The Independent Labour Party found its early strength in northern Britain. It emerged first in 1893 in Bradford, a Yorkshire textile town where industrial troubles were common, and where no less than 23 local labour clubs had been set up. Within two years the ILP had 305 branches, 105 of them in Yorkshire, 73 in Lancashire and Cheshire, and 41 in Scotland. The party stood for practical reforms that would benefit working people. Its leaders were eager to co-operate with trade unions. Because of this it decided to exclude the word 'socialist' from its title, so that it would not frighten away trade unionists who were used to looking to the Liberals as their allies. The ILP programme included demands for an end to child labour, proper provision for the sick, the disabled and the unemployed; and 'the collective ownership of the means of production, distribution and exchange'.

The ILP even had an MP, the Scottish ex-miner Keir Hardie. In 1888 Hardie had tried to win a by-election in Mid Lanark. His experiences convinced him of the need to develop a distinct party for Labour. The Scottish Labour Party emerged from his efforts. Hardie realised the need to win trade union support. He rarely read books of socialist theory. His temperance upbringing, however, remained very much with him, and once he was in parliament, Hardie tried hard to keep fellow Labour MPs away from the bar.

Poster for the Bradford East by-election in November 1896.

Ramsay MacDonald, an equally important figure, was drawn to Labour by a similar feeling of frustration with the Liberal Party. MacDonald came from the Scottish fishing port of Lossiemouth. Like Hardie he had to overcome a background of poverty and illegitimacy.

A third earlier ILP leader, Philip Snowden, recalled:

... many young men who were Nonconformist local preachers were attracted to the movement by the ethical appeal of Socialism. Their experience in speaking was a great help to the Party propaganda. The movement was something new in politics. It was politics inspired by idealism and religious fervour. Vocal Unions were

formed which accompanied cycling corps into the country at weekends and audiences were gathered on village greens by the singing of choirs.

Philip Snowden, *An Autobiography*

In 1892 Hardie won a by-election in West Ham, an area where the SDF were active. Two other ILP men won seats – John Burns in Battersea, and Havelock Wilson in Middlesborough. Hardie always remained loyal to the ILP, but the other two MPs drifted over to the Liberals.

Socialist enthusiasm showed itself in many ways. There were socialist swimming clubs, socialist scouts and socialist cycling clubs. Aided by the invention of the pneumatic tyre in 1888, members of the latter sped about the country combining business with pleasure. Yet parliamentary success was hard to come by. In 1895 all 28 ILP candidates were defeated. The handful of working men who sat in parliament following the break-through by Thomas Burt and Alexander MacDonald in 1874 were likely to be Liberals.

The ILP remained short of money and ramshackle in organisation. Nor were its social reforms necessarily popular. Reforms in Victorian times meant interfering officials, the loss to a family of children's earnings, the burden of school fees, and the hated poor law guardians. The clearance of slums left poorer families more crowded than ever, so inadequate was the building of new homes that they could afford.

It was little wonder that Hardie visited the TUC in 1887 to plead for it to support the separate political organisation that the ILP represented.

Trade union support

In 1900 delegates from some unions met representatives from the ILP, SDF and the Fabians. The result was the setting up of a body for joint political action, the Labour Representation Committee. It was made up of seven trade unionists,

two ILP delegates, two SDF delegates and a Fabian. It represented a triumph for Hardie's efforts to draw unions into backing a separate political organisation. Hardie thwarted SDF efforts to commit the LRC to openly socialist policies, for he felt that such policies might frighten away further union support. Yet the LRC was not strong. Its funds came chiefly from a levy on unions of 10s. for every thousand members. In the 1900 elections only two LRC men – Keir Hardie and Richard Bell – won seats. Bell proved to be a Liberal at heart, and in 1905 was expelled from the LRC.

The emergence of the Labour Party

In 1901 the unions supporting the LRC represented 353 700 workers. By 1908 the number had grown to a million. Fear for their security lay behind this change. In 1901 the House of Lords upheld the Taff Vale Railway Company's case for damages and losses (because of a strike) against the Amalgamated Society of Railway Servants. The union was required to pay the full costs of the strike (totalling £42 000). Other unions were horrified at the implications of this, and the LRC

James Ramsay MacDonald who for a time was secretary of the Labour Representation Committee.

leaders were quick to declare that they would work to reverse this decision. The rush of new members also brought funds to fight elections.

These signs of strength helped the LRC's secretary, Ramsay MacDonald, to organise an electoral pact with the Liberal chief whip, Herbert Gladstone. Gladstone's secretary warned him:

The LRC can directly influence the votes of nearly a million men. They will have a fighting fund of £100 000. Their members are mainly men who have hitherto voted with the Liberal Party. Should they be advised to vote against Liberal candidates and should they act as advised, the Liberal Party would suffer defeat. They would be defeated, but so also would we be defeated.

By-election results seemed to bear out these fears. In 1901 the LRC split the anti-government vote in northeast Lanark and let in a Tory. In 1902–1903 three by-elections (Clitheroe, Barnard Castle and Woolwich) were won by LRC men – David Shackleton, Arthur Henderson and Will Crooks. On major issues of the day, like free trade and Ireland, LRC and Liberals found themselves in agreement (especially since the SDF had left the LRC in 1901). Thus the LRC got a free run in a number of seats; and in return it agreed to give general support to the Liberal Party.

In the general election of 1906, what did LRC men stand for? In the view of one historian:

The typical Labour candidate of the 1900s offered the electorate a battery of proposals including the 8 hour day, reversal of the Taff Vale decision, employers' liability, old age pensions, poor law reform, the feeding of necessitous school children, taxation of land values, free trade, Home Rule, nationalisation of mine royalties, payment of MPs, curtailment of the power of the House of Lords and universal suffrage. There was virtually nothing in this that was not acceptable to the new Liberals, or to the Gladstonians for that matter.

M Pugh, *The Making of Modern British Politics*

Labour and the election of 1906

The election manifesto ran as follows:

This election is to decide whether or not Labour is to be fairly represented in Parliament.

The House of Commons is supposed to be the people's House and yet the people are not there.

Landlords, employers, lawyers, brewers and financiers are there in force. Why not Labour?

The Trade Unions ask the same liberty as capital enjoys.
They are refused.
The aged poor are neglected.
The slums remain; overcrowding continues, while the land goes to waste.

Shopkeepers and traders are overburdened with rates and taxation, whilst increasing land values which should relieve the ratepayers, go to people who have not earned them.

Wars are fought to make the rich richer and underfed school children are still neglected.

The unemployed ask for work, the Government gave them a worthless Act and now the red herring of protection is drawn across your path.

Production, as experience shows, is no remedy for poverty and unemployment. It seems to keep you from dealing with the land, housing, old age and other social problems.

You have in your power to see that Parliament carries out your wishes. The Labour Representation Executive appeals to you in the name of a million Trade Unionists.

Twenty nine candidates met with success, 24 of them in seats where no Liberal opposed them. The movement now changed its name to 'Labour Party' and pressed the Liberals for reforms.

The Liberals of 1905–1914 included men like Lloyd George who were eager to effect a number of reforms anyway. Certainly the 1906 Trade Disputes Act was directed at helping the unions by reversing the Taff Vale decision. Reductions in miners' working hours and control on certain 'sweated' trades – occupations like tailoring that took place in small workshops – pleased Labour too. Other Liberal social reforms were welcomed in general, but often sharply criticised in detail, generally for being too limited and mean.

It would be difficult to argue that the Liberal reforms were chiefly due to Labour pressure. By 1910 Labour found it difficult to know what to do. Elections were expensive, and it did not dare to risk bringing down the Liberals, yet the Liberals seemed chiefly concerned with matters other than those pressed by Labour.

Salaries for MPs

A further threat to Labour came in 1909. A Liberal trade unionist, Walter Osborne, objected to his railway union using part of his union subscription to support Labour. The House of Lords decided in Osborne's favour, thus preventing unions from contributing to political causes from their general funds and threatening the whole financial security of the Labour Party. In 1911 the Liberal Government gave partial relief by introducing salaries of £400 a year for MPs. Lloyd George argued:

The work of Parliament is greater, it is greater in quantity and volume of work, it is very much greater in the attention it demands at the hands of each individual member.

In the old days we had only two classes here. We had the great country families and the legal profession. Since

then you have brought in one class after another – the great middle class – the labouring population and factory representation. There is a large and growing class whose presence in this House is highly desirable, men of wide culture, of high intelligence and of earnest purpose whose services would be invaluable but whose limited means prevent their taking up a political career.

The Times newspaper grumbled:

It is perfectly well known that the Government have no conviction and that payment of members would never have been proposed by them were it not that they do not know how to meet the deficiency of dealing with the Osborne judgement. They know well that their expedient must have permanent and far-reaching consequence which will be evil. The whole thing is merely a gambler's throw. The Labour Party are quite ready to take the payment, but they have made it plain that they do not relinquish their demand for the reversal of the Osborne judgement.

The Times, 10 August 1911

By the end of 1910, a year in which two elections were held, the number of Labour MPs had risen to 42. This growth was especially due to the Miners Federation's decision to join the party. Could Labour look forward to an ever more effective role in the future?

The failure of Labour?

The Labour Party's fortunes from 1910 to 1914 have made historians consider how secure and effective a party it really was. There are a number of points to think about.

Labour's relationship with the Liberals

It took two years for the Liberals to offset partially the Osborne judgement by bringing in MPs' salaries. It took a further two years for them to modify the law itself through the Trade Union Act (1913). Even this did not wholly reverse the

Osborne judgement. Unions that wished to financially back a political party had to keep separate funds for this purpose. However this could only take place after a ballot of their members on whether they wanted their union to affiliate to a party. Indeed members had to give their individual agreement to providing financial support. The Liberal leadership seemed to take little account of Labour needs, yet Labour did not dare to strike out on its own and end its electoral pact.

Election results 1910–1914

In these years Labour fought 14 by-elections and came no higher than third in all of them. These by-elections included four contests for seats Labour had held; as a result the number of Labour MPs had shrunk by 1914.

Quarrels in the Labour Party

The Party seemed divided and quarrelsome, especially on the issue of how far Labour should commit itself to socialism. A typical debate flared up in the Labour Party summer conference in 1907 from which this extract is taken:

W. Atkinson moved

1 *This annual conference of the Labour Party hereby declares that its ultimate object should be the obtaining for the workers the full results of their labour by the overthrow of the present competitive system of capitalism and the institution of a system of public ownership and control of all means of life.*

2 *To organise and maintain a Parliamentary Labour Party with its own whips and whose policy shall be in the direction of attaining the above and also of carrying out the decisions of the annual conference.*

Pete Curran (Gas Workers) said that as a Socialist he opposed this amendment of the constitution. The socialist section was bound in honour to acknowledge that the delegates had not yet declared in favour of class conscious principles. Seven years ago they decided that the Trade Unionists, Socialists and Co-operators should form an alliance for the purpose of brining into existence an independent political party. The idea that permeated this amendment was to switch the movement to what was called class-conscious lines. The Trade Unionists who made up the bulk of the movement and contributed the funds of the Movement would not pledge themselves in this class conscientiousness.

J Keir Hardie (ILP), 'Suppose this amendment were carried? What followed would be that only men who were Socialists could be MPs. Was it desirable that those MPs who were not Socialists should be cleared out?'

A Beattie, *English Party Politics Vol. II*

The outcome was 98 000 voted in favour, 835 000 against.

In 1907 Victor Grayson won Colne Valley for Labour and proceeded to attack MacDonald and his colleagues. In 1911 some frustrated ILP members joined with the SDF to form the British Socialist Party. Yet MacDonald led Labour for most of this period. He had to withstand intense criticism. Ben Tillett, hero of the 1889 dockers' strike wrote:

I do not hesitate to describe the conduct of these blind leaders as nothing short of betrayal. They have displayed greater activity for temperance reform than for labour interests. A great many victims to destitution will be in their graves before the Liberal Government will have approached the subject of unemployment, which they will sandwich between the abolition of the House of Lords and Welsh Disestablishment. The temperance section in particular will be seizing on the other 'red herrings' and the winter will have passed and these unctuous weaklings will go on prattling their nonsense, while thousands are dying of starvation.

Ben Tillett, *Is the Parliamentary Labour Party a Failure?*, 1908

Beatrice Webb, one of the Fabian leaders, complained:

J R MacDonald seems almost preparing for his exit from the ILP. I think he would welcome a really conclusive reason for joining the Liberal Party. Snowden is ill, Keir Hardie 'used up'. The rank and file are puzzled and disheartened. The cold truth is that the Labour members have utterly failed to impress the House of Commons and the constituencies as a live force and have lost confidence in themselves and each other. The Labour Movement rolls on. The Trade Unions are swelling in membership and funds, more candidates are being put forward, but the faith of politically active members is becoming dim or confused whilst the rank and file become every day more restive. There is little leadership but a great deal of anti-leadership.

Beatrice Webb's Diaries, 1914

Trade union developments

The years from 1911 to 1914 were a time of great industrial unrest, with strikes and lockouts on a sizeable scale. During this time trade union membership rose from two to over four million. A number of big unions were formed (like the NUR and the National Transport Workers Federation) and three of the bigger unions – the Miners, the Railwaymen and the Transport Workers – formed a 'Triple Alliance' to support one another. To some, it seemed that this was the way to change society – by the direct action of unions, not through the Labour Party. Tom Mann led such 'syndicalists', borrowing ideas from similar movements in France and Spain. The syndicalist views were expressed in a pamphlet in 1912 backed by the South Wales Miners and partly written by A J Cook, a man who was to trouble Labour leaders in later years. The aim of the authors was to create:

One organisation to cover the whole of the coal, ore, slate, stone, clay, salt, mining and quarrying industry of Great Britain, with one Central Executive . . .

(With the aim) That the organisation shall engage in political action both local and national, on the basis of complete independence of, and hostility to all capitalist parties, with an avowed policy of wresting whatever advantage it can for the working man.

Alliances (are) to be formed and trades organisation favoured with a view to steps being taken to amalgamate all workers into one national and international union to work for the taking over of all industries by the workmen themselves. The suggested organisation is constructed to fight rather than to negotiate.

W H B Court, *British Economic History 1870–1917*, 1965

However, the evidence shows that these years were not entirely gloomy for Labour.

Union affiliation

Despite legal threats, union affiliation to Labour continued, and by 1914 covered a million and a half workers. In addition, the separate political funds required by the 1913 Trade Union Act may in fact have helped Labour. Money for the party was now specially laid aside – it did not have to compete with the other demands on the general fund.

Trade unionists attitudes

Most trade unionists were not syndicalists. The Triple Alliance did not have political aims, and the disputes of the period were about the usual issues of wages, hours and conditions. The tensions of 1910–1914 may even have helped Labour by widening the gulf between the Liberal middle classes and the trade unionists.

Local politics

In local politics Labour was a growing force. As early as 1898 the Party captured West Hammersmith council, and proceeded to give its workers two weeks' annual holiday, eight-hour working days and £1.10s per week minimum wages. Election results show Labour's rise:

Labour in municipal elections			
Year	Candidates		Number
	Labour	SDF/BSP	elected
1907	274	66	86
1908	313	84	109
1909	422	133	122
1910	281	49	113
1911	312	32	157
1912	463	95	161
1913	442	52	196

A new party

Labour was a very new party. Some of its problems were due to its very limited organisation. Paid party agents played a vital part in the complicated electoral procedures of the time by making sure that supporters were properly registered. However in 1912 Labour had only 17 agents, while the Liberals had nearly 300! Given time, and the money that the unions eventually provided, progress might be made. Certainly MacDonald worked hard to develop the party organisation.

The Daily Herald

In 1911 Labour gained the support of a successful popular newspaper – George Lansbury's *Daily Herald*.

Electoral reform

Some people thought that widening the vote to include all adults might benefit Labour. The party supported suffragists, who sought the vote for women by peaceful means. It also demanded the vote for all adults. Yet whether this would really benefit Labour was not clear. MacDonald thought that:

in places like the Potteries where poverty and degradation is of the blackest kind, the Labour Party is bound to be weak.

Quoted in M Pugh, *Modern British Politics*

The Great War, however, was to have a sharp impact on Labour fortunes.

The impact of the First World War

The start of the First World War split the Labour Party. The Party Chairman (MacDonald), Snowden and a cluster of mainly ILP members opposed the war; but the majority of the party supported British involvement in the conflict, and a senior member, Arthur Henderson, even joined the coalition government. Those hostile to the war joined the Union of Democratic Control where they met Liberals who shared their high-minded views on the proper conduct of foreign affairs. They had, at first, a hard time of it, as they were abused at meetings and persecuted by the popular press.

However, the wider Labour movement benefited from the war. Trade union membership stood at 4.145 million in 1914 but by 1919 it had risen to 7.926 million, as unions pulled back from the pre-war years of conflict with the state. Ministers listened more readily to union leaders, negotiated with them to obtain a temporary relaxation of rules about employing skilled men and placed them on committees. Though not all the unions were affiliated to the Labour Party, affiliated members doubled, and this growth greatly helped party finances. Interest in social issues like food and rent prices seemed to come more from the Labour movement than from the Liberals. This helped establish a mood that eventually drew over to Labour several Liberals who cared about social reform, such as Christopher Addison, William Wedgewood Benn, and

Charles Trevelyan. The latter commented, 'All social reformers are bound to gravitate as I have done, to Labour.' Nor were pro and anti-war Labour supporters totally divided. In the War Emergency Workers National Committee, contacts between them were kept, with agreement on issues like the need to raise wages and control rents. Lloyd George's dismissive treatment of Arthur Henderson, who wished to go to Stockholm to a conference of socialist delegates from countries involved on both sides of the conflict, drove that key Labour figure from the government. Henderson now concentrated on reuniting and developing the party. He worked in an optimistic atmosphere, as the Russian Revolution toppled the Czar, and socialism seemed to be on the march.

The 1918 constitution

In 1918 the party created a new constitution for itself. The chief architect of this was the Fabian, Sidney Webb. Webb believed in peaceful social reform, and stressed the importance of the power of the state to transform ordinary lives. Wartime events encouraged him, for state power had expanded to control rents, bring in rationing, and take charge of the economy. The most distinctive feature of the new constitutions was clause 4. In it the party aimed

to secure for the producers by hand or by brain the full fruits of their industry, and the most equitable distribution thereof that may be possible upon the basis of the common ownership of the means of production and the best obtainable system of popular administration and control of each industry or service.

This was the closest Labour came to clearly declaring itself to be a socialist party. Several historians have commented that although Labour included enthusiastic socialists, the bulk of the members were not really very interested in, or

committed to such a creed. As Martin Pugh has written:

Socialism was for Labour a symbol sufficiently vague to be impervious to mere day to day policies and events.

It served as a badge to mark out the party's distinctive character. The historian A R Ball observed,

Ideology was sub-servient to the important tasks of organising electoral success.

British Political Parties, 1981

Before the 1918 election Henderson had set to work to transform the party organisation. He developed local constituency parties and ward party branches based on individual memberships. The party's annual conference elected an executive of 11 representatives from unions, five from constituency parties, and four from women's sections. This cut into the power of the ILP and other socialist groups, for the trade union block vote dominated conferences. Thus equipped, Labour pulled out of the coalition just three days after the armistice ended the war. Although its organisation was just emerging, it managed to field 361 candidates. The newly widened electorate gave it over two million votes, though antiwar candidates like MacDonald tended to suffer defeat. Fifty-one of Labour's 60 MPs were union nominees – 25 of them for the Miner's Federation – and prone to adopt a line as patriotic as Lloyd George's ministry.

Labour also gained support from the Cooperative Movement. In 1917 the movement's annual Congress agreed to found a political party. One Co-op MP triumphed in the 1918 election, and joined the Labour group of MPs. Labour and Co-op candidates avoided fighting one another in elections.

Labour's post-war rise

Although the Labour Party was well organised by 1918, it did not really expect to be in office within six years. In the immediate post-war years it seemed possible that the Labour movement might pursue a different strategy from the slow peaceful route to power advocated by leaders like MacDonald. The years 1919–1921 were marked by widespread major industrial upheavals through strikes by miners, railwaymen, dockers, and even by some members of the police. Voices in the movement were heard to urge 'direct action' by workers as the way to change Britain.

The government was especially alarmed by events on Clydeside. In 1919, six tanks were based in the city and soldiers manned machine-guns at the windows of Glasgow hotels. Behind this fear of 'Red' Clydeside lay a period of upheaval. During the war the rise in house rents had led to strikes by the housewives of Govan and Partick that spread to 20 000 households and had helped to force the stoppage of rent increases during wartime. Local people had suffered a sharp swing in employment. Some employers angered workers by the forceful way in which they tried to break traditional working practices and bring in new machines. Shop stewards in the area began to lead workers' actions when their official union leaders seemed to be too timid. Socialist leaders were active in the area, including James Maxton of the ILP, and John Maclean, a Govan schoolteacher and a member of the Social Democratic Federation (SDF). Maclean had opposed the war and had so alarmed the authorities that he had spent much of the war in prison. But the efforts of the Clyde Workers' Committee (of local shop stewards) to call a general strike in 1919 failed. The ILP certainly did not seek revolution. The upheaval owed much to resentment at the tactless and aggressive behaviour of remote politicians and employers. In 1920 dockers opposed to the government policy of sending weapons to help Poland fight the USSR, refused to load the arms ship *Jolly George*, and thus thwarted Lloyd George's policy.

By 1922 the fear of the Labour Party leaders that the movement they sought to guide might lurch out of control was fading. On 15 April 1921 a key event took place: the miners struck against wage cuts but the other major unions refused to back them, and the miners were eventually compelled to return to work. Rising unemployment helped to dampen union activities too. Many unions reorganised themselves into larger units, such as the Amalgamated Engineering Union (1920) and the Transport and General Workers Union (1921). They strengthened their links with the Labour Party through a National Joint Council representing the TUC General Council, the National Executive of the Labour Party, and the Parliamentary Labour Party. The Liberal Party had no links to workers such as Labour had with the unions.

Labour Party leaders pursued cautious policies, refusing to allow the newly formed British Communist Party affiliate with them, and rejecting involvement with the Third International through which the USSR sought to guide socialists in other lands. Labour was able to exploit Lloyd George's retreat from social reform and his harsh policies towards trade unions.

In addition Labour also offered an idealistic foreign policy, attacking the old system that had led to conflict in 1914. The Labour Party absorbed the old UDC beliefs that the war was due to secret diplomacy, the arms race, and a mistaken pursuit of the theory of the balance of power. Labour stressed the value of the new League of Nations. These were attractive ideas to a war-weary nation. ILP leaders like MacDonald and Snowden returned to Parliament, no longer blamed for opposing a war which was now widely seen as dreadful in its impact. MacDonald's wartime stand helped him to win sufficient left-wing support to secure him the leadership of the Party. The historian Martin Pugh believes that events after 1914 allowed

Labour to inherit the mantle of radicalism and to rally middle class and working class progressives under its wing.

History VI, No. 5

Labour's organisation improved too. Dr Marion Phillips led the new Women's Section. Four Standing Committees served the National Executive, and these dealt with organisation and elections, policies, literature and research, and finance and general purposes. By 1922 the *Daily Herald* relied upon financial support from Labour and preached the party's policies. Henderson's drive to set up local party branches was taking effect in industrial areas. In Bradford, for example, a party branch was formed in 1919 from the ILP, the Trades Council and the Workers' Municipal Federation. Branches like Bradford, Leeds, and Huddersfield were able to support full-time agents. Michael Savage has suggested that:

The Labour Party underwent a fundamental change in character in the early 1920s in many areas; it changed from a party based on certain trade unions to one based on neighbourhood organisations.

The Dynamics of Working Class Politics, 1987

Ramsay MacDonald played a key role in establishing the character of the Labour Party. His aim was to edge out the Liberals and make Labour the second party. His impressive appearance, effective oratory, and winning personality made him the dominant force in the party. MacDonald was adept at describing a socialist utopia, using the vaguest of language, whilst actually advocating the most cautious of policies designed to win the widest support.

Liberal troubles

The 1922 election ended the Liberal Lloyd George's period of political leadership. Several historians maintain that the rise of the Labour Party was, in the period after 1914, partly due to the growing troubles of the Liberal Party. These troubles helped MacDonald's policy of establishing labour.

It was a divided Liberal Party that fought the 1918 election. The results produced 62 MPs who followed Lloyd George's leadership and 54 who still followed Asquith, the man who had been Prime Minister till 1916. But even when the two sections of Liberal MPs were united, they were outnumbered by the 142 Labour MPs elected in 1922. In part, then, Labour owed its rise to Liberal troubles.

War's impact

Some historians see Liberal troubles beginning before 1914 with divisions in the Party and a weakening Liberal grip on local government. The declaration of war on Germany led to a time of increasing division in one party. Two Ministers, Burns and Morley, promptly resigned. Another group that included men like Charles Trevelyan and Arthur Ponsonby felt uneasy about British involvement in the war and helped form the Union of Democratic Control. There they met like-minded Labour men and eventually tended to find a home in the Labour Party. Lloyd George led Liberals who wanted the war conducted vigorously even if it meant going against Liberal principles and using government power to interfere in people's lives. The introduction of conscription proved particularly distressing to Liberal consciences.

Asquith's reluctance to act decisively led to his losing power to Lloyd George in December 1916. A bitter division between them never healed. About 120 Liberals backed the new Prime Minister and until 1922 these Liberals held on to power as a result of joining in close coalition with the Conservatives. This left Asquith's Liberals short of money and lacking in a strong party organisation.

Several historians, seeing the divided state of the Liberals by 1918, have concluded that the Great War did them immense harm. Robert Blake, for example, has written:

The Liberals were fatally handicapped. On almost every issue that came up, Conservative tradition and ideology were better suited than Liberal to meet the needs of the hour ... The necessities of a prolonged war tended to create doubts and divisions in the Liberals.

The Conservative Party from Peel to Churchill, 1970

Even more bluntly, Trevor Wilson has observed:

The Liberal Party can be compared to an individual who, after a period of robust health and great exertion, experienced symptoms of illness (Ireland, Labour unrest, and the suffragettes). Before a thorough diagnosis could be made he was involved in an encounter with a rampant omnibus (the First World War) which mounted the pavement and ran him over. After lingering painfully, he expired.

T Wilson, *The Downfall of the Liberal Party*, 1966

Post war Liberal troubles

The Labour Party was able to reunite after 1918 but the Liberals remained divided. Only 28 Asquith Liberals were successful in the 1918 election whilst 133 Coalition Liberals triumphed and continued, till 1922, to work with the Conservative Party to sustain Lloyd George's Government.

Several of his policies caused further worry and his harsh treatment of his Minister of Health, Christopher Addison, drove the latter over to the Labour Party.

Nor could Liberals rely any longer on Irish Nationalist support, for the 1918 election virtually wiped out that party, replacing it with Sinn Fein, a movement that demanded Irish independence. To add to this, Lloyd George's forceful personal style and the risky foreign policy he pursued in backing Greece over a war with Turkey, eventually pushed his Conservative Coalition parties into mutiny. They rallied behind a junior Minister, Stanley Baldwin, and voted to abandon the Liberal alliance.

Around 29 per cent of the voters chose Liberal candidates in the 1922 election, a figure very similar to Labour's. But the Liberals were split. Their organisation was in poor shape, their leader (Asquith) was seventy in 1922 and far from effective. The historian Martin Pugh suggests the new mass electorate did not mean that the Liberal Party was necessarily doomed, nor unable to cope with new political conditions, but rather that:

Liberal decline must be attributed less to structural changes than to wartime political changes which, by 1918, had began to push existing Liberal supporters towards Labour and indeed towards Conservatism.

History VI, Vol. 5

Liberal loss was Labour's gain and seemed to justify MacDonald's policy of refusing to collaborate with Liberals.

➤ ACTIVITIES

1 Historians have drawn different conclusions about the situation of the Labour Party before 1914. Choose one of the three following views and plan an essay that will discuss it.

a) *'The Labour Party's growth in the early twentieth century was inevitable, given the social and economic issues of the time.'*
K Laybourn, *The Rise of Labour*

b) *'The end of this period (to 1914) found the Labour Party dependent upon the Liberals, dissatisfied with its achievements, unsure of its aim and apparently in decline.'*
C Brand, *The British Labour Party*

c) *'There are no real grounds in voting behaviour for believing Labour to have been poised to take over from the Liberals in 1914, on the contrary, without the protection of the pact the Parliamentary Party would have been reduced to a handful.'*
M Pugh, *Modern British Politics*

2 Do Harry George's views in *Progress and Poverty* 1883, accurately explain the increasing numbers who supported the Labour movement? (Evaluating a source with reference to context.)

Chapter Five

The Changing Political Identity of Britain

Your studies of the widening of the franchise, the coming of female suffrage and the development of the Labour movement already provide evidence of the changing political identity of Britain. This chapter contains further evidence about how this identity changed between mid-Victorian times and 1928.

As a result of studying the material in this chapter you should have a sound understanding of:

◆ The growth of modern political parties.

◆ Ways in which parties tried to win votes.

◆ The different identities of political parties.

◆ Whether Britain, by 1928, can be called a democracy.

By drawing on this chapter and by considering the earlier chapters, you should be in a position to discuss and write about the question:

In what ways did the political identity of Britain change, 1867–1928?

TASK

After studying this chapter plan and write an essay on the following:

'It was during the period 1850–1914 that the modern political party was born in Britain.' Do you agree?

In order to do this, consider and make notes to answer the following questions:

◆ What are the features of a modern political party?

◆ Were any of these features present in the 1850s?

◆ Were they present in 1914?

◆ Why did developments take place between these dates?

◆ Who played a major part in bringing about changes?

◆ Do the changes justify agreement with the essay title?

Once your notes are complete, compare and discuss them with others. Then write out the essay. It may help to refer briefly to or quote from the views of historians and people at the time.

The growth of political parties

Before 1867

Neither the Conservative nor the Whig–Liberal Parties were well organised in the mid-nineteenth century. Both were loose alliances of differing groups. Party leaders had only a very limited control over their followers and could suffer several defeats on their proposed legislation without being unduly worried.

Each party had a London-based club (The Tory Carlton Club and The Liberal Reform Club) and each had set up organisations that made sure those of their followers who qualified were properly registered as voters.

But neither party was well organised in parliament or in the country. There was no real continuity of activity in constituencies between elections and no developed party organisations to make that possible. There were a number of MPs who did not feel strongly bound to either party and for much of the time (the historian Robert Blake suggests) real differences between parties were small. Each group was chiefly concerned with winning the struggle for office rather than carrying out a particular political programme.

However by 1867 developments were taking place that made the emergence of national political parties more feasible. A national network of cheap newspapers (freed from stamp and paper duty and printed on high-speed steam-powered presses) offered opportunities that imaginative party leaders could exploit. There were important educational developments that increased the number of ordinary people who were well able to read. In 1870 in England and 1872 in Scotland, education acts were passed that required all children to attend school and develop their abilities in reading, writing and arithmetic. At the same time libraries developed and by the end of the

century almost all sizeable communities possessed these centres of study.

In many places in industrial Britain, Mechanics Institutes were founded to become centres for discussion and for lectures on issues of the day.

The consequences of widening the franchise

A number of MPs opposed the changing of the country's political identity by giving the vote to many working men. One member of the Liberal Party, Robert Lowe, argued:

If you want ignorance, if you want drunkenness, if you want impulsive and violent people, where do you look for them in the constituencies? Do you go to the top or to the bottom? The working men, finding themselves in a majority will awake to a full sense of their power. They will say 'we can do better for ourselves'.

Robert Lowe lived to see Labour's rise to form a Government in 1924. But the widening of the franchise went ahead, even if the forms it took in 1867 and 1884 were based on taking into the system men who had some sort of stake in society rather than on the principle that all citizens had a right to the franchise.

The widening franchise itself produced social changes. After 1867 even Robert Lowe saw the need for a mass education system; he declared:

From the moment you entrust the masses with power, their education becomes a necessity. You have placed the Government of this country in the hands of the masses and you must therefore give them an education.

Hansard

Britain's changing political identity as a result of the wider franchise alarmed several party leaders.

In 1867 the Conservative politician Lord Carnarvon explained his worry that the 1867 Reform Act would make life impossible for his party:

I am convinced that we are in a very critical position.

Household suffrage will produce a state of things in many boroughs the results of which I defy anyone to predict. In Leeds, for example, the present number of electors are about 8500. With household suffrage they will become about 35 000. Is there anyone who dares to say what will be the character and tendency of that constituency? It may be good or bad; but it is a revolution. The Conservative Party is in imminent danger of going to pieces now if indeed it does not disappear in the deluge that the Government are bringing on.

D G Wright, *Democracy and Reform*

He was right to be concerned. Giving the vote to far more people had a major impact on political parties. Many voters already felt an attachment to a political leader and his party. In the 1860s it was not always easy to see strong policy differences. Both parties favoured free trade and both supported parliamentary reform in the later 1860s. But during the later nineteenth century attempts were made to distinguish between the policies of the two parties. Closely linked to this was a tendency to appeal to some groups in society rather than to others.

1867–1884/5 produced a system that pushed party leaders into policies that might offend the wealthy but were popular with rank and file members. Thus the university Test Acts opened up teaching posts at Oxford and Cambridge to men who were not Anglicans. The practice of allowing men to buy positions as officers in the infantry was stopped. The legal position of trade unions was improved.

Taking the Party to the people

By the 1880s the canvassing of voters in boroughs, and the use of rallies, posters and propaganda were common. Party supporters wore the colour of their party, though there was some confusion in this since neither party had yet developed exclusive claim to one colour in particular. In Suffolk, for example, Conservatives wore blue. Not far away, in Cambridge, Liberals also sported blue. By the late 1880s party leaders were beginning to tour Britain making major speeches, and to have their words not only reported in the provincial press, but also printed for distribution. In 1887 the Marquis of Salisbury, by then leader of the Conservatives, grumbled:

This dirty business of making political speeches is an aggravation of the labours of Your Majesty's servants which we owe entirely to Mr Gladstone.

M Pugh, *The Making of Modern British Politics*, 1982

William Ewart Gladstone had a major impact on the image of the Liberal Party. He served as Chancellor of the Exchequer in 1852 and 1859–1866, and then as Prime Minister (1868–1874, 1880–1885, 1886 and 1892–1894). He brought to politics a deep belief in the importance of moral causes. Gladstone was a very devout Christian. He himself belonged to the Church of England but he also attracted backing from members of other churches who admired his strong religious beliefs. He made political issues into moral causes. He believed in free trade, low taxes and checking government spending. He was very impressed by changes in the labour movement and was ready to extend the vote to the upper working class. He supported peaceful foreign policies and also came to work for home rule for Ireland. He possessed great skill as a speaker and was able to rouse huge gatherings of ordinary people. In 1879–1880 he held his Midlothian campaigns, trying to stir up the country against the Conservative Government by a country-wide rail tour, stopping at key points to address the crowds who had been notified of his coming. One of his supporters. John Morley, later wrote a history of his hero's life in which he described these campaigns:

Nothing like it had been seen before. 'Statesmen' had

enjoyed great popular receptions before, and there had been plenty of cheering and bell ringing and torchlight in individual places before. On this journey ... it seemed as if the whole countryside were up. The stations where the train stopped were crowded, thousands flocked from neighbouring towns and villages to main centres along the line of the route ... All that followed in a week of meetings and speeches was to match. People came from the Hebrides to hear Mr Gladstone speak. Where there were 6000 seats, the applications were 40 or 50 000. The weather was bitter and the hills were covered with snow, but this made no difference in cavalcades, processions and the rest of the outdoor demonstrations.

John Morley, *The Life of William Ewart Gladstone,* 1903

Gladstone's opponents were reluctantly forced to follow suit and the age of the national leader touring the country to make speeches on national issues had been born. The Marquis of Salisbury's early efforts, one observer noted, were not very impressive:

Lord Salisbury was forced to yield to the democratic spirit so far as to 'go on the stump' and address popular audiences in great towns. It was an uncongenial employment ... His voice was clear and penetrating, but there was no popular fibre in his speech. He talked of the things which interested him; but whether or not they interested his hearers he seemed not to care a jot. When he rolled off the platforms and into the carriage which was to carry him away there was a general sense of mutual relief.

George W E Russell, in *F E Higgett*

With time, however, Salisbury's technique improved.

It became important to encourage voters to identify with their leaders and by 1928, with the

Gladstone travelling by train to address the voters during the Midlothian Campaign, 1879.

coming of radio and the setting up of the BBC there were new opportunities for reaching voters. The Conservative Leader, Stanley Baldwin rapidly learned the skill of seeming to be giving a personal and informal chat rather than a big speech.

Party organisation

The increasing number of voters, the secret ballot, and anti-corruption legislation made it vital for a successful political party to develop an efficient and permanent organisation. The old ways of stitching together support were no longer enough. The spreading grip of political parties across the country can be seen in the fall of the number of seats that were not fought. In 1859 there were 383 uncontested constituencies, in January 1910 only 75. The figures fluctuated, partly according to how united the Liberals were and how much money they could raise.

The flight of rich people from the Liberals gave the Conservatives the edge here and Gladstone certainly regarded the heavy-spending pro-Conservative brewers as serious opponents. Some of the uncontested seats were in Ireland where no one was prepared to stand against Nationalists. Nevertheless the general trend was down. More seats were fought regularly after 1880 than before, and such efforts required good organisation.

Voter registration played an important part in stimulating party growth. The electoral roll of voters was compiled in January (in England and Wales) and in November (in Scotland) from figures gathered earlier. When potential voters increased in number, making sure that one's supporters were registered developed into a major job. Registration took place before a revising barrister and with him objections could be raised about the voters one's opponents were attempting to register. In Newcastle in 1888–1891, for example, Conservatives raised objections to 9500 names. Moreover regulations changed from time to time. In 1907 lodgers with their own front door key to a building were allowed to register as householders. Alert party agents were quick to boost their support by exploiting this. It thus became important for parties to have a large network of paid agents for this work, as well as to organise publicity, electioneering, and other tasks. By 1891 the agents of both the parties had formed professional bodies, with examinations, benevolent funds, and minimum salary scales.

Party agents worked alongside an expanding number of party clubs and branch associations. These clubs consisted usually of two or three rooms where drinks were served, billiards were provided and social events were organised. The clubs also served to help morale, recruit members, and provide volunteer labour.

The branch associations were made up of people seriously committed to their party's cause. Thus, while few MPs had to deal with organised parties in their constituencies in the 1860s, the situation had changed enormously by 1914. The Liberal Party especially experienced dramatic developments, which were spearheaded by Joseph Chamberlain's Birmingham Liberals. In 1865 this branch constructed a system of representatives elected by party members in wards, who came together in a general committee to decide policy and select candidates for elections. Since the committee was large, an executive committee was formed, partly by ward-election, and partly from people nominated by the general committee. This was a far more organised system than had hitherto existed; it also threatened to push its policies at the party leadership, rather than doing meekly as it was told. Some leading Liberals were alarmed by it, finding it too American in style, and calling it rule by a caucus (i.e. minority). Nevertheless, numerous other urban Liberal associations copied that of Birmingham. In 1877

Chamberlain called a meeting of all such associations to establish the National Liberal Federation. Ninety-five branches took part. This NLF threatened to be a very different organisation from the Liberal Central Association (set up in 1874 and run by party whips to raise money and to encourage the growth of loyal party branches). In 1877 the Whig leader Hartington complained of the NLF:

It is almost certain to put the management into the hands of the most advanced men because they are the most active ... to the exclusion of the more moderate and easy-going Liberals. There is a good deal of the American caucus system about it.

P Adelman, *Gladstone, Disraeli and Later Victorian Politics*

The Birmingham caucus secretary from 1873, Frank Schnadhorst, emerged as NLF secretary too. Hartington had good reason to fear that the NLF was intended to be a Radical challenge to Whig power in the party. Chamberlain vigorously defended this new development, saying:

Party is an instrument to achieve some more definite results than the return to office of a certain number of persons of undeclared opinions ... At the present moment Liberals are at a loose end, each advocating some favourite reform.

The Liberals of Birmingham have fully recognised the altered conditions under which they have to carry on their work. Owing to various causes, and notably to the extension of the suffrage and to the increased interest taken by the mass of the people in general politics, it is absolutely necessary that the whole of the party should be taken into its counsels and that all its members should share in its control and management. It is no longer safe to (accept) the nominee of a few gentlemen ... willing to subscribe something towards expenses ... The object of a Liberal association should therefore be to secure a perfect representation of the opinions of the whole party.

Conservatism naturally works from above downward while Liberalism best fulfils its mission when it works upwards from below.

A Beattie, *English Party Politics, Vol. 1*

Certainly the Birmingham caucus proved to be very successful at winning all three local seats in general elections and at mounting effective campaigns in local elections. In the 1886 split the NLF remained loyal to Gladstone and drew closer to the Liberal Central Association. In the early twentieth century a new chief party agent, Hudson, emerged, and he worked well with his party's political leaders.

Liberal efforts had alarmed Conservative leaders, and even before the creation of the NLF had led them to form the National Union of Conservative and Constitutional Associations (1867). In 1870 Disraeli placed the very capable John Gorst in charge of this body and he developed the organisation that eventually became the Conservative Central Office. In 1881 he explained some of the work of this organisation:

Enquiries are made as to the residence and qualification of the voters ... Forms, instructions and advice are furnished. Local leaders are assisted in finding suitable candidates. Election literature is supplied. Formation of new associations is promoted and assisted. Speakers and hints for speakers are provided. Pamphlets, important speeches are printed and issued. All bills affecting the interests of the party are circulated amongst the local leaders.

A Beattie, *English Party Politics, Vol. 1*

Whereas Liberal associations developed as organisations seeking at times to influence policy, their Conservative counterparts were developed as a response to orders from above and were expected to do as they were told. In the early 1880s Gorst and Randolph Churchill made an attempt to give the National Union more power to challenge party leadership, but it came to nothing.

In 1881 the Conservatives established the Primrose League, named after what was thought to be Disraeli's favourite flower and colour. By 1910 it had two million subscribing members. The League did not indulge in detailed policy discussions instead it rallied volunteer support for the party and, between elections, organised concerts, fetes, outings and other social occasions. It proved invaluable in holding together party supporters and, especially, in drawing women to the Conservative cause. Nursing a constituency in-between elections had become a very important activity. In 1892 the Wiltshire *County Mirror* observed that candidates won votes by:

. . . the visit to the village feasts, the chat in the village schoolroom, or pleasant friendly musical evenings in the winter.

> H Pelling, *Social Geography of British Elections*, 1967

The voters of the 1850s would scarcely have recognised the activities characteristic of the election in 1910. The number of voters, the relatively humble status of many of these voters, the secret ballot, the party efforts to turn out their supporters, the absence of large-scale open bribery, and the importance attached to party leaders and national issues were all signs of a transformed political world. The massive increase in voter numbers brought about by electoral reform in 1918 and 1928 increased the emphasis on party organisation and leadership.

The identity of political parties

Labour

The emergence of the Labour Party and its struggle to give itself a separate identity has been dealt with in the previous chapter. The 1918 constitution (especially Clause 4) and Labour views on foreign affairs as well as MacDonald's determined refusal to do deals with the Liberal Party, all added up to the establishing in the voters' minds of a distinct identity for the Party. Labour's close links with the trade union movement – indeed its very real need for union organisation and funds – further marked it out as a distinct party by the 1920s. The first Labour Government of 1924 did not last long, but its behaviour and policies helped MacDonald establish Labour's respectability. He said:

They have demonstrated that they, no less than any other party, recognise their duties and responsibilities and have done much to dispel the fantastic and extravagant belief that they were nothing but a band of irresponsible revolutionaries intent on wreckage and destruction.

MacDonald and his followers continued to argue that a better life for working people should be achieved through the Labour Party and not through the direct action urged by some others. In 1926 a General Strike by trade unions in support of coal miners' attempts to resist cuts in wages and an increase in hours seemed to threaten this policy. But the strike failed, Labour returned to office in 1929 and MacDonald seemed to have succeeded in his determination to make the Labour movement fit into the normal peaceful parliamentary system.

Liberals

What did the Victorian Liberal Party stand for? Whose support did it attract? One significant strand of support was provided by the many thousands of devout nonconformist churchgoers. The religious census of 1851 showed that half the country's worshippers were nonconformist (that is, those who did not attend Catholic or Church of England services). The historian Henry Pelling suggests:

In small towns and country villages the ministers and the lay preachers were the backbone of Liberal strength.

H Pelling, *The Social Geography of British Elections*, 1967

This strength was especially to be found in the English Midlands and in Wales and Scotland.

In January 1880 the journal *The Nonconformist* observed that it was the Liberal Party which:

. . . has striven to be 'the party of Christ', the party of moral principles as against that of selfish and corrupt interests, the party of peace as against that of violence, the party of popular improvement and reform as against that of resistance to progress, the party of justice . . . The strength of the Liberal Party is in the force of individual social conscience.

P Adelman, *Gladstone, Disraeli and Later Victorian Politics*, 1970

William Gladstone, the dominant Liberal of the Victorian age, tapped such feelings. Though he was himself Anglican, he was passionately concerned about moral causes. His return to politics (after retiring in 1875) was inspired by his loathing of Conservative foreign policy at a time when Turkish rulers had killed large numbers of Bulgarians living in their empire. Gladstone believed Disraeli was too concerned with propping up Turkey as a barrier to Russian expansion. His views led to the 1880 election involving a much clearer choice for voters than most earlier elections: foreign policy issues dominated. Moreover, Gladstone began to despair of wealthy people's attitudes. He declared during the Midlothian campaigns:

We cannot reckon upon what is called the landed interest, we cannot reckon upon the clergy of the established churches. We cannot reckon on the wealth of the country nor upon the rank of the country.

P Adelman, *Gladstone, Disraeli and later Victorian Politics*

Such views helped to push wealthy Whigs out of the party. This took time, however, and was not really deliberate. Indeed rich titled landowners were more likely to be members of Gladstone's cabinet than were Radicals. When Gladstone retired (temporarily) in 1875, the problem of finding a leader and policies on which the party could agree, was clearly seen by the Whig leader, Hartington. In 1875 he wrote:

My suggestion . . . was not exactly that we should do without a leader; but that the Whigs or moderate Liberals should have one, the Radicals another and the Irishmen a third. I think that there is hardly any important question on which the Whigs and Radicals will not vote against each other; Disestablishment, Household Suffrage in Counties, Education, Land Laws, etc. and the position of a nominal leader seeing his flock all going their own way without attending to him, will not be comfortable. If each section had its own leader and its own organisation, it seems to me that there might be more real union and co-operation on points where we could agree than if we were nominally united; when each section would complain and quarrel every time the party organisation was not used to support its views . . .

M Willis, *Gladstone & Disraeli: Principles & Policies*, 1989

Gladstone himself recognised the problem of presenting a clear Liberal image saying:

The problem for me is to make if possible a statement which will hold through the election and not go into conflict with either the right of the party, for whom Hartington has spoken, or the left for whom Chamberlain spoke.

Joseph Chamberlain had been pushing forward reforms that would have changed the franchise, the distribution of seats, education and taxation. Hartington began to think,

I see nothing for the Whigs but to disappear or turn Tory.

In 1886 Gladstone accelerated the departure of the Whigs by declaring his support for home rule for Ireland. His Irish policy had already upset them by attacking the authority of the landlords. By 1906 only 8 per cent of Liberal MPs were major landowners. Those abandoning Gladstone included Chamberlain who, though a Radical, opposed home rule as a vote-loser and as an attack on the Empire. The Whigs and Chamberlainites became Liberal Unionists. Together they mustered 93 votes, enough to wreck home rule. In 1895 Chamberlain completed this shift in politics by joining a Conservative cabinet.

Home rule provided a simple test as to whether one was a Liberal. It reduced the party to 191 MPs in the 1886 election and left it searching desperately for able leaders behind whom to unite. But it eased the way for those keen on reform. In 1891 the National Liberal Federation put forward its 'Newcastle Programme' which asked for temperance reform, reform of the House of Lords, taxation of land values and mineral royalties, the disestablishment of the Welsh and Scottish churches, and home rule for all appropriate areas of the UK. It was widely accepted in the Party. Liberals still differed on issues – some opposed the Boer War (as did Lloyd George); others were 'Liberal Imperialists' in favour of a vigorous imperial policy. But, from 1903, they were able to rally round a single cause, for as Joseph Chamberlain worked to convert the Tories to taxes on foreign imports (tariff reform), Liberals were able to unite round the policy of free trade. As Lloyd George put it in 1908:

I am standing for Britain and the flag of freedom in her markets. That flag has stood for free trade for 50 years and the results are superb.

Liberals did well in the 1906 elections by denouncing the Tories. But in the 1910 elections they suffered heavy losses and historians debate whether, by this time, Liberalism had based itself on too few sectors of the population to survive as a major party. George Dangerfield speculated whether the problems of the time (the Irish question, the House of Lords, the suffragettes, and industrial troubles) were just too much for it. Others have pointed to the rise of the Labour Party and have noted the reluctance of Liberal constituency parties to rival it by picking working class candidates themselves. Henry Pelling has suggested Liberal decline might be:

The result of long-term social and economic changes that were simultaneously uniting Britain geographically and dividing her inhabitants in terms of class.

H Pelling, *A Short History of the Labour Party*, 1961

But Paul Adelman argues:

There is no hard evidence for the supposed demoralisation of the Liberal Party. Asquith's leadership was unquestioned; his government remained strong, unified and confident. It would be false to conclude that we are faced with a Liberal Party in decline in the years preceding the First World War.

Modern History Review

Liberals stood for home rule, a minimal amount of social reform, and free trade. This was perhaps not enough, when, according to Alan Ball:

At the end of the nineteenth century social class division replaced local issues and religious cleavages as the major dimensions of British politics.

A Ball, *Political Parties*, 1987

The Conservatives

The key figure in the development of the mid-Victorian Conservative Party was Benjamin Disraeli. He appears at first to be an unlikely leader. He was the son of a Jewish literary man, educated at obscure schools (and never went to university), almost arrested for debt and he made such a disastrous maiden speech as an MP that it was howled down. However, Disraeli was very ambitious, he was highly gifted, and he was rather fortunate. He learned how to speak well, he befriended a wealthy Tory MP George Bentick and he married a wealthy lady. His attacks on Robert Peel's decision to scrap the Corn Laws brought him fame and party popularity and helped cause the split that removed the Peelite faction (including Gladstone) who would have barred his own progress. His political skills were displayed from 1867–1868, and in 1874–1880 he finally led a Conservative ministry that had a clear majority. This ministry pushed through social reforms in public health and housing, in the safety of merchant shipping, and in trade union reform. Disraeli made much of his party's enthusiasm for the British Empire and for a vigorous foreign policy that placed British interests first. His biographer, Robert Blake, maintains:

Disraeli made the Conservatives both the party of empire and the party of a strong, or as his enemies would have said, jingoistic foreign policy. There was nothing inevitable about this development. In Palmerston's day those were the attributes of the Whig/Liberal Party ... From the 70s onwards, the Conservatives were identified with the cause of British nationalism, British ascendancy and the pursuit of purely British interests.

R Blake, *Disraeli*, 1969

Another historian sees further importance in Disraeli's career:

Modern Conservatism('s) ... electoral success since 1867 would have been impossible without its capacity to command a significant working class vote, and here it owes something to Disraeli's sense of the necessity of accepting the enlargement of the political nation and making the social condition of the people one of the prime objects of the party's concern.

P Smith, *Disraelian Conservatism & Social Reform*, 1967

However, not all historians are so enthusiastic. One of them has suggested:

Disraeli held the Conservative Party together through a period of confusion in parliament. But the making of the Conservative Party ... had to do with circumstances beyond Disraeli, – with the death of Palmerston and the inevitable shift of his Conservative followers, with the disintegrating effect of Gladstone's leadership on the Liberals.

A Tucker, *Canadian Journal of Economics and Political Science*, 1962

In the 1880s the Conservatives benefited from the continuing drift to their ranks of wealthy men who had once been Whigs. They exploited the Liberal split over home rule and found their ranks swelled by Liberal Unionists. Indeed it has been suggested that the Irish question benefited them in other ways too, bringing support in Glasgow from anti-home rule members of the Orange Order and support in Liverpool from voters opposed to the flood of Irish Roman Catholic immigrants.

Parliamentary reform also helped. The redistribution of seats in 1885 was so managed as to create separate suburban Tory-voting constituencies in urban areas where such voters had once been swamped in larger electorates. As Salisbury himself suggested:

there is a great deal of 'Villa Toryism' that requires organisation.

Conservative leaders continued to stress that their party stood for the British Empire and for a vigorous foreign policy. They exploited Queen Victoria's Jubilee and Britain's eventual success in the Boer War.

But in the twentieth century these causes brought trouble. Firstly, Tories argued that Irish home rule attacked the empire and this led them to back Ulster's resistance to it. Eventually, as the official parliamentary opposition, they seemed to be supporting armed hostility to the policies of Britain's elected (Liberal) government. Then in 1903 Joseph Chamberlain led a campaign for tariff reform, which was intended to bind the British Empire more closely together, while taxing imports from foreign lands in order to protect British industries. But the campaign split the party and led to conflict outside parliament between the Tariff Reform League and the Free Food League.

Yet the Conservatives also remained aware that they needed to stand for reforms. The setting up of county councils, the limiting of shop hours, the Workmen's Compensation Act (for industrial injuries) of 1897, and the Education Act of 1902 were all signs of this continuing desire to be a party for more than just the wealthy.

Radical opponents like Lloyd George attacked the Conservatives as the party of the rich. In 1892 Lloyd George declared:

What are the components of the Tory Party in our country? It contains practically the whole of the members of the privileged classes. Their numbers and far more their wealth and influence constitute the chief ingredients of its power. They must, therefore, wield its policy.

H du Parcq, *Life of Lloyd George*, 1912

It is certainly true that leaders like Lord Salisbury and A J Balfour came from aristocratic backgrounds. About a quarter of Edwardian Conservative MPs were wealthy landed gentry and half came from industry and commerce, especially from certain trades like brewing (the consequence, perhaps, of the long established pressure groups for temperance reform in the Liberal Party). But even the Liberals still had a few landowners and a good many businessmen, and the Conservatives were certainly well aware of the need for wider support. When a genuinely popular and cheap daily newspaper appeared –

The Daily Mail – it supported them. And Salisbury understood the problem of finding policies to hold together the wealthy and the ordinary people. In 1886, he commented:

The Tory Party is comprised of very varying elements and there is trouble and vexation of spirit in trying to make them work together. I think the classes and the dependants of class are the strongest ingredients in our composition, but we have to conduct our legislation so that we shall give some satisfaction to both classes and masses. This is especially difficult with the classes, because all legislation is rather unwelcome to them as tending to disturb the state of things with which they are satisfied.

P Adelman, *Gladstone, Disraeli and Later Victorian Politics*

In fact Salisbury led a party that had been very successful in widening its support from country towns and rural areas to include urban constituencies too. In 1900 Conservatives captured 177 borough seats in England and their strength in England remained formidable. Liberals became very dependent on Scottish and Welsh support. Moreover Liberal decline helped Conservative leaders to rally behind them those who had wealth and property. And although in fact Labour showed few signs of trying to implement socialist policies, Conservatives commonly described Labour leaders as socialists, and exploited fears of Communist Russia by trying to link Labour to that country's beliefs.

The First World War helped Conservatism to recover and to leave behind links to anti-government military movements in Ireland. When Lloyd George's coalition no longer served their party's interest, the Conservatives broke with him in 1922. This divided the Conservatives, but Baldwin's skilful leadership had reunited the party by 1924. Baldwin's character and achievements show another strength of the Conservative Party – it responded effectively to changing social and political conditions. Baldwin and Neville Chamberlain carried out a range of social reforms and preached the merits of the Conservative Party as the party of capable economic management. Baldwin presented his party as a movement concerned with the whole nation, not just the one sector.

The Conservative Party of this period was more affluent than its rivals. It could afford to pay more party agents than either the Liberal or the Labour Party could do; it developed skilful advertising; and its leaders adapted well to the age of radio and the newsreel. The party organisation of the inter-war years improved the pay and training of its party agents, developed a flourishing women's section, and used volunteers to offset the constraints on spending at election time – in short it adapted well to the new conditions in which voter registration was no longer the key.

Although the Conservative Party contained people who had disliked the extension of the franchise in 1918, there is no evidence to show that this harmed the party, and indeed some historians believe that newly enfranchised female voters in particular were inclined to vote Conservative. By 1928 Conservative fears of the impact on them of a wider franchise had gone and it was the Conservative leader, Baldwin, who provided women with the vote on the same terms as men. The struggle between the Liberal and Labour Parties for the anti-Conservative vote helped the party too. The Liberal peer Lord Lothian commented:

Toryism appeals to the instinct for conserving the traditions of the past, it prefers experience to theory . . . it has the immense interests of property and social privilege almost wholly behind it as a source of funds and influence.

J R M Butler, *Lord Lothian*, 1906

A democracy?

One dictionary defines 'democracy' as follows: 'Government by the people or their elected representatives.'

By 1928 Britain had universal adult suffrage. But it also had an hereditary monarchy and a House of Lords that was made up of peers who had inherited their positions, and bishops. This was dominated by Conservatives throughout this period and regularly blocked reforms passed by the House of Commons. In 1909 Lloyd George was the Chancellor of the Exchequer in a Liberal Government. He put forward a budget to pay for social reforms by increasing the higher rates of income tax, introducing a 'super tax' for those earning over £5000 a year and increasing estate duties and stamp duties on shares. He proposed a 20 per cent tax on the unearned value of land whenever it was sold, a small tax on undeveloped

Stanley Baldwin outside Chequers with his family.

land and minerals and a duty on the increased value of leased land whenever a lease was ended.

Furious opposition developed in the Lords, stirred further by Lloyd George who described them as:

500 men, ordinary men chosen accidentally from among the unemployed. Who made 10 000 people owners of the soil and the rest of us trespassers in the land of our birth?

The Lords rejected his budget by 350 votes to 75.

A general election produced reduced Liberal numbers, yet kept them in power. The Lords backed down from the Liberals who were now determined to reform the constitution, and a further election in 1910 sustained them in office. The result was a Parliament Bill to cut the power of the House of Lords which passed into law in 1911 (despite determined hostility from many peers). The reform took from the Lords the power to interfere with any money bill. They could delay other reforms passed by the Commons for two years. In addition the maximum length a parliament could last before a general election had to be held was cut from seven years to five. Did this change make Britain a democracy?

➤ ACTIVITIES

1   Work with a partner to draft a one-sided plan for what to include in an essay titled:
    In what ways did the political identity of Britain change, 1867–1828?

2   Divide into two groups to develop and discuss the points that can be made against the view:
    'In 1928 Britain cannaot be regarded as a genuine democracy.'

3   Account for the views expressed by Lord Carnarvon in 1867 about the effects of the Reform Act of that year. (Evaluating a source in terms of content and context.)

A DEVELOPING DEMOCRACY –
An Overview

Reasons for Change

Economic changes led to the growth of places away from South East England; they wanted to be properly represented in parliament.

There were better off people wanting to take a part in politics.

People in trade, finance and industry wanted to influence politics.

Labour organisations wanted to influence government to protect their rights.

Britain became a more democratic society, 1867-1928

Better communication and improving education increased interest in politics.

Results of Change

Well-organised political parties developed. They included the Labour Party.

Voting became secret in 1872 and there were controls on expenditure.

The House Of Lords' power was reduced in 1911.

Parliamentary reforms, 1867, 1884, 1918, 1928, resulted in all adults having the vote.

The importance of social reforms like education increased.

Political parties offered voters party programmes of reforms that they hoped would be popular.

A series of seat redistributions produced an approximate equality between constituencies.

SECTION B

Government and the People

Introduction

Section A dealt with the changing political identity of Britain. It involved exploring the development of political ideologies and considered how far these changes were due to the country's changing social and economic identity.

This section deals with how social and economic factors brought about problems in Britain and considers the ways in which the government used its authority to tackle the problem of poverty in particular. The ways in which the government acted were shaped by the ideology of those politicians who happened to be in power.

This section deals especially with the period from around 1900–1951. The Higher course requires a careful study of three periods in particular, i.e.:

◆ The Liberal Government of 1906–1914.

◆ The 'Great Depression' of 1929–1931 and the response to it of the National Government of 1931–1939.

◆ The Labour Government of 1945–1951.

These periods cannot be studied in isolation. The situation before 1906 has to be understood if Liberal actions are to make sense, and similarly circumstances before the other two governments, must be studied. This means that this section will also cover all that is needed for the Intermediate unit 'From the Cradle to the Grave? Social Welfare in Britain 1890s–1951.' This unit requires a study of:

◆ The problem of poverty around 1900.

◆ The Liberal reforms, 1906–1914.

◆ The Labour Government of 1945–1951.

Higher students will need to prepare for essays that include such titles as:

◆ Discuss the view that the Liberal reforms of 1906–1914 represented the foundation of the Welfare State.

◆ How successful were the policies of the National Government (1931–1939) in solving the economic and social problems created by the Depression?

◆ Did the Liberal government of 1906–1914 or the Labour government of 1945–1951 do more to promote social welfare in Britain?

◆ How true is it to say that the Labour government of 1945–1951 set up the Welfare State?

It will help to bear these titles in mind when studying this section. Intermediate 2 students may well choose to produce their Extended Response from this unit and titles like those above may be worth considering. The Intermediate 2 examination, however, consists of sources and questions like this:

Source A, from a book by Jack London, *The People of the Abyss*, 1903.

Five minutes walk from almost any point will bring one to a slum. Here and there lurched a drunken man or woman and the air was obscene with the sound of squabbling. At a market old men and women were searching in the garbage, thrown in the mud, for rotten potatoes, while children clustered like flies around a rotting mass of fruit . . . which they ate on the spot.

Question: Describe what it was like to be poor in Britain in 1900. (Use Source A and recalled knowledge.)

This section includes source-based questions that cover the kinds of activities required for the Intermediate 2 examination.

As a result of studying this section you should have a sound knowledge and understanding of:

◆ Poverty in Britain in the 1900s, including evidence from enquiries into it.

◆ Ways in which help was already being provided for the poor.

◆ The Liberal reforms tackling poverty 1906–1914.

◆ Why poverty was still an issue by 1931, including the problem of unemployment and its causes.

◆ National Government responses, 1931–1939.

◆ The reasons why Labour reforms 1945–1951 took place.

◆ The reforms of the Labour Government 1945–1951.

Chapter Six

The Problem of Poverty in 1900

In 1900 the average life expectancy for men and women was nearly 30 years less than by 1998. Of every 1000 babies born in 1900, 163 failed to reach the age of one. In 1980 the equivalent figure was 12. A high death rate persisted for children and young adults. British people in 1900 were smaller than they are today too.

In the late nineteenth century and the early twentieth century a growing amount of evidence emerged of the extent of poverty in Britain and of the desperate misery of the lives of the poor. This chapter explores this evidence and deals with the way that the evidence began to change attitudes towards the problem of poverty. In particular, governments had to consider whether they were prepared to use their authority to increase the extent of help provided for the poor.

As a result of studying the material in this chapter you should have a sound knowledge and understanding of:

- The evidence that showed the extent and severity of poverty around the year 1900.

- The ways in which the very poor were helped at this time.

- The reasons why attitudes were changing towards providing further help for the poor.

TASK

Work through the material in this chapter and:

- List the reasons why so many people lived in such poverty.

- List the ways in which the poor were helped.

- Explain why many were coming to think that more should be done.

Evidence of poverty

The investigators

Pressure for action came from a number of different directions. By late Victorian times a more literate public with better access to newspapers and magazines could be reached by investigators eager to enlighten richer people about the misery in which many poor people lived. A whole range of people explored the distinct slum areas that had developed in cities after those who could

afford it had moved out to the suburbs. Some of these explorers compared their journeys to those being made by other Europeans 'in darkest Africa'. William Booth (1829–1919), the founder of the Salvation Army, drew such comparisons; he demanded for the people he had encountered a standard of living at least equal to that enjoyed by cab horses.

Children queueing for dinner in a soup kitchen.

The Reverend Andrew Mearns's pamphlet, *The Bitter Cry of Outcast London*, made an especially powerful impact in 1883. He went to:

pestilential human rookeries where tens of thousands are crowded together amidst the horrors which call to mind what we have heard of the middle passage of a slave ship. To get into them you have to penetrate courts reeking with poisonous gases rising from accumulations of sewage and refuse, courts which rarely know the virtues of a drop of cleansing water, every room on these rotten and reeking tenements houses a family, often two … The State must secure for the poorest the rights of citizenship, the right to live in something better than fever dens.

A queue of Londoners waiting for their Salvation Army breakfast.

In 1889 G R Sims tried to stir the consciences of the wealthy by reporting on his exploration of a part of London in which the poor lived, an area he called a

dark continent that is within easy walking distance of the General Post Office.

His report was full of descriptions of individual homes like this:

What a room! The walls are damp and crumbling, the ceiling is black and peeling off. The floor is rotten and broken away in places and the wind and rain sweep in through gaps. The woman, her husband and her six children live and sleep in this one room.

Some investigators not only described poverty but also tried to establish reasons for it. Above all, they found, that without steady work, life could become a nightmare. There were those who were too old, too ill, too tied up by very young children, or even too young to work. Those able to work could not always rely on steady employment. William Booth interviewed a man found wandering by the Thames in London and wrote down the man's story:

I'm a confectioner by trade. I come from Dartford. I got turned off (i.e. dismissed) because I'm getting elderly. They can get young men cheaper and I have the rheumatism so bad. I've earned nothing these days. I thought I could get a job at Woolwich so I walked there but could get nothing. I found a bit of bread in the road wrapped in newspaper. That did me yesterday. I'm 54 years old.

Darkest England and the Way Out 1890

There was no unemployment benefit for those without work, just as there was no pension for the elderly, or state payments to people who were sick or injured. Yet many people were put out of work if trade in their business was not doing well and many worked at jobs (like building) where bad weather could stop their employment.

Wage levels were often very low making it difficult for many families to live a reasonable life even when there was a wage earner. In 1897 Robert Sherard, a journalist, interviewed workers in the English Midlands and noted down stories like this one from a chain-maker:

This woman had six children to keep and her husband, for he had been out of work since Christmas. Most often she had to beg dripping (i.e. animal fat) as a relish to the insufficient bread. Her children had been weaned on 'sop', a preparation of bread and hot water flavoured with the drippings of the teapot. For clothes she depended on charity.

Booth and Rowntree

At the end of the century came two investigations into poverty that were so detailed and so carefully researched that it was impossible to ignore their great weight of evidence. The pioneer in this scientific investigation was Charles Booth, a wealthy Liverpool ship owner who came to London to open offices and heard socialist claims that a quarter of Londoners lived in great poverty. Doubtful of this, he began his own enquiries. His work took up 17 years of his life from the mid–1880s, and he filled 17 books with findings which greatly altered his views. The evidence was published as *Life & Labour of the People of London*. Booth tried to proceed calmly and scientifically, finding classifications for the many people he interviewed:

A	The lowest class – occasional labourers, loafers and semi-criminals.
B	The very poor – casual labour, hand-to-mouth existence, chronic want.
C and **D**	The poor – including alike those whose earnings are small, because of irregularity of employment, and those whose work, though regular, is ill-paid.
E and **F**	The regularly employed and fairly paid working class of all grades.

The proportions of the different classes shown for all London are as follows:

A (lowest)	37 610	or	0.9%	In poverty 30.7%
B (very poor)	316 834	or	7.5%	
C and **D** (poor)	939 293	or	22.3%	
E and **F** (working class, comfortable)	2 166 303	or	51.5%	In comfort 69.3%
G and **H** (middle class and above)	749 930	or	17.8%	
	4 209 970		100%	
Inmates of Institutions	99 830			
	4 309 800			

Booth concluded:

What might be an admissible state of things in days past is admissible no longer. It drags us back and has become a question of the first importance.

Booth showed that low pay, lack of regular work, supporting large families, illness, and old age, were major causes of poverty. (Around 15 per cent of the very poor were so placed, he suggested, because of drink, laziness and character defects.) Booth became an advocate of government action, such as the introduction of pensions for all. His evidence, however, was built up from the impressions of poverty noted by school board visitors, clergy and charity workers.

Other investigators wondered whether London's conditions were unique. Seebohm Rowntree, a member of the wealthy York chocolate-manufacturing family, explored his native town.

He concluded in 1901 in *Poverty, A Study of Town Life*:

We have been accustomed to look upon poverty in London as exceptional, but when the result of careful investigation shows that the proportion of poverty in London is practically equalled in what may be regarded as a typical provincial town, we are faced by the startling probability that from 25 per cent to 30 per cent of the town populations of the United Kingdom are living in poverty.

However, some historians have suggested that generalising on the basis of York is dangerous.

Rowntree made careful use of recent scientific work to establish what a family needed to earn to buy adequate food and fuel and to pay the rent. He concluded that 52 per cent of the very poor were paid wages too low to sustain an adequate life. Around 21 per cent of families lived in misery because the chief wage earner had died, or was too ill or too old to work. Rowntree's statistics showed 2229 houses sharing 155 water taps, 353 houses sharing 58 closets, and 247 infants per 1000 people in poor areas dying before the age of one, compared with 94 infants per 1000 in families wealthy enough to hire servants.

Rowntree's work enabled him to sketch out the typical life of a working man, pointing to the times when poverty was most likely to affect him.

The life of a labourer is marked by five alternating periods of want and comparative plenty. During early childhood, unless his father is a skilled worker, he probably will be in poverty; this will last until he or she or some of his brothers or sisters begin to earn money and thus augment their father's wages sufficiently to raise the family above the poverty line. Then follows the period during which he is earning money and living under his parents' roof. This is his chance to save money ... this period of comparative prosperity may continue after marriage until he has two or three children, when poverty will again overtake him. This will last until the first child is 14 years old and begins to earn wages. While the children are earning and before they leave home, the man enjoys another period of prosperity – possibly only to sink back again into poverty when his children have married and he himself is too old to work, for his income has never permitted his saving enough for him and his wife to live upon for more than a very short time.

B S Rowntree, *Poverty: A Study of Town Life*, 1901

Booth and Rowntree's researches turned them against those who argued that the poor were to blame for their misery and that they should save money to cope with times of crisis. As Rowntree noted:

Wages paid for unskilled labour in York are insufficient to provide food, shelter and clothing adequate to maintain a family in a state of bare physical efficiency. And let us be clear what mere physical efficiency means. A family must never spend a penny on railway fare or omnibus, they cannot save, nor can they join a sick club or Trade Union. The children must have no pocket money. Should a child fall ill it must be attended by the parish doctor. The wage earner must never be absent from his work for a single day.

B S Rowntree, *Poverty: A Study of Town Life*, 1901

Booth and Rowntree established the huge scale of poverty and clearly identified its causes. Further work by A L Bowley in five different towns pointed to low wages as especially important as a cause of poverty.

The officials

Officials employed to make sure that factory or health regulations were obeyed, doctors hired as medical officers of health by local authorities, and school inspectors, all added their evidence to the case that more should be done.

Medical officers of health, for example, drew up reports like this one in Salford:

Our medical officer's report to the education committee in 1905 noted outbreaks among children of 'small-pox, typhus fever, enteric fever, scarlet fever and diphtheria', (being) only a few of the diseases mentioned. 'A large proportion of the pupils', the report added, 'show signs of rickets'. There has been considerable distress during the winter, but the children had 'much appreciated the free breakfasts provided'. Some went hungry every day.

R Roberts, *The Classic Slum*, 1971

A Lambeth Schools inspector commented that in his view:

Want of food, irregularity and unsuitability of food taken together are the cause of degeneracy in children. The breakfast that these children get is normally bread and tea, if they get it at all. There is bread and margarine for lunch and dinner is normally nothing but what a copper coin can purchase at the local fried fish shop. They supplement this with rotten fruit, which they collect beneath barrows. One of the most important points is the absence of fresh milk.

Quoted in T Barker (ed), *The Long March of Everyman*, 1975

Parliament itself ordered a number of enquiries into social problems that were carried out by groups of experts called Royal Commissions. In 1894 a Royal Commission investigating working conditions produced two reports. The majority of members reached an optimistic conclusion, stating:

The general impression left by the information before us is that the level of wage rates has risen considerably during the last 50 years in respect of (and with the exception of house rents in large towns) their power of purchasing commodities. The daily hours of labour have, during the same period, been in most cases shortened and the sanitary conditions of work have improved.

A minority of members produced their own report. Whilst not disagreeing with the evidence of greater prosperity, they pointed to the kind of lives endured by many people, maintaining:

Notwithstanding the great increase in national wealth, whole sections of the population – at least five million – are unable to obtain a subsistence compatible with health or efficiency. Probably two million are, every year, driven to accept Poor Relief, and even in well-organised and skilled trades where the normal working day is often nine hours, an excessive amount of overtime is systematically worked. Many thousands of workers still toil under circumstances which make disease and accident an inevitable accompaniment of their lives.

By the beginning of the twentieth century, then, all sorts of evidence had emerged of the huge scale of poverty in Britain. A better educated population, with access to a growing number of newspapers and magazines were able to read about the problem. And politicians had to take account of the fact that nearly two thirds of adult males now had the vote.

What help was already available?

Self-help?

A number of people in nineteenth century Britain believed it was wrong to encourage people to believe that they could always count on government help were they in difficulties. The philosopher, John Stuart Mill, suggested the state should not interfere in peoples' lives:

Letting alone should be the general practice, every departure from it, unless required by some good, is a certain evil.

Victorians were fond of reading a book entitled *Self-Help* that had been written in 1859 by a Scot, Samuel Smiles, from Haddington. Smiles was not totally opposed to all state action and was certainly not a supporter of *The Times* journalist who wrote it was better:

to run the risk of cholera and the rest than to be bullied into health.

Smiles supported laws that would prevent the spread of disease and cruelty and that encouraged a better educational system. A total policy of 'letting alone' (or laissez-faire) did not seem to Smiles to be sensible. What he did believe is indicated by the following extract from his famous book.

'Heaven helps those who help themselves' is a well-tried maxim, embodying in a small compass the results of vast human experience. The spirit of self-help is the root of all genuine growth in the individual; and exhibited in the lives of many, it constitutes the true course of national vigour and strength. Help from without is often enfeebling in its effects, but help from within invariably invigorates. Whatever is done for men or classes, to a certain extent takes away the stimulus and necessity of doing for themselves; and where men are subjected to over-guidance and over-government the inevitable tendency is to render them comparatively helpless.

Even the best institutions can give a man no active help. Perhaps the most they can do is, to leave him free to develop and improve his individual condition. But in all times men have been prone to believe that their happiness and well-being (would be best) secured by means of institutions rather than by their own conduct. Hence the value of legislation as an agent in human advancement has usually been much over-estimated. No laws, however, stringent, can make the idle industrious, the thriftless provident, or the drunken sober. Such reforms can only be effected by means of individual action, economy, and self-denial; by better habits, rather than by greater rights.

By the 1900s there clearly were ways in which ordinary people tried to protect themselves from times of desperate poverty. Trade unions for skilled workers able to afford their subscriptions provided funds to help members in times of need for example. Friendly Societies grew up to help people to save in case of sickness, old age and widowhood. By 1910 Friendly Societies had 13 million members. The savings in union and Friendly Society accounts totalled 40 million pounds. Though most workers could not afford this kind of self-help, by 1900 Friendly Societies were not sympathetic to state support of the poor. In 1894 one of the largest Friendly Societies, the Foresters, argued:

The aim of the working class ought to be to bring about economic conditions in which there should be no need for distribution of state alms. The establishment of a great scheme of state pensions would legalise and stamp as a permanent feature of our social life the chronic poverty of the age. The desire of the best reformers is to remove the conditions that make that poverty so that every citizen shall have a fair chance not only of earning a decent wage for today but such a wage as should enable him to provide for the future . . . Man is a responsible being. To rob him of his responsibilities is to degrade him. The working class should . . . insist upon being capable of using their own wages to their own advantage.

In J R Hay, *The Development of the British Welfare State*

A number of people believed that people who were very poor lived in this condition because of their weakness of character. Norman Pearson, for example, wrote an account, *The Idle Poor*, that maintained:

It is a mistake to suppose that the typical pauper is merely an ordinary person who has fallen into distress through adverse circumstances. As a rule he is not an ordinary person, but one who is constitutionally a pauper, a pauper in his blood and bones. He is made of inferior material, and therefore cannot be improved up to the level of the ordinary person . . . Speaking broadly, pauperism is a token of the inferior capacity which belongs to an inferior stock. The hereditary nature of this incapacity may lighten the moral reproach against the loafer and the vagrant, but emphasises the necessity of protecting the community against them, and in particular, of protecting it against the perpetuation of the degenerate stocks which they represent. This is really the most important factor in the problem, seeing that it affects not only ourselves but our prosperity. On this ground alone the proper authorities should be invested with the power of segregating and detaining – permanently, if necessary – those who burden the present and imperil the future of our race.

Quoted in J R Hay, *The Development of the British Welfare State*

Some of those holding harsh views about the personalities of the poor pointed in particular to how much they drank. Even Seebohm Rowntree, who was sympathetic to the plight of the needy, noted that in York there was a public house to every 230 people. In fact there was probably a gentle downward trend in drinking alcohol during Victorian times. An average of around 162 litres of beer per person a year in the 1850s had fallen to about 135 litres by the end of the century. Scottish temperance workers spread a vigorous anti-alcohol campaign across Britain. Some who believed the poor to be weak-minded tried to cut temptation by such reforms as limiting the opening hours of public houses or by banning betting off race courses (in 1906). Yet Booth and Rowntree's work clearly showed that blaming poverty on personal weakness simply would not do.

Charities and voluntary organisations

Numerous wealthy people worked hard to raise money to help the poor. Some of them felt this charitable approach was the only correct one to pursue, and that even it had to be carefully handled. The Charity Organisation Society tried to co-ordinate the work of different groups. In its report of 1876 it suggested:

. . . it is a hurtful misuse of money to spend it on assisting the labouring classes to meet emergencies which they should themselves have anticipated and provided for. The working man does not require to be told that temporary sickness is likely now and then to visit his household; that time of slackness will occasionally come; that if he marries early and has a large family, his resources will be taxed to the uttermost; that if he lives long enough, old age will render him more or less incapable of toil – all these are the ordinary contingencies of a labourer's life, and if he is taught that as they arise they will be met by State relief or private charity, he will assuredly make no effort to meet them himself. A spirit of dependence, fatal to all progress, will be engendered in him, he will not concern himself with the causes of his distress or consider at all how the condition of his class may be improved; the road to idleness and drunkenness will be made easy to him . . . One thing there is which true charity does require the working man to be told. We desire to tell him that those who are born to easier circumstances sympathise with the severe toil and self-denial which his lot imposes upon him; that many are standing beside him ready and even eager to help if

proper occasion should arise; and that if he, or wife, or child should be stricken with protracted sickness, or with some special infirmity, there are those at hand who will gladly minister to his necessities.

Octavia Hill spent much of her life trying to provide decent homes for poorly paid workers. Yet in 1888 she argued that the idea that charity was readily available could be harmful because:

You discourage the habit of belonging to clubs, the habit of saving, the habit of purchasing things: you bring side by side the man who had laid by nothing, and is well cared for at a time when misfortune comes to him, and the man who has sacrificed something through his time of steady work ... people should keep clear from any danger of holding out to the poor hopes that something can be done for them that cannot be done; even inquiries set on foot by the Government raise very great hopes in the people ... The people are exceedingly sharp and the more their homes look miserable, the more they expect to get ...

Evidence to the House of Lords Select Committee on Poor Relief

By 1900, the large sums given to charity were increasingly seen as simply not enough. Worthy bodies existed throughout the country providing coal, clothing, bedding and soup. None of these activities solved the causes of poverty. None were sufficient to really drag the poor out of a life of misery. Even Octavia Hill admitted that the housing she and others had worked for 30 years to provide had created homes for just 26 000 people. London's population rose by that number in six months.

Official support for the poor

Many of the leaders of Victorian society did not wish to see governments use their authority to regulate people's lives any more than was necessary. 'Laissez-faire' was a widely held ideology; when action had to be taken to improve the nation's health or education it was done rather reluctantly and often against strong criticism. Political leaders like Gladstone believed that taxes should be as low as possible and social reforms were usually expensive. Terrible diseases like cholera and typhoid compelled politicians to pass health reform acts that increased the power of local authorities to improve street cleaning and water supply services, and to clear away slums. Yet when the Conservative, Richard Cross, introduced his 1875 Artisans Dwelling Act which allowed local councils to purchase compulsorily and clear away unhealthy housing areas, he declared:

I take it as a starting point that it is not the duty of the

Mealtime at a Dr Barnardo's orphanage.

Government to provide any class of citizen with any of the necessaries of life, and among (these) we must include ... good and habitable dwellings. That is not the duty of the state because if it did so it would inevitably tend to make that class depend not on themselves but upon what was done for them elsewhere. Nor is it wise to encourage large bodies to provide the working classes with habitations at greatly lower rents than the market value paid elsewhere ... there is another point of view from which we may look. No one will doubt the propriety and right of the state to interfere in matters relating to sanitary laws.

Hansard

As a result some city centres became more pleasant as slum housing was cleared away; but working class urban lives became more cramped, confined and overcrowded than ever before.

The problem of poverty had forced the state to act long before 1900. The action that was taken in 1834 in England and 1845 in Scotland illustrates the growth of the authority of various forms of local government during the nineteenth century. In the words of the historian Martin Pugh:

Victorian governments increasingly wanted local bodies to assume responsibilities they themselves shirked (avoided) and so in spite of their misgivings they significantly extended local democracy after 1870.

M Pugh, *State and Society*, 1994, *Arnold*

By 1900 there were town councils, county councils and smaller rural district and urban district councils all elected by ratepayers (including some unmarried and widowed women). There were also locally elected boards looking after education and trying to cope with the problem of poverty. These parochial boards, like all other elected bodies, struggled to keep their costs as low as possible so that the amount of money they raised from local ratepayers would be as small as possible. Furthermore the parochial

boards were required to make sure that what they offered the poor would be so bleak that no one would be tempted to try to avoid work and live off ratepayers instead.

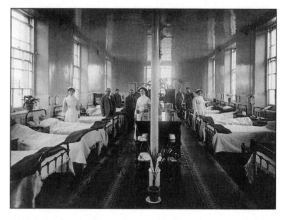

The Men's Ward at the Greenlea Poor House in Edinburgh, 1905.

The very poor in England were offered places in workhouses. Able-bodied poor people were expected to work for their keep. By 1900 the initially very harsh conditions in these places had been somewhat modified. Elderly couples were no longer separated, the aged were allowed the comfort of a little tea and tobacco and few able-bodied people were confined within them. Parochial boards increasingly used 'outdoor relief' i.e., they provided support for people in their own homes. A Royal Commission on the Aged Poor (1895) encouraged the use of outdoor relief to sustain the elderly too. This strategy was widely implemented in Scotland; poorhouses, chiefly for the aged and for young orphans were built here rather than workhouses. In Scotland, however, the able-bodied rendered poor by unemployment were not entitled to any sort of help. In reality help was often provided in a crisis on the grounds that otherwise illness would develop. By the 1900s some better-off workhouses had begun to build hospitals. In Bradford the parochial board guardians even built houses for the elderly.

Staff and residents of 'Arthurville', the Easter Ross Union Poorhouse outside Tain in 1910.

ployed never touched poor relief despite the grim state of their lives. Charles Booth noted:

Aversion to the 'house' is absolutely universal and almost any amount of suffering . . . will be endured by the people rather than go into it.

Royal Commission on the Aged Poor 1895

The Labour politician George Lansbury visited the Popular Workhouse in 1892 and wrote:

It was easy for me to understand why the poor dreaded and hated these places, all these prison sort of surroundings were organised for the purpose of making decent people endure any suffering rather than enter.

Despite these improvements the workhouse–poorhouse system was loathed. Seeking help from the poor law system meant loss of reputation, possible loss of freedom and loss of the right to vote. Around 90 per cent of the unem-

Changing attitudes to poverty

By the end of the century a vigorous debate was under way as to how to tackle the problem. The poor law system was hated, charities could not cope, and Friendly Societies only aided the

Inside the Poplar Workhouse, London 1905.

better-off and had their failings (such as concentrating money on a respectable funeral but doing nothing for the deceased's family). Charles Booth helped lead a campaign for an old age pension provided by the state, despite the eventual refusal of the 1895 Royal Commission to agree to this for fears that money might be paid to people who were not wholly destitute, and that the existence of a pension would stop people saving for their old age and encourage wastefulness and drunkenness. The growing evidence that most people simply could not set aside enough to provide for their needs could not be ignored. There were other pressures too.

Employers

Some employers were persuaded of the need for action, including members of the Rowntree and Cadbury families, William Lever, a soap maker; and Sir John Brunner, a chemical manufacturer. For some it was a matter of Christian conscience; but others felt that having a capable, peaceful workforce meant making sure that workers were healthy and well cared for. Thus John Macauley, the manager of docks in south Wales, argued in 1907:

A great deal could also be done to lessen the effect of occasional unemployment by making insurance against sickness and old age compulsory to the extent of a definite percentage of a man's or woman's earnings. For this purpose the many friendly societies might with advantage be amalgamated and placed under the control of the state. All forms of sweating labour should be abolished, as well as the employment of child labour.

Royal Commission on the Poor Laws 1905–1909

Politicians

There were an increasing number of politicians ready to support state action to tackle poverty. The socialist and labour societies were particu-

larly keen on state action. Sidney Webb, a leading member of the Fabian Society, believed that by 1902 a great deal had been done (perhaps by accident) as a result of piecemeal steps taken to increase the power of local authorities. He described how it was possible for a councillor to:

. . . walk along the municipal pavement, lit by municipal gas and cleansed by municipal brooms with municipal water and seeing by the municipal clock in the municipal market that he is too early to meet his children coming from the municipal school hard by the municipal hospital will use the national telegraph system to tell them not to walk through the municipal park but to come by the municipal tramway to meet him in the municipal reading room by the municipal art gallery, museum and library.

D Fraser, *The Evolution of the British Welfare State*, 1973

Webb regarded these as strong foundations on which to build. But, in 1902 at least, he expected little from the Liberals. He saw their leadership as still living in the past, unable:

to turn over a new leaf and devote themselves to obtaining the greatest possible development of municipal activity, the most comprehensive extension of the Factory Acts, or the fullest utilisation of the Government departments in the service of the public. They are aiming at something else, namely the abstract right of the individual to lead exactly the kind of life that he likes (and can pay for) unpenalised by any taxation for purposes of which he individually disapproves.

K O Morgan, *The Age of Lloyd George*, 1971

Eagerness for action was not simply felt by socialists. As early as 1885 Joseph Chamberlain had put forward a Radical Programme in which it was argued:

The evil effects of overcrowding upon the poorer classes of our large towns is now generally recognised, . . . (and) it is to the interest of all in the community to do away with these evils. It is in the interest of all in the community that the workman should become a better instrument of production, that his dwelling should not be a hotbed of disease, that his degradation and misery should not be a constant source of danger to the state. The warning of Danton must be heeded, 'If you suffer the poor to grow up as animals they may chance to become wild beasts to render you'. The State has too long made itself the champion of the rights of the individual; it must assert the rights of the many – of all. It is apparent that in open competition the fittest obtain more than they deserve, and the less fit come too near perishing. The generation of workmen now coming to manhood will at least be able to read; no doubt they will quickly learn that their claims were long ago admitted to be right and equitable. For the privileged classes long to refuse payment of these claims is impossible; to refuse by instalments is equally impolitic and unjust.

Ed H W Lucy, *Speeches of Rt Hon Joseph Chamberlain*, 1885

In 1886 Chamberlain was in power, in charge of the Local Government Board whose task it was to oversee the work of local boards and councils. It was a period of high unemployment, and he urged local councils to run public work schemes that would provide paid employment for the out-of-work, free of the shame of the poor law. This marked a tendency that was to develop in later years.

The debate over how the poor should be helped was, by 1905, clearly expressed in the arguments offered to and by a Royal Commission that spent the next four years studying poverty, its causes and its remedies. Even at this late date it was possible to hear arguments that had raged through late Victorian times. J S Davy, head of the Poor Law division of the local Government Board spoke for the old system and its 'less eligibility' requirement. Paupers should suffer, he said:

the loss of personal reputation, second the loss of personal freedom which is secured by detention in a workhouse and third the loss of political freedom by suffering disenfranchisement.

Royal Commission on The Poor Laws, 1905–1909

On the other hand a Royal Commission minority made up of a church minister, a trade unionist, a Labour politician and Beatrice Webb, (Sidney's wife), wanted the old system swept away; the setting up of a Ministry of Labour; the organising of labour exchanges, retraining and public works programmes in times of depression; and local authority control over a range of welfare provisions.

A growing number of Liberals raged against evidence that could not be denied. Charles Masterman wrote:

Public penury, private ostentation – that perhaps is the heart of the complaint. A nation with the wealth of England can afford to spend, and spend royally. The spectacle of a huge urban poverty confronts all this waste energy. The only justification for the present unnatural heaping up of great possessions in the control of the very few would be some return in leisure and cultivation of the arts. We have called into existence quick travelling. We have converted half the Highlands into deer forests for our sport. We fling away in ugly white hotels and in elaborate banquets of which everyone is weary, the price of many poor men's yearly income.

C F G Masterman, *The Condition of England*, 1909

The Liberal MP, Leo Chiozza Money, reckoned there were 1.25 million rich, 3.75 million comfortably off and 38 million poor people in Britain. He complained:

We purchased a great commerce at the price of crowding our population into the cities. We have given our children what we grimly call elementary education and robbed them of the elements of a natural life. All this has been done that a few of us may enjoy a superfluity of goods and services. Deprivation for the many and luxury for the few have degraded our national life at both ends of the scale.

Leo Chiozza Money, *Riches and Poverty*, 1909

Liberal leaders knew that men like these expected social reforms and might drift over to the Labour Party if nothing was done. (In fact Leo Chiozza Money did join the Labour Party in 1918.) By the 1900s politicians had to recognise the results of the wider franchise that they had introduced and modify their laissez-faire ideology to provide changes that many voters expected. The Conservatives, by 1906, were dominated by Joseph Chamberlain's argument that Britain should end its free trade policy and tax foreign imports. Behind this wall of 'tariffs' Britain and her Empire would prosper, wealth would grow and unemployment be cut. If Liberals wished to cling to free trade, they had to find some other way of improving people's lives, and there were a whole group of 'New Liberals' ready to urge their leaders to use the power of the state. One of them, Herbert Samuel, explained the causes that:

combined to convert Liberalism from the principle of state abstention. It was seen that the State had become more efficient and its legislation more competent. It was realised that the conditions of society were so bad that to tolerate them longer was impossible and that the laissez-faire policy was not likely to bring the cure.

Quoted in K Morgan, *The Age of Lloyd George*

Another Liberal MP, J M Robertson, proclaimed:

Laissez-faire ... is quite done with as a pretext for leaving uncured deadly social evils which admit of curative treatment by state action.

Quoted in M Pugh, *The Making of Modern British Politics*

Prominent among such men were the surprising allies, David Lloyd George (who came from humble origins) and the recent convert from Conservatism, Winston Churchill (who was born in Blenheim Palace). The latter commented, bleakly:

I see little glory in an Empire which can rule the waves and is unable to flush its own sewers.

S H Wood, *The British Welfare State*

These Liberals saw social reform as a way of heading off socialism. They hoped that a system that gave people a degree of social and economic independence would be an insurance against the spread of socialist ideas. In this way they were at one with Conservatives like A J Balfour who believed:

Social legislation is not merely to be distinguished from Socialist legislation but it is its most direct opposite and its most effective antidote. Socialism will never get possession of the great body of public opinion among the working class or any other class, if those who wield the collective forces of the community show themselves desirous to ameliorate every legitimate grievance.

In 1906, Lloyd George told a crowded meeting of Liberals:

If, at the end of an average term of office, it was found that the Liberal Party had done nothing to cope seriously with the social condition of people, to remove the national degradation of slums and widespread poverty in a land glittering with wealth and that they had shrunk from attacking boldly the main causes of this wretchedness, then would a real cry arise in this land for a new party and many of us here in this room would join in that cry.

Quoted in S H Wood, *The British Welfare State*, 1982

Behind Liberal politicians stood liberal thinkers like the Oxford philosopher T H Green (who taught Asquith) and J A Hobson. They argued for state action to secure a minimum standard of living for all citizens. They maintained that reforms could be financed by taxing land that had risen in value, perhaps because of urban development, and by other sorts of unearned income.

Fear for Britain's place in the world

The Boer War that ended in 1902 had shown up in horrifying detail the poor state of health of many people in Britain. A quarter of the urban male population were unfit to serve in the armed forces. In Manchester, 8000 of the men who volunteered for the army had to be rejected as physically unsuitable at once; only 1200 were eventually accepted. At a time when other countries were building up their armed forces, Britain seemed potentially weak. The founder of the Boy Scout movement, Robert Baden-Powell, who was one of the Boer War's heroes, warned:

recent reports on the deterioration of our race ought to act as a warning to be taken in time before it goes too far. One cause which contributed to the downfall of the Roman Empire was the fact that the soldiers fell away from the standard of their forefathers in bodily strength.

Others were concerned that in the economic battle with rivals like Germany and the USA, Britain's workers were insufficiently energetic and educated. In 1905 a group of experts reported:

No country can permanently hold its own in the race of international competition if hampered by an increasing load of this dead weight of poverty.

Those who believed it was morally wrong to allow widespread poverty to exist in Britain were therefore joined by others who saw the scale of poverty as weakening Britain's place in the world, at a time of growing international tension and increasing foreign challenges to Britain's economic power. It was a Liberal Government that had to respond to the problem.

➤ ACTIVITIES

1 Read the source in which William Booth talked to an unemployed man (Page 81). Use the source and your own knowledge to describe the main causes of poverty in 1900. (Demonstrate knowledge and understanding of historical developments, events and issues.)

2 Read Seebohm Rowntree's account of the life of a working man (Page 83). Use the source and your own knowledge to explain why the work of Charles Booth and Seebohm Rowntree were so important. (Explain historical developments and events.)

3 Read Norman Pearson's account *The Idle Poor* (Page 86). What is the value of this source to someone studying the treatment of poverty at this time? (Evaluate historical sources with reference to their origin, purpose, content and historical context.)

4 Compare the views on dealing with poverty expressed by the Charity Organisation Society (Page 86) and Seebohm Rowntree's report on wages in York (Page 83). (Comparison between sources.)

5 Account for changes in attitudes to poverty in the late nineteenth and early twentieth centuries. (Essay)

Chapter Seven
Liberal Reforms 1906–1914

On 4 December 1905, the Conservative Government that had been in office for ten years, resigned. In the general election that took place in January 1906, the Liberals won 400 seats, a huge majority in the House of Commons. The Liberals did not, however, control the House of Lords.

The material in this chapter deals with the use that the Liberal Government made of its authority to reform British society and thus change its identity. The Liberal Party had not been wholly won over by the views of 'New Liberals' however, indeed the new Chancellor of the Exchequer, H H Asquith, had declared, two years before the election:

If a Liberal Government came into power, the first duty they set before themselves would be a reduction in the country's expenditure.

The ideology of the Liberal Party was not united behind a policy of vigorous social reform that would, inevitably, cost money.

As a result of studying this chapter's content you should have a sound knowledge and understanding of:

- The main reforms that were carried out by the Liberal Government.

- How far these reforms solved the problem of poverty in Britain.

TASK

How might a 'New Liberal' have reviewed the work of his Government by 1914 in a speech to voters in his constituency?

To do this:

- Build up a clear and full list of the reforms, using sub-headings for each one.

- Consider the problems and difficulties faced by the Government that might explain why more had not been done. List these.

- Consider the beliefs of many Liberals and explain why these limited reforms.

What had the Liberals the ability to do?

Despite all the evidence already available about poverty, even more was added to it by a Royal Commission set up in 1905 to study the Poor Laws. The Commission produced its report in 1909 and set out a great deal more evidence, though it was divided as to how best to tackle the problem. Yet a vigorous policy of social reform faced a number of obstacles, despite the Liberals' majority in the House of Commons.

Political attitudes

Until 1908 the Government was led by the amiable figure of Sir Henry Campbell-Bannerman, thereafter the Prime Minister was Herbert Henry Asquith. Both men were very concerned with holding together a Liberal Party that contained widely differing views. Two general elections in January and December 1910 cut the Liberal numbers in Parliament very sharply, this made holding the party together even more urgent. Many Liberals were far from eager to see changes to the existing ways of helping the poor and even the Minister who was President of the Local Government Board, John Burns, defended the existing system as:

Sympathetic, reasonable and adaptable to any sensible demand that may be made on it.

The Royal Commission produced a majority report which accepted the views of Helen Bosanquet of the Charity Organisation Society to keep the Poor Law structure (though shifting many of its powers to specialised agencies). Beatrice Webb led those who wrote a minority report demanding that the current system be scrapped and that the State should guarantee a minimum level of support for the poor.

Faced with such a division and with a party far from agreed on vigorous reform, it is not surprising that the Liberals proceeded cautiously.

Cost

The traditional Liberal financial policy of the nineteenth century was to keep taxes as low as possible. Since the Liberals also supported free trade rather than taxing imports, it was not easy to see where revenue for reforms would come from. Moreover, by 1909, the Government was engaged in an expensive naval arms race with Germany, urged on by the press and by popular demands that Britain retain control of the seas by building far more of the new and very expensive 'Dreadnought' class battleships than Germany.

Parliament

Reforms would have to pass parliament. The Liberals lost their huge majority in the Commons in two elections held in 1910, but their Labour and Irish allies still gave them an overall lead. However, in the House of Lords, the Conservatives dominated politics with a permanent majority.

Asquith raged against this declaring:

We are living under a system of false balances and loaded dice. When the democracy votes Tory we are submitted to the uncontrolled domination of a single Chamber. When the democracy votes Liberal, a dormant Second Chamber wakes up from its slumbers and is able to frustrate and nullify the clearest and most plainly expressed intention of the elective House.

In 1909 the House of Lords went beyond all its previous actions and rejected the budget put forward by Lloyd George to find £16 million to finance social reforms (£8 million for pensions alone) and a naval rebuilding programme. The budget sought to raise revenue in ways that New Liberals had been advocating for some years:

- Income tax was to rise on a sliding scale from 9d. to 1s. 2d. in the pound.

- A 'super-tax' of 6d. in the pound was to be levied on incomes over £5000 a year (in 1914 this figure became £3000).

- Duties on tobacco, beer, spirits and petrol were increased.

- A tax of 20 per cent of the unearned increased value of land was to be levied when land changed hands, plus a duty of a halfpenny in the pound on the value of undeveloped land and minerals. These taxes meant that a survey and valuation of land was required. This upset landowners as much as the taxes did.

- Those earning less than £500 a year were allowed £10 tax free per child.

The Lords could not amend the bill introducing the budget but they could in theory reject it. They now did so. Asquith declared war on them, calling an election and asserting:

The House of Lords have deliberately chosen their ground. They have elected to set at nought in regard to finance the unwritten and time-honoured conventions of our Constitution.

Lloyd George dismissed the Lords as '500 men chosen accidentally from among the unemployed'. The election of 1910 produced 275 Liberal MPs and 273 Conservatives, with Labour and Irish Nationalists votes increasing the Liberal grip on office. The Lords gave way and passed the budget.

But the Liberals were now bent on cutting the power of the Lords. A second election in 1910 was fought on the issue of the power of the House of Lords. The upper house finally gave way when faced with the threat that the king would create new Liberal peers sufficient in number to swamp the Conservative majority, and passed the Parliament Act (1911) which reduced its own authority. Henceforth the Lords could only delay bills passed by the Commons for two years, and they lost all power to alter or reject money bills.

Thus social reform had contributed to bringing about constitutional change.

Officials

Social reforms also required officials to carry them out. By Edwardian times Britain possessed far more people in paid public service than had been the case in the mid-nineteenth century. In 1841 there were 40 000 men and 3000 women engaged in such work. By 1911 the numbers had risen to 271 000 and 50 000 respectively. Moreover from 1870 admission to the civil service had to be by an examination and this ended the old system of obtaining office by influence and seniority. (The Queen wondered if men recruited under the new system would really be gentlemen!)

By Edwardian times too, a range of local government services overseen by local government officials had emerged. The Victorians had reformed local government, creating elected councils in cities and towns, setting up county councils (1888), and parish and district councils (1894). It was these bodies which were given many of the tasks of earlier social reforms either directly, or (as in the 1902 Education Act) by shifting the work of separately elected boards to them. Whole armies of officials bustled about Edwardian Britain. One of the problems of the Liberals was that such officials were not necessarily popular with ordinary people. One historian has suggested that, in Victorian times at least:

It would not be far wrong to argue that the postman was the only representative of authority encountered in ordinary daily experience who was generally regarded as benign and helpful.

F M L Thompson, *The Rise of Respectable Society*

Governments had cleared away slum housing but without providing replacement homes. They had forced children to go to school from the age of five to 12 or 13 denying their much needed earnings to their parents, and for a time they even charged fees for this compulsory education. They had put controls on working hours for women and thus limited their earnings.

The Liberal Government could not assume that social reforms would be popular, indeed the historian Martin Pugh suggests:

Much of the State's activity in connection with children – vaccination, medical inspection, school meals, arrangements for taking them into care was resented by parents as an infringement of their role.

M Pugh, 'State & Society', 1994, *Arnold*

Reforms (1) School Meals, Medical Inspections and the 'Children's Charter'

During the 1906 election, social reform was not a major issue. Instead the Liberals preferred to defend free trade against Chamberlain's proposed tariffs. Nevertheless the pressures of the time and the views of the New Liberals led to legislation. Evidence turned up by the members of a committee examining the 'physical deterioration' of British people, led the committee to propose that school meals should be provided for needy children and that medical inspections of school children should be carried out. In 1906, therefore, when a Labour MP proposed a bill allowing local authorities to provide school meals, Liberal support enabled it to become law. Parents able to afford to pay were expected to do so. But:

where children are unable by reason of lack of food to take full advantage of education, they (i.e. the local authorities) may apply to the Board of Education and spend out of the rates.

Parliamentary Papers

This rate could amount to a halfpenny in the pound. In 1914 the government agreed to supply grants to meet half the costs, yet by this date at least half the local authorities had still to respond to the opportunity of providing meals. In 1914, then, the State made the provision of school meals compulsory.

The medical inspection of school children was required by a law which was passed in 1907. The Board of Education set up a medical department, and the gloomy reports sent in by doctors checking children's health led to the introduction of school clinics from 1912. Identifying problems was easy, but curing them was sometimes impossible. The costs of medicines, hospital care, spectacles, even of travel to a hospital were heavy burdens for many parents. A pair of spectacles could well cost a quarter of the weekly income of families on around £1 a week. Where ill-health was a consequence of dreadful housing conditions and a wretched diet, doctors could only despair. Some workhouses had developed infirmaries, and in 1886 it had been agreed that visiting them for treatment did not make one, officially, into a pauper. Charities and voluntary societies created a number of clinics and hospitals, but constantly struggled for money. Not till 1914 did maternity and child welfare clinics get any government money.

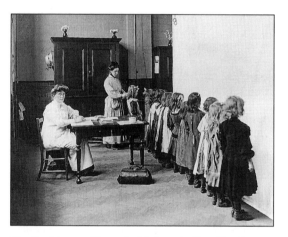

Medical inspection of children in Deptford, 1911.

In 1908 the Liberal MP Herbert Samuel put forward a bill that gathered together a number of measures that dealt with the welfare of children. The law this bill became was commonly called the 'Children's Charter'. It meant that children were not allowed to beg, could be tried for offences in special courts and could be sent not to prisons, but to 'borstals' away from adult criminals. A probation service was introduced. Children under 16 years old were not to purchase cigarettes or to enter public houses.

Social reformers welcomed the measures but others grumbled that too many rules and regulations were being imposed on people's lives.

Forbidding the young alcohol seemed to one worker to be a mistake:

Tis just the way to drive them to drink, to make a forbidden mystery of it. Children's Charter do they call it? Mischief-makers opportunity, I say.

Reforms (2) Old Age Pensions

Charles Booth was just one of the influential people who belonged to a pressure group that demanded that pensions should be paid to the elderly, to help them to continue to live outside workhouses (and the Scottish poor houses). However, Liberal ministers hesitated because the costs of the reform alarmed them. A series of by-elections in which Labour candidates defeated Liberals may well have helped persuade Liberal ministers to act in 1908.

Pensions were made available to those who were over 70, had lived in Britain for at least 20 years and had been out of prison for the last ten of these (later shortened to two years). The pensions were paid through post offices, places free of the stigma of the old poor law. Entitlement, however, depended on income. A pensioner with a yearly income of up to £21 received the full 5s. a week. Those living on £31 10s. 0d. a year were not entitled to a pension. Between those two, a sliding scale adjusted the pension – 2s. for those incomes up to £28 17s. 6d.; 3s. for those receiving up £26 5s. 0d.; or 4s. for those living on incomes up to £23 12s. 6d. It was not generous, yet the £8 million it cost to provide for 668 000 people helped to precipitate the budget crisis of 1909.

A working class boy, whose family kept a tiny shop, observed:

even these small doles meant life itself for many among the elderly poor. Old folk, my mother said, spending their allowance at the shop, 'would bless the name of Lloyd George as if he were a saint from heaven'. The

government met with much opposition to the introduction of a pension scheme at all from both the middle and working classes. Free gifts of money, many urged, would dishearten the thrifty who saved for their old age, and encourage the idle.

Quoted in R Roberts, *The Classic Slum*

THE NEW YEAR'S GIFT.

Punch cartoon showing the year bringing relief to an elderly couple. The paying of pensions to people over 70 meant they no longer had to ask for help.

The historian Peter Clarke has pointed out how cautious this reform was:

Anyone on poor relief was initially ineligible for a pension … (yet) paupers were the one group of old people manifestly in greatest need, but a wish to discriminate between the deserving and undeserving died hard.

P Clarke, *Hope & Glory*, 1996, *Penguin*

Government backbenchers soon succeeded in removing this clause in 1911. The task of funding this reform fell on David Lloyd George for, in 1908, he became Chancellor of the Exchequer. Lloyd George came from humble origins and was a witty and highly intelligent lawyer. He brought a passion to causes that he supported that helped sweep others along. He also delighted in provoking his opponents. Since, from time to time, the Conservative, Joseph Chamberlain had spoken of the need for pensions, Lloyd George claimed that what Liberals were doing was not a radical new policy.

Reforms (3) Employment

Surveys like Booth's and Rowntree's had shown that low wages, unemployment or irregular earnings were major causes of poverty. Other investigators commented on the damage done to health by the hours and conditions in which some people worked. In 1908 the actual working time in coal mines was limited to eight hours a day. In 1909 the Trade Boards Act set up boards to control wages and working conditions in the sweated trades. In 1911 the Shop Act introduced a legal weekly half-day holiday for shop workers (whose hours of work were usually very long).

Winston Churchill, President of the Board of Trade in 1908, took a keen interest in such reforms. To aid him in his work, he recruited the support of an Oxford academic, William Beveridge. Beveridge (like Lloyd George) visited Germany, and admired the arrangements in place there that required workers and employers to set money aside regularly as an insurance against accident and unemployment. Beveridge believed:

The problem of unemployment lies at the root of most other social problems. Society is built up on labour; it lays upon its members responsibilities which in the vast majority of cases can be met only from the reward of labour; it imprisons for beggary and brands for pau-

perism; its ideal unit is the household of man, wife and children maintained by the earnings of the first alone. The household should have at all times sufficient room and air – but how, if the income is too irregular always to pay the rent? The children should be supported by the parents – but how, unless the father has employment? The wife, so long at least as she is bearing and bringing up children, should have no other task – but how, if the husband's earnings fail and she has to go out to work?

Everywhere the same difficulty occurs. Reasonable security of employment for the bread-winner is the basis of all private duties and all sound social action.

Some workers in Britain earned enough to be able to save through their trade unions. Around one and a half million managed this. The rest of the country's workforce made no provision at all for times of hardship. In 1905 the Conservatives allowed local authorities to raise rates of up to a penny in the pound to be used to provide work for the unemployed when conditions (in winter especially) ended their usual occupations. Churchill and Beveridge wished to do more.

Labour exchanges

Labour exchanges provided one answer. The necessary legislation in 1909 allowed 83 such places to open their doors in 1910 (and more

Workmen at the labour exchange in Camberwell, February 1910.

were set up in succeeding years). But workers were not required to register there nor were employers compelled to notify the exchanges of any vacancies. The provision of washing facilities, clothes-mending services and refreshments were designed to make the exchanges attractive to workers. To the skilled they were probably very helpful but for the unskilled they had far less to offer.

Insurance

Insurance was the other major policy initiative. Churchill argued that his 1911 bill offered a lifebelt to save those in temporary trouble but it did not rescue the long-term unemployed and it excluded many occupations. Churchill explained:

To what trades ought we as a beginning to apply our system of compulsory contributory unemployment insurance? There are trades in which seasonal unemployment is not only high, but chronic, marked by seasonal fluctuations: house-building and workers of construction, engineering, machine and tool makers, ship and boat building, sawyers and general labourers. They comprise two and a quarter million workers. We propose to follow the German example of insurance cards to which stamps will be affixed each week.

The contributions came from employees ($2\frac{1}{2}$d. a week), employers ($2\frac{1}{2}$d. a week) and the State ($1\frac{2}{3}$d.). The benefits amounted to 7s. a week, payable for up to 15 weeks, with the entitlement to one week's payment for every five weeks' contributions. Workers who did not come into the scheme, or who had used up all their entitlement, were still driven, in the end, to turn to the poor law for relief. But the insurance fund prospered, and by 1914 it had a surplus of £23 million in it.

Reforms (4) Health Insurance

Lloyd George had good reasons to feel strongly about the need for health insurance. Tuberculosis, a disease that flourished in deprived environments, claimed 75 000 lives a year. One of the victims had been his own father. Around six million people continued to set aside money for times of illness by saving with Friendly Societies and insurance companies. These organisations fiercely opposed insurance proposals that involved the State, fearing for their own survival. Yet Lloyd George was determined to do something for:

people who cannot be persuaded or cannot afford systematic contributions. No plan can hope to be really comprehensive which does not include an element of compulsion.

He raged against:

The bitter hostility of powerful organisations like the Prudential, the Pearl, with an army numbering scores, if not hundreds of thousands of agents and collectors who make a living out of collecting a few pence a week from millions of households.

An insurance scheme in operation in Germany influenced his thinking. So too did the view he shared with Churchill that insurance schemes gave workers a sense of self-respect. He felt that dependence on State handouts was both very costly and damaging to workers' morale.

The insurance societies were won over when Lloyd George modified his plans by reducing their threat to private insurance. Pensions for widows and orphans, for example, were scrapped. Moreover insurance societies that were 'approved' became the means (under state supervision) by which the 1911 insurance provisions were administered.

There were other critics too. On the one hand some of the wealthy objected to the insurance scheme in principle, and the Conservative Party delayed it as far as they were able; on the other hand Labour critics attacked the scheme as wholly insufficient. The Labour leader, Keir Hardie called it 'a porous plaster to cover the disease that poverty causes'. The final form of the act entitled insured workers to 10s. a week for a period off work for health reasons of up to 26 weeks. They were permitted a free medical examination by doctors who agreed to care for a 'panel' of insured workers, and who in return received payment from the state. The funds for these benefits came in part from the workers themselves (4d. a week from those earning under £160 a year, employers 3d. a week, and the State 2d. a week). The scheme excluded insured workers' families, though it did allow a payment of 30s. for the birth of each child. It was intended to maintain an income for the breadwinner, not to provide a national health service. Nor did the scheme offer free hospital, dental, or other specialist services. The wealthier were still expected to provide for their own needs. And the insured who used up their 26 weeks' entitlement were compelled to seek poor law help.

The strategy of using insurance meant that the highly unpopular poor law system was by-passed.

How successful were Liberal reforms?

All the Liberal reforms offered levels of support that were confined to the poor and gave low levels of aid that were really only a supplement to other resources. Supporting a family on 7s. or 10s. a week, or existing in old age on 5s. a week alone, was well nigh impossible. Nevertheless the Liberals had built up a network of support that did not involve people seeking poor law relief. Lloyd George and Churchill continued to consider further reforms that included a state housebuilding programme to free farm workers from living in tied cottages.

The historian, A J P Taylor has stressed how limited the welfare programme was that the Liberals carried out. The State:

provided a meagre pension for the needy over the age of 70. Since 1911 it helped to insure certain classes of workers against sickness and unemployment. Expenditure on the social services had roughly doubled since the Liberals took office. Still, broadly speaking, the state acted only to help those who could not help themselves. It left the adult citizen alone.

A J P Taylor, *English History 1914–1945*, 1965, Oxford

The historian, Peter Clarke has argued that, though limited, the way that the Liberals carried out welfare reform was very skilful for it by-passed the poor law and brought in a system that won popular approval.

The unconditionality of insurance benefits, to which workers felt they had earned the right, was a means of winning assent for state intervention. Liberal collectivism thus made an appeal to Labour, by-passing socialist objections, which surely explains why the British Welfare State was built on the foundation of National Insurance.

P Clarke, *Hope and Glory*

Lloyd George's insurance scheme was less radical than he would have wished, but he had to take account of opposition and had to carry his fellow Liberals along with him. A huge crisis in Ireland seemed to threaten a possible civil war and there was the never-ending expense of the naval arms race, as well as the distractions of the tense situation abroad which eventually led to war in 1914. These might all be offered as reasons why Liberal social reform was not more extensive. The historian, Martin Pugh concludes:

The Edwardian social reforms were in no sense a welfare state, though they enjoyed an important link with the post 1945 system in the shape of the insurance principle. The Liberal measures were not intended as a comprehensive or uniform system of welfare provision. Rather, they involved targeting certain discrete parts of the problem of poverty. Those not included continued to require a safety net, which meant that it was necessary to leave the poor law, though it clearly had a diminishing role to play.

M Pugh, *State & Society*

► ACTIVITIES

1   In 1911 Lloyd George declared: 'I am in the Ambulance Corps. I am engaged to drive a wagon through the twisting and turnings and ruts of the Parliamentary road. I am in a hurry for I can hear the moaning of the wounded and I want to carry relief to them in the alleys, the homes, where they lie stricken.' Describe the ways in which the Liberal Government 1906–1914 provided help for the sick. (Demonstrate knowledge and understanding of historical development, events and issues.)

2   Read Churchill's explanation of insurance for the unemployed (Page 100). Explain why the Liberals used this policy to deal with unemployment. (Explain historical developments and events.)

3   Look at the cartoon entitled 'The New Years Gift'. What was the cartoonist's purpose in drawing this scene? (Evaluate sources taking account of origin, purpose, context and content.)

4   Look at the cartoon above. How far does it express a different point of view from the source used in question 3?

THE PHILANTHROPIC HIGHWAYMAN.

Mr. Lloyd-George. "I'LL MAKE 'EM PITY THE AGED POOR!"

5   'Broadly speaking the state acted only to help those who could not help themselves. It left the ordinary citizen alone.' (A J P Taylor). Is this all that social reform had achieved by 1914?

6   Should we blame the Liberals for not doing more?

Liberal Reforms – An Outline Summary

Liberal reforms for children

1906   Education (Provision of Meals) Act. Local councils allowed to provide meals and help pay for them from rates.
1907   Education Act. Medical inspection of all children.
1908   Children Act. New rules protecting children

1908 Labour Exchange Act

A national system was begun, though workers and employers were not compelled to use them.

Liberal laws to improve working conditions

1908   8 hour working day at the coal face for miners.
1909   Trade Boards Act. Controlled wages and working conditions in small workshop activities like tailoring.
1911   The Shop Act. Introduced a legal weekly half-day holiday.

1908 Old Age Pensions Act

		Pension per week
Paid to people over 70 years old		
Where yearly means do not exceed:	£21	5s
Where yearly means exceed £21 but do not exceed:	£23 12s 6d	4s
	£26 5s 0d	3s
	£28 17s 6d	2s
	£31 10s 0d	1s
Pension for a married couple		10s

The 1911 Insurance Act. Sickness Benefits

Payments	4d	a week from workers earning under £160 a year
	3d	a week from employers
	2d	a week from the state
Benefits	10s	a week when ill for 26 weeks; free medical treatment from a doctor chosen by a local Insurance Commission and paid a fee according to the number of free (or 'panel') patients he had.
	30s	maternity benefit for the birth of each child

The 1911 Insurance Act. Unemployment Benefit

Weekly contributions	from the employer $2\frac{1}{2}$d
	from the employee $2\frac{1}{2}$d
	from the state $1\frac{2}{3}$d
Benefits	7s a week for up to 15 weeks on the basis of one week's benefit for every five weeks contributions. No extra payments for dependants.

Chapter Eight

Depression and the National Government

Post 1918 British Governments faced serious problems for which the pre-war Liberal reforms were not a sufficient cure. Moreover politicians were now very aware that they were answerable to a mass electorate who increasingly seemed to expect their leaders to do something about major issues, and not to leave them to be resolved by private actions. The ways in which politicians approached social questions provides evidence of their beliefs and ideology. Their ability to act effectively offers insights into the authority they were able to command, and the consequences of their actions contributed to the changing identity of twentieth century Britain.

During the period between the ending of the First World War in 1918 and the beginning of the Second World War in 1939 the biggest problem of all that faced the Government was one of large scale unemployment. From 1931 the ministers who tackled the problem were part of a National Government, i.e. its members were drawn from several political parties not just one. The material in this chapter deals with the problems faced by this Government and the ways in which it responded.

As a result of working through this chapter you should have a sound knowledge and understanding of:

◆ The reasons why the National Government faced social problems.

◆ The ways in which it tackled these problems.

◆ The extent to which it can be seen as successful in its achievements.

This topic forms an essential part of the Higher course. It is not required for the Intermediate course, but it is still worth studying since it connects two major parts of the Intermediate course.

TASK

Work in pairs to gather information for and against the view that the National Government failed to tackle the social problems of the time adequately. This requires the build up of notes on:

◆ The reasons for social distress.

◆ The possible solutions available at the time.

◆ What the National Government actually did.

The inter-war years – an age of contrasts

Prosperity

During the inter-war years the British economy expanded. By 1938 total industrial production was 63 per cent above the levels of 1913. In many ways the British people became more prosperous. By 1939 two out of every three houses had been wired up to the electricity grid – in 1920 the figure had been one in 17. In the ten years after 1924 the number of licensed motor vehicles on Britain's roads rose from 1.3 million to 2.4 million. By 1939 over 11 million people were enjoying paid holidays, compared to 1930 when the figure had been a mere one and a half million. Britain's towns and cities still bear witness to the surge of home-building that took place in these years, as both council housing and private house-building activities expanded vigorously. When Seebohm Rowntree returned to study York in 1935–1936, he found a better housed population with more homes having their own bathroom. Certain industries expanded. The number working in the electricity industry more than doubled between 1924 and 1938 to reach nearly a third of a million. The building industry employed 840 000 in 1920 but 1 159 000 in 1937. Motor vehicle production, aircraft manufacture, chemicals, banking, insurance and distributive trades all took on more workers.

The inter-war population of Britain benefited from a fall in the price of many goods. Food prices in particular fell sharply. Also the behavioural patterns of Britain's more prosperous people were changing. Church attendances continued to fall. The spread of methods of birth control meant that couples deferred having children and limited the number of them. This made it easier for families to buy houses and to purchase the increasing number of electrical gadgets that were easing the burdens of housework. Drunkenness declined, but smoking increased. Families living in their more comfortable and hygienic homes were able to enjoy listening to gramophone records (from 6d. each), listening to the radio (by 1939 nearly three quarters of all homes had radio licences), and reading from the great range of cheap newspapers and magazines. The cinema developed into an enormously popular attraction, allowing people to escape into imaginary worlds, but also providing newsreels of events taking place all round the world.

Poverty

To be prosperous it was necessary to have a job. From 1921 until the outbreak of the Second World War in 1939, about 14 per cent of the insured workforce were, on average, out of work. Unemployment was not, of course, a new feature of life in Britain, but its long-term persistence was one part of the problem, and the other was its depth in the early 1930s. In 1932 it plunged to a figure of over 22 per cent. As a result, in these inter-war years there were always a million people out of work, and in January 1933 as many as

almost three million. Moreover some unemployed workers did not register as out of work, so the actual figure was certainly higher than the official one. In a new survey in 1936 Rowntree found that of those York inhabitants living in poverty, 28.6 per cent were so placed because of unemployment. There were parts of Britain where in the early 1930s, 50 per cent, 60 per cent or even more of the workforce had no job. The scale of unemployment went far beyond the scope of the Liberal insurance scheme which excluded some workers and gave the insured a very limited period of entitlement. Nor could the old poor law system cope with such huge numbers.

Why was there so much unemployment?

Behind those high levels of unemployment lay factors that contemporaries wrestled to understand. In 1931 a foreign visitor to Britain commented:

manufacturing costs are among the highest in the world. If this situation continues, any economic structure based on exports is faced with inevitable ruin. Old England has been living in a fool's paradise, fondly imagining that she could still rely on the spirit and methods of the nineteenth century. Such reforms as have been attempted are insignificant; at any rate, up to the War no serious efforts were made to transform coal mining, the metal industry, or textiles – the three bases on which exports and prosperity were founded. England is like a venerable mansion which though well and solidly built, has for years lacked repairs both in and out.

André Siegfried, *England's Crisis*, 1931

Export industries were particularly hard hit. In 1913 Britain had taken over 25 per cent of world trade in manufacturers but by 1937 this share had slumped to 19.1 per cent. Coal production fell from 287 million tonnes in 1913 to 227 million tonnes in 1938. The amount of shipping tonnage produced halved from 1913–1938 and the cotton industry's output fell drastically. Unemployment, therefore, was heavily concentrated in certain areas. In 1932 a third of all coal miners were without work, whilst 43 per cent of the cotton workers, 48 per cent of the iron and steel workers, and 62 per cent of the shipyard workers also had no employment. All these were industries that had relied heavily upon export markets.

The decline was, to some extent, inevitable. The war had damaged British exports and helped those less heavily involved, or neutral, to take advantage. By 1914 several other countries had more than caught up with the industrial lead Britain had once possessed, and this trend was bound to continue after the First World War. Moreover world conditions for trade were not consistently healthy during these years. The 'Great Depression' of 1929–1933 was a world-wide phenomenon that hit the USA severely, struck a number of European countries harder than Britain, and even reached the Far East. The boom enjoyed by many lands (though not Britain) in the later twenties had depended far too much on borrowed money. In 1929 confidence in business and banks began to collapse. As banks and businesses failed, trade slumped, unemployment rose and Americans called in the money they had been lending abroad, money that had done much to prevent economic depression in Europe. It was reckoned that by the middle of 1930 the number of unemployed in 33 countries had doubled in a year.

The slump hit Europe in 1931. The failure of the Vienna Bank was followed by financial and business failures across the continent. Countries that depended heavily on selling food and raw materials for industry ('primary' providers) found they were trying to market more than they could sell. The result was that they earned less with which to buy goods from countries like Britain. World trade shrank 25 per cent in three years. The collapse of banks, of share values and of companies led many countries to erect tariff barriers. Trade in the mid-1930s was even more difficult, as governments tried to protect their economies by taxing imports.

Historians have tended to conclude that despite this British industry did not perform well. G E Mingay has suggested:

In the end, it seems likely that at bottom there was a fatal weakness in the attitudes and values of British industrialists. They were cautious, attached to familiar forms of production, and fearful of risks that might jeopardise their control of the business. Few, if any, had technical training.

The Transformation of Britain

Contemporaries also struggled to understand what was happening. The writer J B Priestley travelled round the country in 1934 noting over and over again circumstances like these:

The export trade of such places as Bradford was declining long before the war. We used to sell textile machinery to other countries and send out managers and mechanics with those machines. You cannot expect to teach other people to make goods and then expect them to go on still buying those goods from you. The war was a sharp break in those processes of decline, a brief golden age of profits. Then reality broke in again in the early nineteen-twenties. The export trade, dependent on countries that had not the money to spend, rapidly dwindled. The very tide of fashion turned against the West Riding, which was still making solid fabrics for the world that wanted flimsy ones. Prices sank lower and lower. One firm after another staggered and then crashed.

J B Priestley, *English Journey*, 1934

The contrast between the prosperity in some parts of Britain and the poverty in others meant that politicians of the inter-war period were faced with a massive challenge.

Government actions before 1931

The reaction of politicians in the 1920s was to hope that the problem was short-term, and to work to restore pre-war economic conditions. Ministers did not seek to spend money to revive the economy, instead they cut expenditure, believing that finance should flow to the private sector. Between 1920 and 1925 government spending fell by a quarter in real terms. In 1925 Winston Churchill, Chancellor of the Exchequer, restored the gold standard, thus making sterling freely convertible into gold and fixing its value at the pre-war figure of £1 = 4.86 US$. Foreign policy was aimed at settling differences, restoring harmony, and thus reviving trade.

This still left the problem of what to do about those with no income to provide for themselves. In the 1920s ministers edged towards introducing a broader system of support that relied increasingly on the Treasury rather than on local money. The Unemployment Insurance Act (1920) increased the number of workers able to draw unemployment insurance to include 12 million workers. Domestic servants and agricultural workers were the only major groups still left out. The number of contributions required for them to become entitled to help were cut. In the following year, as unemployment figures climbed to over two million, the government authorised the continuation of payment to people who had used up the 26 weeks' payment to which they were entitled. 'Uncovenanted' or 'transitional' payments were made, and these took account of family needs with a system of payments for dependants. The alternative which was to continue with the old system of sending the 'out of benefit' workers to the Poor Law Guardians, was no longer possible. Guardians were already struggling to cope with those who had no insurance

entitlement. Given the very intense localised nature of unemployment, with its focus in areas where old export industries (like cotton and coal) were in recession, the arrival of workers who had used up their 26 weeks' entitlement would have swamped the system. So the Insurance Fund took the burden, and was soon heavily in debt. It had been planned on the basis of unemployment figures that were low and short-term. Contributions from those in work no longer provided enough to sustain the unemployed. The State was drawn in.

By 1929 politicians and economists were arguing over how best to tackle the problem. The Conservative Minister of Health, Neville Chamberlain, swept away the old Poor Law and placed its duties on large-sized local authorities. Their Public Assistance Committees now dealt with those not entitled either to insurance payments or to unconvenanted benefits. In 1930 Labour shifted the burden of the latter on to the Treasury. Conservative and Labour alike relied chiefly on the revival of the economy to solve the problems but led by Lloyd George, the Liberals began to argue that the state must intervene. Lloyd George drew on the thinking of the economist John Maynard Keynes to offer the electorate the slogan 'We can conquer unemployment'. Keynes was one of the outstanding economic thinkers of the twentieth century. He argued that the government should intervene more and spend public money on projects like road building that would provide jobs and improve Britain. Moreover, he suggested the increased number of people with wages to spend would be able to buy more goods and services and thus create yet more jobs. In 1936 Keynes published his most famous work *The General Theory of Employment, Interest and Money* and won increasing support, but without converting those who were actually in power. In 1929, Lloyd George argued that by borrowing £300 million the state could fund public works

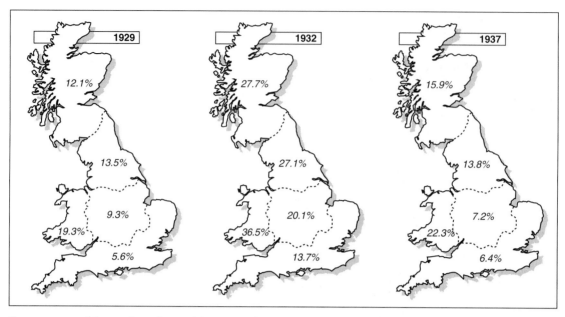

Percentages of insured workers without employment in different parts of Britain, 1929–1937.

like roads and house-building that would provide work and improve the country. Since far too few Liberals were elected in 1929 it is impossible to know if this would have worked. It may be that Lloyd George underestimated the administrative difficulties involved.

The Labour Ministry from 1929 to 1931 tinkered with welfare provision and began a very tiny public works programme, but it spurned the ideas of one of its number, Oswald Mosley, to act more boldly by using state power to revive the economy. As a world trade depression hit Britain too, unemployment rose, confidence in sterling fell, and gold began to flood out of the country. The unemployment insurance fund debt had risen to £100 million by the end of 1930. Although they agreed that public spending cuts were needed, ministers could not agree on a 10 per cent reduction in unemployment benefit. The ministry collapsed, and was replaced by a coalition of Conservatives, Liberals and a handful of Labour politicians headed by Ramsay MacDonald. In front of it lay the problems of a financial crisis, of a shrinkage of exports, and of the growing numbers of unemployed.

The national government's policies

Though no election was needed, the government began by calling one. The Conservative leader Stanley Baldwin, especially wanted to exploit the opportunity of establishing his grip on his party. Liberal constituency withdrawals helped about a hundred Conservatives to Westminster. Baldwin's strategy worked. Though led by MacDonald till 1935, Martin Pugh suggests that the National Government was 'in policy and tone, if not in personnel, thoroughly Conservative'. In general, according to the historians, Chris Cook and John Stevenson:

the main objectives of the Government were to balance budgets and restore business confidence, a view that was shared by the great majority of economists and Treasury advisers.

The Slump, 1977

Ramsay MacDonald addressing an audience at Work Street Recreation Ground in Leeds on 25 May 1929.

Certainly Conservatives dominated the Government providing 470 of its 554 MPs. The Labour Party split, with some following MacDonald and others turning to opposition. Liberals were even more fragmented for some joined the Government as National Liberals led by John Simon. Some soon turned to opposition and Lloyd George led his little family group of four MPs.

Financial measures

The Labour Chancellor of the Exchequer, Philip Snowden, remained in office for a short while. He had long been a stern opponent of heavy Government spending. Now he applied the cuts over which his former colleagues had quarrelled. Teachers and armed service personnel had their pay reduced by 15 per cent, the police suffered 5 per

cent cuts and other public pay was lopped too, including unemployment benefit. Weekly amounts to an out-of-work man fell from 17s. to 15s. 3d.

The historian A J P Taylor commented:

The members of the National Government may be seen in a newsreel assembled for discussion, stern features, teeth clenched as they face the crisis. They would hesitate at nothing to save the country, to save the pound. The result of their courage was that the children of the unemployed had less margarine on their bread. After this resolute decision Ministers dispersed to their warm comfortable homes and ate substantial meals.

English History, 1914–1915, 1970

In fact not even all the cuts survived. The fleet, anchored at Invergordon, mutinied. Their pay cut had to be modified to 10 per cent. Snowden also added 6d. to income tax and 1d. duty on a pint of beer. More dramatically, Britain followed the lead of other countries by abandoning the gold standard, and began to manage its currency instead of leaving its level for the markets to determine. The value of the pound fell by the end of 1931 to $3.40. Fifteen million pounds were placed in an Exchange Equalisation Account to be used for buying and selling currency to keep the pound stable. A J P Taylor noted:

A few days before, a managed currency had seemed as wicked as family planning. Now, like contraception, it became commonplace.

Deals with France and the USA in 1936 settled that the three countries would not alter their rates without consulting one another.

The National Government also reduced the bank rate. Snowden left office in 1932, and was replaced by Chamberlain (till the latter became Prime Minister in 1937, following Baldwin's leadership from 1935 to 1937). Both men were equally committed to containing government spending and the interest payments on money borrowed by the government were adjusted downwards as a result of the bank rate falling to 2 per cent. This policy alone saved £86 million a year of ministry expenditure. In addition, low interest levels encouraged private borrowing, helping firms and individuals to finance their efforts. Cheap money played a big part in the 1930s housing boom, funding both construction work and mortgages for house purchase. The crisis jolted the thinking of politicians, and it even led to Keynes joining the official Committee on Economic Information, but it did not radically alter the official view that heavy state spending to revive the economy was not desirable. Supporters of this view can be found in all three political parties. Critics were present in all three too, though their numbers in the Conservative Party were small. By 1936 the tense state of foreign affairs meant that spending on rearmament could not be avoided, but even here Chamberlain's desire for a balanced budget chopped back the £97 million sought by the RAF to £59 million. The modern four-engined bomber building programme was held back, while cheaper fighters rolled off production lines.

Trade

In 1932 Philip Snowden resigned from office, so too did half the Liberal group, led by Herbert Samuel. What drove them out was the long-term commitment of the government to taxing imports. Baldwin had long been under pressure from some of his party to introduce tariffs – indeed he had offered this policy to the electorate in the early 1920s only to see most voters plump for free trade candidates from other parties. By 1931 he had agreed to make tariffs official policy, for the circumstances of the time seemed to suit this move. British producers feared that the country would be a dumping ground for cheap foreign goods sent here by countries that taxed imports into their own lands. The campaign waged by Lord Beaverbrooke's paper, the *Daily Express*, from 1929 onwards for

imperial free trade formed another aspect of a policy of tariffs. Ever since Joseph Chamberlain had produced his proposal in Edwardian times, some Conservatives had argued that a prosperous British economy could best be obtained by tying together the different parts of the Empire as an economic unit, while taxing non-imperial goods.

The 1932 Import Duties Act imposed taxes on around three quarters of imports at levels of around 20 per cent, though in the case of iron and steel it was $33\frac{1}{3}$ per cent. A conference in 1932 was held at Ottawa to discuss trade between Empire and Commonwealth lands. Britain guaranteed free entry to her markets for most dominion goods, and got minor tariff concessions in return. In fact dominion governments were determined to protect their own farmers and industrialists, so the idea of a vast imperial free trade area proved to be unrealistic. In any case the Government was not wholly committed to the idea. In 1933 MacDonald held a World Economic Conference in London to try to liberalise trade and to stabilise exchange rates. It failed to live up to his hopes, though tariffs did prove to be a helpful bargaining counter in doing deals with other states. Between 1933–1938, 20 bilateral trade agreements were signed. The enthusiasts for imperial free trade were not happy about this approach, but during this period there was certainly a drift to more trade with the Empire. By 1938 47 per cent of exports from Britain went to the Empire and Commonwealth and 39 per cent of imports into Britain came from there. The adoption of protection was a major shift in British policy, though the historian Trevor May suggests:

The slow process of recovery which began in the 1930s seems to have owed little to protection, for one of the features of the inter-war economy was the decline in the importance of international trade and the growth of the home market.

An Economic and Social History of Britain, 1760–1970, 1987

Reforming the British economy

Stephen Constantine has suggested that:

the timidity of ministers was not due to the absence of alternative economic theories but to a failure of political will.

Unemployment in Britain between the wars, 1980

Not all historians agree with the critical implications of this view. Chris Cook and John Stevenson maintain:

It is a harsh judgement which condemns the National Government for failing to alter the regional imbalance of unemployment at a time of world recession and when the problem still remains.

The Slump

There were plenty of critics at the time. Oswald Mosley built up the British Union of Fascists, pointed to the Italian and German governments' efforts, and argued for more state controls and spending. In 1935 Lloyd George repeated his earlier proposals, modifying them in the light of US government policies, and calling them a 'new deal'. Keynes published his major work, *The General Theory of Employment Interest and Money* in 1936, arguing that full employment would not come from the automatic operation of market forces, and that state action was needed to affect both investment and consumption. Yet no one can tell if these ideas would have worked, and most advisers urged ministers to follow traditionally cautious policies. Nor did the government control the huge bureaucracy of modern times. It is not clear that large-scale peace-time state intervention would have been either practical or politically acceptable. The National Government had a huge majority in 1931 and a very comfortable one in 1935.

Initial policies were negative. Labour's subsidies for public works were ended, for fear of channelling resources away from private ventures.

Ministers grumbled at local authorities that spent on public works, complaining they were wasteful. As signs of recovery appeared and public pressures were felt, so the Government edged cautiously into a number of initiatives. Ministers were aware of political upheaval in other lands and were nervous of similar events in Britain. During the 1930s there were a number of marches and protests, the most famous being the 1936 Jarrow March, of men from a town ruined by the closure of Palmer's shipyard. Over 11 000 signed a petition starting:

Whereas for 15 years Jarrow had endured industrial depression without parallel in the town's history, all efforts for the resuscitation of industry have failed and the future holds no prospect of work for the many thousands unemployed. Therefore the petitioners humbly pray that the necessary active assistance be given by the Government for the provision of work in the town of Jarrow.

Baldwin had no time for this form of pressure. He observed:

In the opinion of H M Government such marches can do no good to the causes for which they are represented to be undertaken, are liable to cause unnecessary hardship to those taking part in them and are altogether undesirable in this country governed by a Parliamentary system where every area has its representative in the House of Commons to put forward grievances and suggest remedies, processions to London cannot claim to have any constitutional influence on policy. Ministers cannot consent to receive any deputation of Marchers.

The Times, 15 October, 1936

Branch of the NUWM on the march in the 1930s.

What the National Government actually did may have been reluctantly undertaken, and was certainly a piecemeal strategy rather than a clearly thought out coherent one; but it showed signs of a commitment to manage the economy that bears out Stephen Constantine's view:

In the new thinking which emerged between the wars, government was given an increasingly predominant role. For this the unemployment problem was largely responsible.

Government backing went to railway building, and London Transport and road building (from 1935). Government loans made possible the resumption of work on the half-built luxury liner *Queen Mary* on the Clyde. When rearmament began, contracts were placed in depressed areas to help the iron, steel and shipbuilding industries. The 1929–1931 Labour Government had established government-backed agricultural marketing boards that the National Government developed. Separate boards for milk, hops, potatoes and meat, together with support for the sugar-beet industries, ate up 40 million pounds a year in subsidies by 1936, and people approved. One farmer commented:

The Milk Marketing Board started in 1933. My father kept bullocks, milked a few cows, and mother took butter to Exeter and sold it for about 1/10d. a pound. We probably took £5 a week. It was not a very good way of making a living. But through the formation of the Milk Board everybody was paid the same price for milk throughout the country. We were then getting the equivalent of double the price for liquid milk ... and this stabilised Devon farming in particular because here was an ideal grass-growing area, and we could keep cows and it could be profitable.

Quoted in Pagnamenta and Overy, *All Our Working Lives*, 1984

Some effort was made to overhaul and reduce the capacity of old-fashioned industries. Attempts to rationalise the coal industry came to little, though royalties paid to landowners where pits were developed were nationalised. The 1935 Finance Act offered tax relief to industries that were reorganised to shed excessive capacity. Iron and steel in particular received a high level of tariff protection in return for promises to reform. An Act of 1936 attacked the problem of surplus cotton-spinning capacity, by setting up a Spindles Board which bought up and scrapped cotton-spinning machinery, using money raised by levies on existing machines. The formation of the National Shipbuilders Security Ltd, led to the closure of 28 antiquated yards by 1937, and this was paid for by a 1 per cent levy on members. Government loans encouraged owners of tramp-steamers to scrap old vessels and build new ones.

By 1934 the evidence of severe long-term unemployment in certain parts of the country led to the Special Areas Act. Two commissioners were allowed to spend two million pounds a year to encourage employment in the designated districts of south Wales, southern Scotland, north east England and western Cumberland. But the tiny amounts of money involved made it difficult to do much. The commissioners supported local amenity schemes, encouraged land settlement, and tried to draw in new businesses. In his 1936 report, the commissioner responsible for England and Wales stated:

It has to be admitted that no appreciable reduction of the number of those unemployed has been effected. Such increased employment as is likely to result from the operation of the many schemes initiated will prove altogether insufficient, in the absence of a spontaneous growth of new industries and expansion of existing industries, to offset the release of labour brought about by increased mechanisation and rationalisation . . .

The all-important question that arises from a study of the results obtained from its administration is whether the time is now ripe for a second experiment which, whilst continuing work already embarked upon, would make an attempt to deal more directly with the problem of unemployment. My recommendation is that by means of State-provided inducements a determined attempt should be made to attract industrialists to the Special Areas.

Third Report of the Commissioner for the Special Areas, 1936

In 1937 the money involved was increased, and the Treasury was given power to aid companies ready to move into distressed areas. Some 121 new firms did start businesses, including a new steel works at Ebbw Vale, yet the overall effect of the commissioners' work was the creation of, at most, 50 000 new jobs.

The Drummond Street Occupational Centre in Bradford put men to work on allotments.

Welfare

By 1931 governments had accepted that it was their responsibility to help the unemployed. Perhaps this in part was motivated by the desire to keep protest down to modest levels. In fact Britain in the 1930s remained mainly peaceful, helped by the absence of inflation (which so upset the middle classes in Germany by destroying their savings) and by a significant fall in the cost of living. Only about 18 000 people joined the Communist Party. The British Union of Fascists attracted about 40 000 but by 1936 ministers felt confident enough to clamp controls on its uniform wearing and marching. The National Union of Unemployed Workers recruited 50 000 members.

Some contemporaries wondered why protests did not take place on a bigger scale. The writer George Orwell suggested:

The post-war development of cheap luxuries has been a very fortunate thing for our rulers. It is quite likely that fish and chips, art, silk stockings, tinned salmon, cut price chocolate, the movie, the radio, strong tea and the football pools have, between them, averted revolution.

G Orwell, *The Road to Wigan Pier*, 1937

The historian Keith Laybourn suggests:

Many of the unemployed expected to find work. When this did not occur ... unemployment became almost institutionalised and absorbed within the framework of the community ... the struggle for existence consumed most of the efforts of the working class poor and appears to have contributed to the feeling of apathy and futility.

Britain on the Breadline, 1998, Sutton

And an ordinary inhabitant of Ashton under Lyne thought:

At that time there was that Victorian hangover and people were that cowed, they were afraid of authority.

N Gray, *The Worst of Times*, 1985

One historian has argued that voluntary efforts to aid the needy played a significant part. Charitable bodies (as well as local authorities) provided clothes, food, allotments and centres where the unemployed were offered recreations. In the late 1930s such centres had a membership of 200 000 and R H C Hayburn suggests that:

In alleviating the suffering of those out of work, the state's efforts were overshadowed by those of a voluntary nature.

Journal of Contemporary History, VI, 1971

In 1936 Seebohm Rowntree re-examined York, and found significant improvements in the lives of people, when compared with his findings in 1899. He offered an analysis of the reasons for this:

The first is the reduction in the size of family. The second reason is the increase in real wages, probably amounting on the average to about 35 per cent. The effect of this would have been greater but for the heavy unemployment in 1936. A third cause is the remarkable growth of social services during the period under review. In 1899 the only financial aid given from public sources to persons living in their homes was Poor Relief, the acceptance of which rendered the recipients paupers; they lost their rights as citizens, for they could not vote.

Our schedules show that in 1936 no less than £5309 was paid out weekly for the following social services:

	£	s.	d.
Unemployment benefit	1801	18	5
Health benefit	113	7	6
Old age pensions and pensions for widows and orphans	2624	10	3
Public assistance	753	5	9
Milk and/or meals for school children	16	14	9

£5309 is equal to 6s. 6d. per working class family and to 1s. 11d. per head of the working class population. Of this total, £3412 went to the 5088 families living below the minimum. This is an average of 13s. 5d. per family and 3s. 11d. per head

S Rowntree, Poverty and Progress

Certainly ministers were bombarded with data and reports from all sorts of pressure groups who believed that the state should act to improve health care, housing and diet, and to bring in family allowances. As Stephen Constantine notes:

The origins of the post-war welfare state were to be found in the discourses and proposals which inter-war unemployment, not exclusively but substantially, generated.

S Constantine, Unemployment in Britain Between the Wars

The 10 per cent cut in unemployment benefit of 1931 was accompanied by a close scrutiny of the income of the household in which the unemployed person resided. It involved an examination of savings, pensions, lodgers' rents, and income from other family members. This was much resented. George Orwell claimed that it broke up families as elderly and young people left home rather than see payments reduced or stopped to an unemployed family member. Though the 10 per cent cut was restored in 1934, the hated means test remained.

Unemployed Alfred Smith, gives his wife the week's housekeeping money, 1939.

In 1934 Chamberlain introduced the Unemployment Act to rationalise support of the needy. He disliked the way Public Assistance Committees treated requests in a fashion that varied from place to place. PACs in Rotherham and County Durham were considered to be so over-generous that Ministry of Labour Commissioners replaced them. Now Chamberlain proposed to reorganise the unemployment insurance scheme by tightening its operations, widening its scope (to include farm workers, for instance) and confining its task to those whose contributions provided a genuine 26-week entitlement. William Beveridge was put in charge of a Statutory Committee to run the operation. It prospered and was soon able to increase dependants' allowances, though Rowntree reckoned that insurance income of 35s. a week for a family of five fell well below his figure (43s. 6d.) of what such a family needed to stay out of real poverty.

The burden of supporting those who had used up their insurance entitlement, or who had never had any entitlement, was shifted from PACs to a new Treasury-funded body, the Unemployment Assistance Board, which distributed standard rates of support through local Labour Exchanges. When rates were announced, there was uproar. So many PAC rates were higher than UAB figures that the Government had to delay introducing the new rates until 1937. Till then current PAC rates, or UAB rates (whichever were higher) were paid. The reform left the PACs to deal with the elderly, sick, widowed, or very young who were in desperate need.

Some historians' views on the National Government

Martin Pugh has written of the National Government:

In several ways it abandoned the policies it had been established to defend in 1931 ... it was responsible for major infringements of laissez faire. Unquestionably the greatest gain was that the National Government, in spite of itself, abandoned the gold standard and effectively devalued the pound. The structural problems of British industry remained. Such success as the National Government had enjoyed reflected the adoption of parts of Keynesian economics more by force of events than out of conviction.

State & Society, 1994, Arnold

Malcolm Pearce and Geoffrey Stewart offer the following view:

The National Government did not solve the problem of the distressed areas but it eased their plight and made the painful process of economic adjustment bearable whilst preserving the decencies of a democratic and tolerant society.

British Political History 1867–1995, Democracy and Decline, 1996, Routledge

Keith Laybourn argues:

The National Government became more liberal in their provision of relief as time went on and provided a modest amount of special aid to overcome some of the worst excesses of regional mass unemployment. Yet this was achieved within the confines of balanced budgets. There was little evidence that they were ever seriously interested in introducing the more expansionary policies of J M Keynes. It remains debatable as to whether or not Keynesian ideas could have solved the problems of the 1930s. It seems likely that factors other than government policy helped to improve employment prospects and reduce unemployment.

Britain on the Breadline, 1998, Sutton

➤ ACTIVITIES

1 Plan and write an essay on the following title:

'We should praise the National Government for doing as much as it did for the economy and the unemployed, not blame it for not doing more.' Do you agree?

2 Read the visitor's comments on British economic troubles (Page 105). Use the source and your knowledge to explain why there was so much unemployment at this time. (Explain historical developments and events.)

Chapter Nine

The Labour Government 1945–1951 and the Welfare State

Between 1945 and 1951 a Labour Government led by Clement Attlee carried out a series of reforms that are often seen as creating a 'welfare state' in Britain, i.e. all people's major needs were met from the cradle to the grave. The material in this chapter deals with these reforms, with the factors that brought them about, and considers their importance.

As a result of studying this chapter you should have a sound knowledge and understanding of:

◆ The various reasons for the Labour Government's social reforms.

◆ The main reforms.

◆ How far these reforms can be seen as successful.

This topic forms part of both the Higher and Intermediate courses.

Attlee and supporters celebrating the Labour election victory.

TASK

Use the material you have already studied and add to it from this chapter in order to draw up a detailed plan for answering the question:
'The Welfare State of 1945–1951 was less a socialist achievement than the ending of a process owing much to Liberals and Conservatives.' Do you agree?

To develop such a plan:

✦ Look back over your work so far to list the reforms already carried out.

✦ List in detail the wartime reforms.

✦ List in detail the post war Labour reforms.

✦ List your conclusions.

Wartime and welfare

From 1 September 1939–14 August 1945 Britain was again at war. The fight against Germany, Italy and Japan took British servicemen all over the world.

The speedy success of German forces in 1940 drove the British out of mainland Europe. For the army at least there were not to be the huge and costly conflicts of the First World War, but for Britain's airmen and sailors the war was at times desperate. They fought to prevent invasion in 1940, to reduce German air-raids on Britain and to stop German ships and submarines starving Britain into defeat by sinking shipping. 270 000 members of the armed forces and 35 000 merchant seamen were killed in the conflict.

The bombing of Britain meant that 60 000 civilians died. Many factories and shipyards, railways and bridges were damaged. Air-raids totally wrecked 475 000 houses, and badly damaged around four million more.

The struggle demanded great sacrifices by the British people. By 1945 nearly eight million Britons were in the armed forces or in the uniformed groups who supported the forces. Government spending and borrowing rose sharply. In 1937–1938 defence took £197.3 million, 21.5 per cent of total spending. By 1944–1945 defence costs had climbed to £5125 million, 82.94 per cent of total spending.

From 1940 the Conservative Winston Churchill led the Government. Its power increased by means of an Emergency Powers Act (1938). New ministries of food, supply, economic warfare and information were established and the numbers of civil servants swelled from 387 000 in 1939 to 704 700 by the end of the war. Conscription for those not in employment defined as essential came promptly in 1939. A new Minister of Labour, the trade union leader Ernest Bevin, took responsibility for the huge task of organising the British people for the war effort. The conscription of men aged between 18 and 41 was extended to unmarried childless women aged between 20 and 30, and by 1943 the age range for women had been widened to between 18 and 50 years old. Some women joined the forces, and thousands were drafted into jobs left vacant by men recruited to fight, or into jobs created by new demands on production in wartime.

The economy

Taxes rose. Income tax reached 10s. in the pound. Even this yielded insufficient money, and so the government plunged Britain more deeply into debt, increasing the pre-war figure sevenfold.

Some industries suffered. Activities regarded as less urgent, like building new houses and making clothes, suffered a 50 per cent fall in labour force size. Other industries boomed, including chemicals, aircraft manufacture, farming (the total tilled area increased 66 per cent) and machine tools. The war stimulated scientific research and its practical application, as in the development of jet engines, better radar, and antibiotics. The old industries like coal, iron and steel, and shipbuilding found their products once more in demand, but their out-of-date working conditions were ill-suited to the pressures of a crisis which left no time for modernisation.

The war severely damaged trade. Britain had to concentrate on meeting urgent wartime needs of food, raw materials for industry, oil and military products. Earnings from exports slumped.

Bombing

In 1939, terrified of the slaughter they feared would come, the government organised the evacuation of 1 500 000 children from places likely to be targets of bombing to more remote areas.

Another two million children were moved privately. By the end of 1939, 900 000 had drifted back to the towns as the German bombers failed to come – they were busy in Poland. Many children from city slums had habits that horrified their new hosts. The writer-diplomat Harold Nicolson noted in his diary:

many of the children are verminous and have disgusting habits ... This is a perplexing social event. The effect will be to demonstrate to people how deplorable is the standard of life and civilisation among the urban proletariat.

Quoted in A Kendall, *Their Finest Hour*, 1972

During 1939 and 1945 cities were more likely to be bombed than remote parts of the country; many children were evacuated by train from the cities.

Though the Luftwaffe's raids did not devastate Britain as dreadfully as pre-war politicians had feared, life in target areas (like major cities) became a tense and often distressing experience – though some felt that, in curious ways, life improved.

A Londoner observed:

People were much more together. They met in the air-raid shelters, in the tubes at night, they were in the Home Guard, or they queued for spam or whatever it was they could get hold of, one egg a week. Everybody really lost a lot of their inhibitions about talking to their next-door neighbours. When the raids were over they used to almost celebrate in the early morning and this was the spirit that I think a lot of people hoped would continue after the war ...

P Addison, *Now The War is Over*, 1985

Although wages rose and unemployment virtually vanished, there was little for the population to spend their wages on, as rationing was introduced and then spread to cover clothing, petrol, and many items of food. It continued after the war, indeed in 1948 it became more severe.

Mrs Whitham working out her ration quota for the family.

Women's work

Once again, as in the First World War, women found that their labour was urgently required. The number of women working in vehicle building and engineering, for example, rose by 770 000. 65 000 women joined the Land Army to help with farm work, and they had to be allowed to carry out jobs that had hitherto been the exclusive preserve of men. Many women hoped these new opportunities would continue in peacetime. This was not necessarily what their employers wished, as this factory manager's comment on one employee indicates:

This girl has so taken to machines that she'd like to become an apprentice and go right through the works. This of course is not possible on account of Union agreements. There's a feeling among the men at the moment women must be in the factory solely because of the war but really women's place is the home.

The end of the war found British people subject to higher taxes and more extensive government controls than ever before. War had damaged and distorted the economy, wrecked overseas trade and drastically cut overseas investment. Yet the war had also brought an unprecedented awareness of the need for social reform and a sense that such reforms were needed urgently.

Labour enters the Government

The Second World War ended the unemployment crisis and brought Labour leaders into office. Although Churchill was Prime Minister and kept control of defence, Labour Ministers occupied key posts in home affairs. Attlee became Deputy Prime Minister and Herbert Morrison, Arthur Greenwood, Stafford Cripps and Ernest Bevin all obtained important positions. The Labour Party made clear its view that:

After the war, the national war effort must be turned to the building of a new Britain. While planning the war, the Government must plan for peace and a new society. Instead of regarding each item of state control as a temporary infringement of the normal, the occasion should be seized to lay the foundations of an efficient economic system.

The wartime ministry, led by Winston Churchill, brought Keynes into the Treasury and absorbed his ideas. In 1944 a white paper *Full Employment in a Free Society* showed that all members of the coalition were committed to using the power of the state to prevent the return of the 1930s. Memories of this time may have helped Labour win power in 1945, for they at least had been out of office then and could claim to be blameless. The huge issues raised by total war had made massive government intervention in daily life inevitable as people were conscripted for the forces and for civilian work, food was rationed, and the economy managed by new ministries.

Welfare Reforms (1) Diet

Once more war highlighted some of the flaws in British society. The Ministry of Food planned the rationing scheme with a view to improving the nation's health. Calcium, iron, minerals and vitamins had to be added to certain foods. The Emergency Milk and Meals scheme of 1941 supplemented basic rations with extra items for expectant mothers and young children. Cheap milk, cod liver oil and orange juice went to mothers, whilst the price of milk and school meals was kept low by government subsidies. Children unable to afford even subsidised foods, were given them free and by 1945, 1.65 million children were served with school meals daily. Churchill approved of this policy: 'There is no finer investment for any community than putting milk into babies,' he said.

Welfare Reforms (2) Health

Pre-war medical care still excluded over half

the population, i.e. those who were not part of the 1911 insurance scheme. It was therefore particularly severe on women. Doctors charged fees to those outside the scheme, and in any case it did not cover specialist treatment, or dental and eye care. Pre-war hospitals were not part of a co-ordinated system. About 1000 were voluntary organisations depending on fund-raising, bequests, and contributions from patients, whilst about 2000 were local authority hospitals (often developed first by Poor Law Guardians) which relied partly on fees. The war shook up this confused muddle. Hospital care had to be extended to cope with the war-wounded who were given free treatment. The war-wounded could also include civilians injured by bombs. The local authority hospitals, and the hospitals set up by voluntary charities, soon had many 'emergency beds' whose occupants received treatment paid for by the state. A free immunisation programme soon produced a sizeable fall in deaths from diphtheria from nearly 3000 in 1938 to 818 in 1945.

Welfare Reforms (3) Helping the Needy

During the war prices rose quite sharply. The government tried to keep them down by paying subsidies to food producers, but old age pensioners found it especially hard to manage. In 1940 the Unemployment Assistance Board was given power to pay supplementary amounts to needy elderly folk, a step which widened the work of the Board and made it more popular. The Board also helped bombed families who could not support themselves in the disastrous circumstances following the destruction of their homes. In 1941, as a result of pressure from Ernest Bevin, the Board abolished the household means test.

These were separate welfare reforms, which came at a time when there was a growing awareness among politicians that war would produce an overhaul of welfare. In addition, a planning group that included Conservatives produced this statement for the Ministry of Information:

Wartime conditions have already compelled us to make sure, not only that the rich do not consume too much, but that others get enough. The needs of war production call for new measures for improving the housing, welfare and transport of workers. The evacuation scheme should give the impetus to radical improvements in our educational system and social services. The wartime measures to protect the standard of living point the way to a planned population policy. The mobilisation of manpower should spell the end of mass unemployment. War measures for rationalising the distribution of various products should lead to a remodelling of distribution as a whole, so as to transform increased productivity into increased consumption on a higher standard.

Quoted in P Addison, *The Road to 1945*

By 1942 the Ministry of Health anticipated a new kind of post-war hospital service:

In the last year or so the numerous organisations and authorities whose interests lie in the hospital world have been giving increasing thought to the future. All start from the accepted premise that there can be no return to the pre-war position of unrelated hospital units pursuing independent and often wastefully competitive courses.

Quoted in A Marwick, *Britain in a Century of Total War*

The Beveridge Report

In 1942 an overall welfare plan was published. It was written by Sir William Beveridge. The Beveridge Report was the result of pressure from the TUC, which told the Labour minister, Arthur Greenwood:

We are definitely of the opinion that the country cannot continue to afford the inefficient and incomplete services rendered to insured workers together with the expensive muddle and waste associated with it. We ask the Minister of Health to take the lead in an examination of the whole position with a view to plans being produced which would provide a properly balanced scheme.

Memorandum by the TUC in J R Hay, *The Development of the British Welfare State*, 1978

Beveridge's suggestions were the response to this pressure. Greenwood gave him the task of leading a committee to study insurance, and the resulting ideas were very much Beveridge's own notions. He wanted to see the whole system made much more simple and more efficient. He believed that insurance should protect people against all the serious hardships of life, and thought that the scheme should cover the whole population of the country. The insurance payments he planned were seen as the rightful due of all, not money to be doled out carefully in differing amounts according to a means test. But he did not think payments should be generous. Beveridge was a Liberal, a believer in the principle of people contributing to the savings organised by the state, and if people wished to make more generous provision for themselves, then he believed that they should turn to private insurance schemes.

He did not confine himself simply to looking at insurance. He argued that:

the organisation of social insurance should be treated as one part only of a comprehensive policy of social progress. Social insurance may provide income security, it is an attack on Want. But Want is one only of five giants. The others are Disease, Ignorance, Squalor, and Idleness.

To fight these giants, Beveridge stated that it would be necessary to have a proper national health service, a policy of full employment, and allowances paid to families with children. He said of his ideas:

The scheme proposed here is in some ways a revolution but in more important ways it is a natural development from the past. It is a British Revolution.

TRANSFORMATION SCENE

"Avaunt, foul sprite! and be no longer seen
I'll have you know I am the Fairy Queen!"

William Beveridge drew up a welfare plan to provide insurance to protect people against serious hardship.

The main points of the Beveridge Report

1 The appointment of a minister to control all the insurance schemes.

2 A standard weekly payment by people in work as a contribution to the insurance fund.

3 The right to payments for an indefinite period for people out of work.

4 Old age pensions, maternity grants, funeral grants, pensions for widows and for people injured at work.

5 Payments at a standard rate, the same for all whatever their private means, paid without a means test.

6 Family allowances to be introduced.

7 A national health service to be set up.

Beveridge was criticised by the private insurance companies, who felt that his plans would hurt their business. One of their officials declared of the report, 'The author is an economist turned spendthrift, destroying every vestige of self-reliance and self-help.' And the Prime Minister, Churchill, was worried about the cost of the proposals. The war was hurting Britain, but Churchill believed that post-war Britain needed strong defence forces to prevent another war. He wrote:

A dangerous optimism is growing up about the conditions it will be possible to establish after the war. Our foreign investments have almost disappeared. The United States will be a strong competitor. The question steals across the mind whether we are not committing our people to tasks beyond their capacity to bear.

W S Churchill, *Cabinet notes in the Second World War IV*, 1951

But there was no doubt about the general reaction to the Beveridge Report. Though it was written in dry and difficult language, it became a bestseller. The Labour Party and the trade unions welcomed it with enthusiasm. The Ministry of Information found it to be a major topic of conversation, its officials on Clydeside, for instance, reported:

Interest in the Beveridge Plan on its publication was really tremendous. For a week or two the war news tended to take a back seat. Practically everyone approved of the underlying principles. Soldiers writing home spoke of their pleasure at the Scheme.

In Parliament, 97 Labour and 22 Conservative and Liberal MPs voted that the report should be put into operation as soon as possible. One of them, the Labour MP James Griffiths, told the House:

It is by acceptance or rejection of the plan that we shall be judged by the nation. I suggest that the question which we ought to ask ourselves is not whether we can

afford the plan, but whether we can afford to face the post-war period without it.

In contrast, the *Daily Mirror* refused to get excited:

Too much has been made of the Beveridge Report. It is no revolutionary document. Mainly it is a co-ordination of existing services with certain modest additions thereto. It is a beginning, not an end, and it must not be confused with reconstruction in the larger sense.

Quoted in A Marwick, *Britain in a Century of Total War*

Further wartime reforms

But even before the Coalition had come to an end, work had begun on some of Beveridge's ideas.

In 1943 a ministry to supervise insurance was set up, and in 1945 family allowances were agreed. These allowances were less generous than Beveridge had proposed, being 5s. a week for every child after the first one, not 8s. for every child without exception. The payment of these sums did not begin for another year.

The Coalition had also created a Ministry of Town and Country Planning (1943). One of its first reports suggested the setting up of new towns to reduce congestion in London. Temporary homes were built, at state expense, for some of Britain's homeless, and the price of building materials was controlled to stop house prices getting out of hand.

In 1944 a Conservative, R A Butler, piloted through parliament a new Education Act. The act provided for free secondary education for all from the age of 11 (12 in Scotland) up to the age of 15.

These were real achievements, and there were also government White Papers showing what was planned in the near future. There were statements to show that a high and stable level of employment, and the creation of a national health service, were matters to which the Government was committed. If the Coalition could agree on so much, then both the Labour and the Conservative Parties felt that social welfare policies must be pursued after the war, even though the two parties ended their coalition in 1945.

The veteran social reformer Seebohm Rowntree summed up the situation, saying:

The whole of the social and economic life of the nation has been uprooted by the war as by an earthquake. When peace comes, the social and economic evils and injustices for which the community suffered before the war must not be permitted in the new world which has to be created.

But Winston Churchill again worried that too much was being expected of post-war Britain. He did not attack Beveridge in principle, but rather concerned himself with the cost of welfare when there were other burdens to be borne after the economy had been so badly hurt by warfare.

Labour's welfare policies from 1945–1951

Throughout the 1945-1951 period the country was free of serious unemployment problems save those temporarily caused by the exceptionally severe winter of 1946-1947. However, the government's determination to keep Britain militarily strong did mean that social welfare reforms were not the only call upon the country's limited resources. Britain at this time supported a large army, air force and navy; she kept bases across the world; and she developed atomic bombs. There were also conflicts into which Britain was drawn. To push vigorously ahead in such times required both courage and optimism, but at least British people seemed much more ready than

they had been after 1918 to wait for reforms to come and to accept the continuation of wartime controls in peacetime.

The government kept a very tight grip on consumer spending, maintaining rationing and many controls. By nationalising coal, electricity, gas, the airways, the Bank of England, the railways and the waterways the government kept a firm grip on a substantial part of the economy.

Help came from abroad. The economist J M Keynes was sent to the USA to negotiate a loan. Not only did he obtain such a loan, the Americans also agreed to cancel some of the wartime debt Britain had built up with the USA. Further American aid flowed to Britain between 1948 and 1951 as the USA adopted a policy of reviving West European prosperity as a barrier to the spread of communism from Russia. Canada too provided a generous loan of $1500 million.

Insurance

James Griffiths was in charge of converting Beveridge's plans for a simple comprehensive scheme of insurance into reality. Like Attlee, Griffiths saw his work as the completion of a process that had been going on for many years. A speech by the Conservative R A Butler showed that there were no big differences between Labour and Conservatives on this issue, for Butler welcomed the scheme, declaring:

I think we should take pride that the British race has been able, shortly after the terrible period through which we have all passed together, to show the whole world that we are able to produce a social insurance scheme of this character.

Quoted in S H Wood, *The British Welfare State*, 1982

As Beveridge had suggested, the scheme put into place involved weekly contributions from employees, employers and the state, and it paid benefits at standard rates. The cost of old age pensions had particularly worried Beveridge. He had suggested that there might even be a 20-year delay in bringing in pensions for men at 65 and for women at 60 years, but Griffiths did not delay. He brought in the measure at once. As Beveridge had suggested, a scheme was introduced to provide compensation for people who were injured at work. The Industrial Injuries Act provided payments to those temporarily hurt and long term payments for those put permanently out of a job. For the latter group, because an injured person might have extra expenses, the rates of payment were more generous than for the unemployed.

In 1948 a National Assistance Board was set up to help people for whom the insurance scheme did not provide enough help, or the right kind of help. For some people the insurance benefits were simply not enough, and as time passed this problem became increasingly serious. The insurance benefits did not rise sufficiently often to keep up with the now steadily rising cost of living, and old people in particular had to turn to the Assistance Board for further help. This help was given only to the needy and the Board's officials had to question the applicant to make sure that they were dealing with a genuine claim. This 'needs test' was less harsh than the old means test for it did not include a check on the earnings of other members of the claimant's family. The Board's help might consist of weekly payments, but it could also give single payments to solve a particular problem (such as an urgent need for bedding or clothing).

The insurance and national assistance schemes were huge undertakings. Thousands of new staff were needed, new offices had to be built, and the files and records of information about Britain's citizens began to grow.

Insurance Reform

1946 26s. a week for a single person, 42s. for a married man, at times of old age, unemployment (up to 180 days), and illness.

1946 Compensation for people injured at work – 45s. a week, a further 16s. if married. Maternity grants and allowances. Death grant of £20. Payments to widows. No means test. Standard weekly contribution for those in work.

1948 National Assistance Board set up, to help those for whom insurance did not do enough (e.g. pensioners whose pensions did not keep up with the rise in the cost of living). Old age pensions were paid to men over 65 and to women over 60. The government found that old age pensions were soon eating up two thirds of all insurance spending.

The National Health Service

The new Minister of Health was Aneurin Bevan. Bevan was a coal-miner's son who had worked down a coal pit before making a career in the Labour movement. By 1945 Bevan had won himself a considerable reputation as a very forthright speaker who held strong socialist views. During the war he had been Churchill's most determined and persistent critic in parliament, and Conservative politicians regarded him as a person of extreme views. His task of building a national health service meant that he had to win the co-operation of doctors. A great many of them, already worried about what a health service might do to their jobs, were even more concerned when faced by Aneurin Bevan. What doctors feared was that they would be turned into state officials, would lose independence, and would be sent to work wherever the government chose to place them.

Bevan brought in a bill in 1946 to outline the features of the health service he wished to set up, and allowed a two year delay before the service would begin. During that time he hoped to win over the majority of doctors. In introducing his bill, Bevan pointed out that the old health insurance system:

covered only 21 million, the rest of the population have to pay whenever they desire the services of a doctor; the National Health Insurance scheme does not provide for the self-employed nor the families of dependants. It gives no backing to the doctor in the form of special services. Our hospital organisation had grown up with no plan. This Bill provides a universal health service with no insurance qualifications of any sort. It is intended that there shall be no limitations on the kind of assistance given – general practitioners' service, specialists, hospitals, eye treatment, dental treatment, hearing facilities.

The detailed arrangements for the health service were then worked out during two years of discussion. When doctors actually met the man they had thought of as a fierce Welsh socialist, they found him charming, witty, and ready to negotiate. Hospital staff were won over quite readily. Their buildings and medical equipment were so expensive and so much in need of overhaul and additions that they realised only the government could provide what they needed. Bevan agreed that hospital doctors could continue to treat private patients as well as working for the health service, and that hospitals should have a number of beds for patients who wanted to be treated privately and could afford to pay. The hospitals were organised in groups, and each group was controlled by a Regional Board appointed by the minister. Each hospital had a management committee to watch over its affairs. Major hospitals which were centres for the training of new doctors had their own separate governors whom the minister himself appointed.

Winning over GPs was not so easy. In 1946 a poll amongst them showed that 64 per cent were

'Just spots before the eyes. . . . Don't worry, we'll soon cure that!'

Cartoon of Bevan placating the concerns of doctors.

opposed to Bevan's plans. The British Medical Association organised and led a campaign that argued that what was proposed would destroy doctors' freedom to treat patients as they thought right. But the doctors became increasingly isolated, for popular opinion ran very strongly in favour of the health service. Lord Moran, President of the Royal College of Physicians, helped Bevan to gradually calm doctors' fears, although at times the discussion between the two sides became quite angry. (Bevan once called the BMA 'a small body of politically poisoned people'!) By 1948 the detailed arrangements the minister was ready to make had persuaded a quarter of the doctors in England and a third of those in Wales and Scotland to sign on for the new service. Early in 1948 organised opposition collapsed, and the health service was able to come into operation on 5 July 1948.

Its impact was enormous, as illustrated by this example. In 1948 Alice Law lived in Manchester. When the NHS began, her mother:

went to the optician's, obviously she'd got the prescription from the doctor, she went and she got tested for new glasses, then she went further down the road . . . for the chiropodist, she had her feet done, then she went back to the doctor's because she'd been having trouble with her ears and the doctor said . . . he would fix her up with a hearing aid, and I remember, me mother was a very funny woman, I remember her saying to the doctor on the way out. 'Well the undertaker's is on the way home, everything's going on, I might as well call in there on the way home!'

Quoted in P Addison, *Now the War is Over*

The service that emerged was paid for, very largely, by taxes. The weekly insurance stamp did include a little for health insurance, but enough to pay only 9 per cent of its cost in 1949, and 10 per cent by 1954. Bevan calmed the doctors' worries about becoming state officials by agreeing not to pay them by direct salary. New doctors received some direct salary from the government, but in general the pay that doctors received depended on the number of patients on their lists. When medical practices had been private, doctors had bought and sold them. Bevan insisted that this must stop, arguing that patients were being treated like cattle. But he did set aside £66 million for doctors to draw upon when they retired, to compensate them for no longer being able to sell practices they had spent lifetimes building up. The work of GPs was henceforth watched over by executive councils set up in each county and borough, and these were made up of equal numbers of medical and lay people.

Some aspects of health care were kept by local authorities. Their Medical Officers supervised services such as vaccination, immunisation, health visiting, child care, and provision for the destitute (especially the elderly).

When the health service started, it brought such a flood of people seeking treatment that Bevan himself declared, 'I shudder to think of the ceaseless cascade of medicines which is pouring down British throats at the present time.' Prescriptions had cost about £7 million a month before the health service was created. Within three months

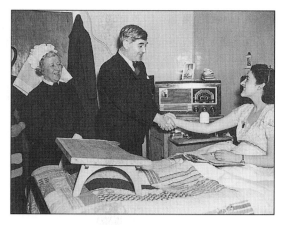

Bevan, Minister of Health meeting a patient at Papworth Village Hospital.

they cost twice that figure, and they continued to rise. Dentists had expected about 4 million patients a year, yet twice that number sought treatment. The National Health Service became an increasingly heavy burden on British finances and, much as Bevan and some of his colleagues resented it, charges for some of its services were introduced by 1951.

Housing

Post-war Britain faced a huge shortage of housing. The war had damaged and destroyed thousands of homes and had prevented normal house-building work from going ahead. Moreover the slum-clearing programme of the 1930s had barely begun to touch the problem of substandard housing. The burden of tackling the problem fell upon Bevan's Ministry of Health, but the ministry had already more than enough to do in attempting to set up the National Health Service.

The ministry's first task was to house the homeless, and to this end it continued the Coalition policy of putting up temporary factory-made 'pre-fabricated' homes. This provided 157 000 dwellings, far too few to satisfy the country's needs. The fact that building supplies and skilled labour were not plentiful compelled Bevan to choose where to concentrate conventional house-building. He put the emphasis on the building of council houses for rent, placing severe restrictions on private building. People in homes that needed considerable spending to raise them to a decent level received help from the Treasury, but the fact remained that by 1951 there was still a very serious shortage of housing in Britain.

The government's housing policy did show concern for the future, as well as efforts to meet an immediate need. Bevan insisted that the council houses must satisfy quite a high standard. In 1946 the New Towns Act set out plans for dealing with overcrowding in older cities. New communities were to be carefully designed and built, with government help; 12 were planned by 1950. In 1947 the Town and Country Planning Act gave counties and county boroughs much more power to plan their communities, and to buy up properties in areas that they wanted to redevelop.

The government's life ended before really massive signs of what it proposed were visible, but in the following years the rebuilding of old communities and the creation of new ones went ahead on the basis of these post-war plans.

Child welfare

By 1947 the Education Act of 1944 was in operation. The government raised the age at which children could leave school to 15, at a time when the country was short of workers. It also had to spend more of its precious resources on building schools and on an emergency programme to train enough teachers to staff the schools. Schools were organised so that at age 11 (12 in Scotland) children were examined and divided

up between grammar schools for the most able and secondary modern schools for the majority. The Education Act proposed a third kind of school, technical schools, but not many of these were provided.

The idea of sorting children into different schools on the basis of an examination did arouse a little criticism at the time and by 1947 the London County Council in particular had become unhappy about the system and planned comprehensive schools instead. London's first comprehensive, Kidbrooke School, opened in 1954.

The government also planned a big increase in opportunities in higher education. Universities and colleges were to be expanded and there was to be a system of grants from the state or the local authority so that students able to win higher education places could accept them even if their parents had little money.

In 1948 the Children's Act tried to provide a better service for children who needed special care and protection. Local authorities were now required to appoint Children's Officers, whose job it would be to see that children taken into care by the local authorities were decently housed and properly cared for.

The range of reforms carried through by 1950 adds up to a system that is generally called 'the welfare state'. The closing stages of this work were supervised by Labour Party ministers, but they knew very well that what they were doing was building on foundations laid by the Liberals and the Conservatives. The care of people in need and the improvement of people's health, housing and education were policies that statesmen of all three parties had at times thought necessary. When a Conservative government replaced Labour in 1951, it did not at once start attacking the social reforms of the previous five years, but accepted these reforms and even added further improvements.

Certainly the health, housing and education of the British people have been much improved during the twentieth century. In 1950 Seebohm Rowntree carried out a third study of York, and found far less overcrowding and poverty. Whereas those on poor pay and those who were unemployed had once been the main victims of poverty, by 1950 it was the elderly who formed the main group of the poor. But even for them life was far more comfortable than it had been 50 years earlier. A great deal of money had been spent, and large numbers of officials had been appointed to make the system work. Far more people paid taxes, and taxes were fixed at higher rates. Controls over people's lives were more detailed and numerous, and the power of the government was increased. But everyday life, for the majority of people, was vastly improved.

Historians' views on Labour's achievement

Historians have especially considered two issues. Firstly, how much of a break with past policies Labour reforms represent. Secondly, whether such a bold and costly programme ought to have been followed at this time. David Dutton has written:

The major achievement of the Labour Party after 1945 was to complete and consolidate the work of the war-time coalition.

British Politics since 1945, 1990

Kathleen Woodroofe notes how state action created a system, in which welfare support was believed to be a right, free of the shame of the old poor law.

By government policy and a network of social services she (i.e. Britain) hoped to provide employment for those who were unemployed, to insure her citizens against the major hazards of life and eventually to give them a national minimum of health, wealth and well-being. These were social rights ... to accept assistance no longer meant loss of personal liberty or disenfranchisement.

Twentieth Century Britain – National Power and Social Welfare, 1976

Several historians have commented on the Conservatives' ready acceptance of Labour's programme, with the exception of aspects of the NHS. Nevertheless, Arthur Marwick believes Labour's achievements:

were not simply the inevitable response that any government would have made to the particular historical circumstances of 1945. They were the endeavors of a political party that, over a long period of time, had thought hard, if unevenly, about the issues of welfare policy.

Modern History Review, Vol 2 No 1, 1990

To support his case he points to Labour policy proposals in the early twentieth century, to some of its activities when briefly in office and particularly to the boldness of Bevan's plans for health and housing.

Kenneth Morgan's work, *The People's Peace* (1990), includes observations on Churchill's very suspicious view of the cost of Beveridge, and of aspects of health service ideas. Churchill's interests lay in visions of world affairs that might well have severely constrained welfare reforms had he led the post-war government. Certainly at the time Bevan believed this to be the case.

Martin Pugh believes:

Some critics have claimed that the welfare state was a hugely expensive burden which damaged the British economy in the long term. Obviously large sums of money were involved, notably in health. The total expenditure on health was put at £478 million by 1951, about five times the 1938 level ... that expenditure rose after 1945 indicated that a great deal of ill-

health had gone untreated – with very damaging effects on the economy. Any genuine audit of welfare policies would have to include some assessment of the economic gain from a more fit and healthy labour force. Many of the welfare benefits such as family allowances, were very cost-effective ways of relieving hardship. Rowntree's study of poverty in York was repeated in 1950, the conclusion it reached was that only 2.77 per cent of the working class suffered from poverty. If the welfare state did not abolish poverty altogether, it represented the most effective single campaign against it . . . Any suggestion that state welfare expenditure got out of control has no basis in fact.

M Pugh, *State & Society*, 1994

➤ ACTIVITIES

1   Read Harold Nicolson's account of evacuees (Page 119). Use the source and your knowledge to answer the question:
    In what ways did the Second World War make further social reforms more likely?
    (Demonstrate knowledge and understanding of historical developments, events and issues.)

2   Read Churchill's worries about the Beveridge Report (Page 123). Use the source and your knowledge to answer the question:
    Why were some people not eager to see the Beveridge Report put into operation?
    (Explain historical developments and events.)

3   Look at the cartoon showing Bevan as a doctor (Page 126). What light does this source shed on Bevan's struggles to create the National Health Service? (Evaluate sources, taking account of content, origin or purpose.)

4   In what ways does James Griffiths' speech (Page 123) differ from Churchill's views on Beveridge? (A comparison is made between two sources.)

7   Discuss the conclusions you have reached from the task at the beginning of this chapter. Use your notes and from your discussion plan and write the following essay:
    How true is it to say that the Labour Government of 1945–1951 set up the Welfare State.

GOVERNMENT AND THE PEOPLE –
An Overview

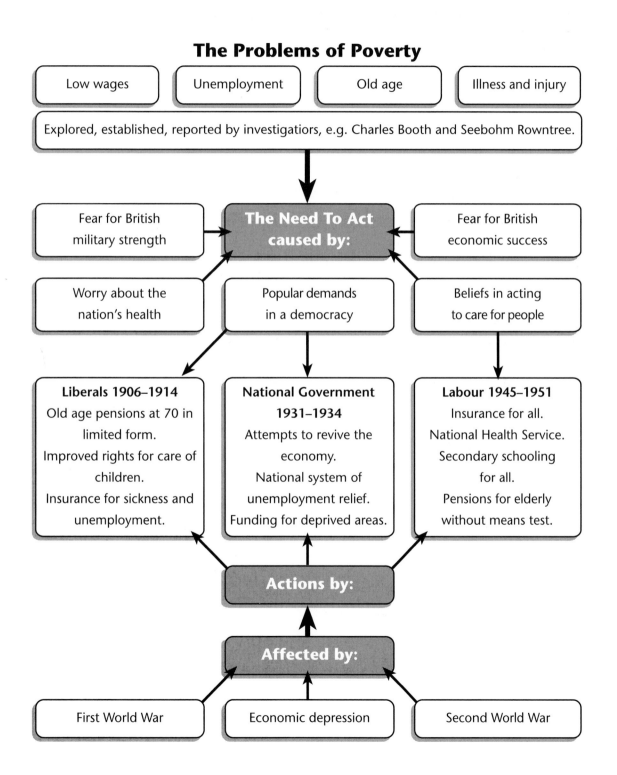

The Problems of Poverty

| Low wages | Unemployment | Old age | Illness and injury |

Explored, established, reported by investigatiors, e.g. Charles Booth and Seebohm Rowntree.

The Need To Act caused by:

Fear for British military strength

Fear for British economic success

Worry about the nation's health

Popular demands in a democracy

Beliefs in acting to care for people

Liberals 1906–1914
Old age pensions at 70 in limited form.
Improved rights for care of children.
Insurance for sickness and unemployment.

National Government 1931–1934
Attempts to revive the economy.
National system of unemployment relief.
Funding for deprived areas.

Labour 1945–1951
Insurance for all.
National Health Service.
Secondary schooling for all.
Pensions for elderly without means test.

Actions by:

Affected by:

First World War

Economic depression

Second World War

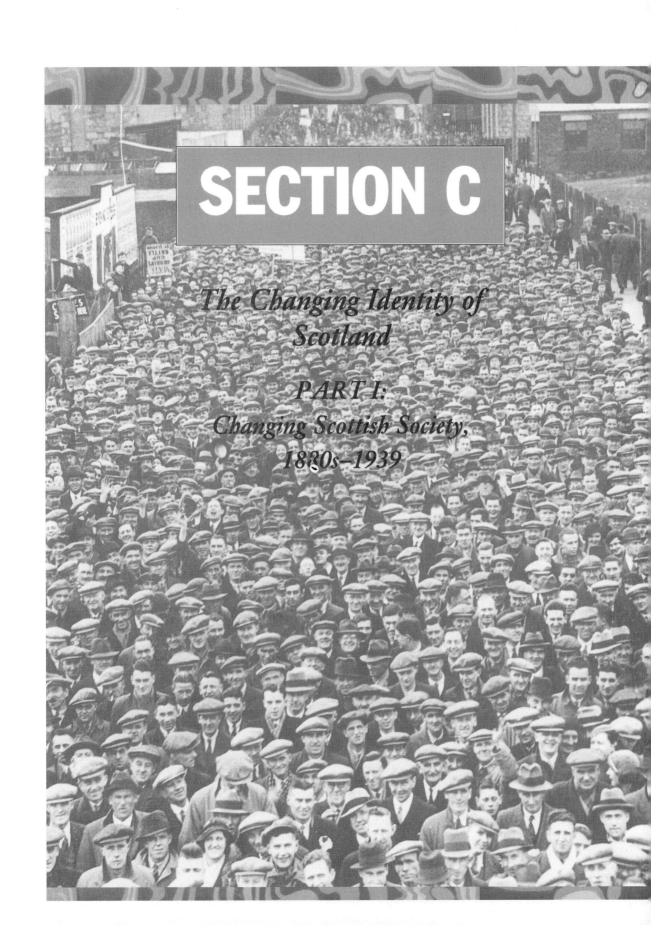

SECTION C

The Changing Identity of Scotland

PART I:
Changing Scottish Society, 1880s–1939

Introduction

Like the rest of Britain, Scotland's identity was shaped at this time by:

◆ The growth of trade and industry in the nineteenth century.

◆ The economic troubles and effects of two world wars on the twentieth century.

◆ The growth of towns and cities, i.e. urbanisation.

◆ The development of a more democratic political system and of political parties.

◆ The increasing role of government in shaping people's lives.

The material in this section focuses on how ordinary people's lives were affected by a much more urbanised existence. It deals especially with the period when a very successful Scottish economy began to face difficulties that caused large-scale unemployment. The main aspects that will be explored deal with how people spent their spare time, the part that religion played in people's lives, and the educational system that their children and young people experienced at this time.

As a result of studying the material in this option you should have a sound knowledge and understanding of the impact of urbanisation 1880s–1939, with reference to:

◆ Leisure.

◆ Popular culture.

◆ Religion.

◆ Education.

This option forms a key part of the Higher History course. It also covers a major part of the Intermediate 2 topic *Campaigning for Change: Social Change in Scotland*.

The material in this option will prepare you for such questions as:

◆ In what ways did the urbanisation of Scotland shape popular leisure pursuits?

◆ What part did religious organisations play in everyday life in Scotland?

◆ *'The approach in the Scottish classroom remained . . . grimly authoritarian and narrow'*

(T C Smout).

Is this an accurate analysis of education at this time?

Chapter Ten
Urbanisation

The inhabitants of Scotland in the 1880s were as likely to live in a town or city as the countryside. By 1939 most Scots had become urban dwellers. This process of urbanisation affected the lives of ordinary people in all sorts of ways. The material in this chapter deals with this major development and provides an essential background to understanding the aspects of everyday life that are required by the curriculum.

As a result of studying this chapter you should have a sound understanding of

◆ Reasons for urbanisation.

◆ The kinds of houses in which most people lived.

◆ The growth of local government.

◆ Everyday living conditions.

TASK

'Between 1880–1939 urbanisation changed the identity of Scotland.' Do you agree?

Investigate this issue by making notes using each of the key aspects listed above as a subheading, producing a brief half-page final report and discussing it with others.

Urban growth

If we take an urban area to be a place where at least 5000 people lived, then in 1881 48.9 per cent of a population of 3 735 573 lived in an urban environment. By 1939, however, 63.4 per cent of a population of just over five million were urban dwellers. The four main cities of Aberdeen, Dundee, Edinburgh and Glasgow were

especially important, indeed by the time of the First World War a third of the country's population lived in these places. Glasgow grew especially rapidly, increasing in population from a little over half a million in 1880 to over a million by the 1930s. The other three cities all expanded rapidly too. City growth was driven forward by a number of factors which differed between each place. Edinburgh attracted bankers and financiers, lawyers and administrators and had a higher proportion of professional people than the other three. The number of well-to-do families in Edinburgh can be seen through the percentage of female workers who were domestic servants, for the figure of 40 per cent was twice that of Glasgow's.

There were industries in Edinburgh too, but it was Glasgow which formed the main focus of engineering, shipbuilding, railway works and other such enterprises. The sheer size of employers like Fairfields shipyards, Templetons carpets and Springburn Railway Works shows the need for numbers of people to live nearby. Moreover great enterprises attracted all sorts of supply and service works to cluster around them.

Aberdeen acted as a regional service centre as well as having granite yards, fishing, shipbuilding and a variety of other works. Like the other cities it benefited from the railway revolution which drew people into it and enabled it to send its produce to distant markets. Dundee had become very dependent on the jute industry and consequently had a higher proportion of women at work than the other Scottish cities. All the cities were able to support shops, entertainments and schools that increased their attraction.

But Scotland was also a country of many smaller towns. In 1911 there were no less than 75 burghs with populations of over 5000. Many different factors shaped the emergence of smaller towns including fishing (for example at Peterhead), heavy industry (as at Coatbridge), woollen textiles (for example Galashiels), floor coverings, especially linoleum (at Kircaldy), and agricultural and service centres (such as Dumfries). Like the cities, these places tended to spread outwards over the 1880s–1930s period, as the better transport offered by trams (horse-drawn at first, then electrified from the 1890s) then motor traffic and in a few cases, local railways, allowed suburbs to grow.

The result worried some. In 1934 George Blake complained:

considering its size, Scotland is overweighed with cities . . . Glasgow is larger in the Scottish scale than London is in the English . . . The size of cities is the most obvious symptom of the hopeless lack of balance in Scottish life. The influence of the cities is too great.

G Blake, *The Heart of Scotland*, Batsford

A more organised age

Urban growth produced problems of health, law and order, and cleanliness that, by the 1880s, were being tackled in each community by ratepayer-elected bodies called 'Police Commissioners'. A Police Act in 1892 and a Public Health Act in 1897 further increased the power of local government under the supervision of the Local Government Board.

Across Scotland, urban areas built town and city halls to house increasing numbers of officials. These local authorities busied themselves not only with law and order but with the provision of pavements and street lighting, with covering road surfaces with cobblestones and constructing under them a network of drains, sewers, gas pipes and pipes to carry clean water. Scotland, by the 1900s, was a country in which local authorities provided numerous services as cheaply as possible and played a crucial part in everyday lives. A Glasgow citizen illustrated this point in 1903 when he wrote that a Glaswegian:

May live in a municipal house, he may walk along a municipal street and ride in the municipal tramcar and watch the municipal dustcart collecting the refuse. Then he may turn into the municipal market, buy a steak from an animal killed in the municipal slaughterhouse and cook it by the municipal gas stove. He can choose among municipal libraries, art galleries, and music in municipal parks.

T C Smout, *A Century of the Scottish People*, 1986

Amid the urban townscape of the period many large buildings stood out. There were the schools to which Scotland's children were now required to go. Numerous churches drew in large congregations. Places of entertainment like theatres, dance halls, music halls and by the 1920s and 1930s, cinemas attracted huge numbers of people. The inhabitants of urban Scotland were provided with far more organised ways of spending their time than had ever been the case before.

Housing

In 1918 a Royal Commission on housing in Scotland provided its report. It had found:

Unsatisfactory sites of houses . . . insufficient supplies of water, unsatisfactory provision of drainage, grossly inadequate provision for the removal of refuse, widespread absence of decent sanitary conveniences, filthy privy-middens in many of the mining areas . . . occupation of one room houses by large families, groups of lightless and unventilated houses in the older burghs, masses of slums in the cities . . . ill-planned houses that must become slums in a few years, old houses converted without the necessary sanitary appliances into tenements for many families.

Report by the Royal Commission on Housing 1918

**The Gorbals, Glasgow C. 1870.
Tenements are being built behind a public house.**

Although there were improvements between 1880–1939, large numbers of ordinary people throughout the period lived in cramped and overcrowded accommodation. The rapid growth of buildings to house the workers in Scotland's expanding nineteenth century industries led, especially, to the construction of four and five storey tenement blocks. Entry by a common stair led, in those buildings, to homes that might well consist of just one or two rooms. In 1911 over half of the country's urban dwellers were crammed into these tiny properties, indeed in Glasgow two thirds of the city's population inhabited one or two roomed homes. In 1888 the City's Medical Officer of Health, Dr Russell, explained these homes:

Produce the high death rate of Glasgow. Their exhausted air and poor and perverse feeding fill our streets with bandy-legged children. Of all the children who die in Glasgow before they complete their fifth year, 32 per cent die in houses of one apartment and not 2 per cent in houses of five apartments and above.

J B Russell, *Life in One Room*, 1888

These wretched conditions reflected poverty and the high cost of paying rents and feu duties to landlords. They produced conditions in which privacy was impossible and disease spread easily. They also meant that people had to live in co-operation with others, supporting one another and sharing amenities like toilets and wash-houses.

After the First World War new types of homes were built, helped by a series of Housing Acts which provided local authorities with government help to build houses to rent, and to clear slums. This development of council housing produced two and three storey properties in which families had their own front doors and their own bathrooms and toilets. The period also saw the construction of privately paid-for bungalows around the outskirts of urban areas. Helpful though these developments were, they still left Scotland in the 1930s as a place where overcrowding in housing was dramatically worse than it was in England. Many urban dwellers of the 1930s lived in conditions like those recalled by Mrs Cockburn.

Dundee was a poor class o'people. Folk didna hae much. We (lived) *in an attic and there was my mother and father and four o'us, two rooms, that was all. Beds were all over the place, and toilets on the stairs. If you had a toilet in the house you were a toff.*

Billy Kay, *Odyssey*, 1980

An urban way of life

Most people in urban Scotland lived their lives in very confined areas. They walked to work, to school and to the shops, though the better off might use the trams. Over the period 1920–1939 the cost of living fell by a third enabling those with jobs to enjoy some improvements in what they could afford, including leisure activities that required expenditure (like entrance fees). The mass production of clothing, footwear and some foods helped too. So too did shorter working hours, better diet, health and welfare provision. Many Scots had time and energy to spare. But those urban dwellers hit by the economic depression of the inter-war years continued to find life a

Post-war housing in Drumogne.

desperate struggle. Managing on a very limited income meant that housewives had to be skilled at mending, making do and managing on a tiny budget.

The kitchen range stood at the centre of tenement life, its coal fire providing warmth, hot water and the means of cooking. Gas lights illuminated many dwellings though the period saw the spread of electricity into more and more homes. Shopping was a frequent activity since the absence of refrigerators meant that food could not be stored for long. For many urban Scots, the local Co-operative Store provided one of the key focal points of life. Mollie Weir, who lived in a Springburn (Glasgow) tenement in the inter-war years recalled:

The Co-operative Store was the hub of our shopping activities. Along one side ran the long mahogany counter with female clerks perched on high stools whose job it was to write down our orders. Along the opposite side ran the long wooden counter attended by the serving grocers, usually male ... Eggs were very precious ... Two doors down was the drapery department

Mrs Thomas cooking at the range in her kitchen in Gourlay Street, Glasgow in the 1930s.

Shop assistants in the Cowlairs Co-operative, 1932.

which also sold shoes. Shoes were worn only on Sundays. There was a Co-op about every 500 yards in our district.

M Weir, *Shoes were for Sunday*, Hutchison

Washday meant sharing a washhouse in a back-yard with many other families, or using one of the 'steamies', washhouses provided by local councils.

The urbanisation of Scotland produced a daily life in which people crowded together in work-places, in homes, in the streets and on public transport. There was little opportunity to escape from others: a communal life was almost unavoidable.

Dundee street scene in the 1900s: bare-footed children and evidence of rickets.

➤ ACTIVITIES

The following source by Jimmie MacGregor recalls a childhood in a Glasgow tenement.

Its fashionable now to sigh over the lost warmth and community of the tenement, but it is noticeable that the sighers are usually of an age to have spent only their childhood there. An older generation remembers also dirt, poverty and inconvenience as well as the continual struggle to protect their children from those realities. The success of that struggle is what allows people like me to look back through rose-tinted glasses. There was, nevertheless, a real sense of belonging. Neighbours were always at hand. Doors remained unlocked and few secrets survived for long.

Sunday Mail

1. What evidence is there in it of the disadvantages of tenement life?

2. What evidence is there of benefits?

3. Do you agree that people are now likely to look back on this life 'through rose-tinted glasses'?

Chapter Eleven

Leisure and Popular Culture

The growth of urban areas helped to change the ways in which people spent their spare time. Streets and back yards, not fields, provided play areas for children. Informal contacts between people crowded together were inescapable. Mass entertainments were now possible when so huge a potential audience was available. The technology that had changed work and travel causing urban areas to grow, changed leisure too, bringing entertainment through the radio and the cinema, for example. The better-off worried about the behaviour of the large numbers of working people crowded in their communities and tried to make it more orderly as well as offering 'improving' ways of spending leisure. Urban life encouraged many to welcome chances to escape to coast and country.

But Scotland was far from unique in developing urban areas and it can be argued that, in some ways at least, urbanisation shaped Scottish identity to make it more like that of urban dwellers elsewhere in Britain. A dictionary's definitions of 'culture' include:

'The total range of activities and ideas of a people.'
'Artistic and social pursuits, expression and tastes valued by a society or class.'

The New Collins Concise English Dictionary, 1982

The material in this chapter deals with how urbanisation shaped people's activities, ideas and tastes. The emphasis is on the lives lived by most people rather than the highly educated élite and the wealthy. As a result of studying this chapter you should have a sound understanding of:

◆ Ways of spending spare time at home.

◆ Public houses and morals.

◆ Gambling and attempts to control it.

◆ Attempts by authorities to improve people's lives.

◆ Commercial entertainments.

◆ The issue of Scottish identity.

TASK

Make notes to answer the question:
In what ways did urbanisation affect leisure and popular culture?

Use the sub-headings in this chapter and note down key points under each.

Spare time at home

We had a lot of visitors. That's something that we miss, but people nowadays are too tied up in this television ... they all visited each other's houses, the families were all very close knit. Not like now. They used tae come, mainly on a Sunday night ... playing cards jist for ha'pennies

Up oor Close, Jean Faley 1990 *White Cockade*

This reminiscence of life in early nineteenth century Glasgow illustrates the importance of socialising. Chatting with neighbours, friends and relatives provided free entertainment for people with little money to spare. The crowded nature of urban housing and the relative freedom from dangerous traffic, meant that socialising often took place in the street or back yard.

'Pitch and Toss' – an Edinburgh street scene in the 1900s.

Children played outside using the street as their playground as in this memory of childhood play in Edinburgh:

You widnae see a wee girl now playing at shops. We made our own. Our butter was earth made up with water and patted down. Broken leaves for cabbages, champit stones for sugar, potato – you were to cut it up very thinly for bacon. You'd play for hours.

Friday Night was Brasso Night, Workers Education Association

Families lacked the money to buy many toys nor did they have a wide range of equipment to provide entertainment in the home, though from the 1900s the 'wind up' gramophone was available to provide short bursts of poorly reproduced music. Radio broadcasting developed in the early twentieth century. In 1926 the British Broadcasting Corporation was established under the stern eye of Sir John Reith, a Scot of strict principles and strong religious belief. Early broadcasts consisted chiefly of plays and classical music. Until 1938 no broadcast took place before midday on Sundays lest it interfere with attendance at church. 'Wirelesses' were not cheap, in 1939 they cost around £3 and annual licenses cost 50 pence, but they became genuinely popular and brought news of great events directly into people's homes.

Drink and temperance

Everyday spare-time activities around the home were the concern of women and children especially. Men tended to spend spare-time away from home, as explained in 1903 by Renfrew's Medical Officer of Health.

A man has finished his day's work and has had his ill-cooked tea. His education has stopped short of making reading a pleasure to him. The children are noisy. There is little room to move. Perhaps there is washing hanging around to dry. He might talk to his wife. Or he might play with the children. But for every day, all year round, it is impossible. He puts on his hat and goes out . . . the public house is warm and bright and where else is he to go?

Quoted T C Smout, *A Century of the Scottish People*

Public houses were very numerous but varied greatly. Some were well lit, comfortable and attractive. Others were bleak and cheerless rooms. Scots had a reputation as heavy drinkers, especially of whisky. In 1914 the average annual consumption of it stood at around a gallon a head. In 1886 an observer of the drinking scene blamed heavy drinking not only on miserable

housing and the desire to forget a life of endless work, but also on the strict beliefs of the Protestant churches in Scotland. He said:

Austerity and joyless gloom on the one hand produce their national corrective in dissolute mirth and defiant licence on the other . . . I could lay my finger on half a dozen small Scottish towns in which, for sheer lack of theatre or any other recreation, a large proportion of youths become sottish (i.e. drunk) and dissolute.

J M Robertson, *The Perversion of Scotland*, 1886

In 1932 the Scots writer Edwin Muir commented:

Scottish streets are given an atmosphere of their own simply by the number of drunk people that one encounters in them . . . Scottish people drink spasmodically and intensely for the sake of a momentary but complete release.

Edwin Muir, *Scottish Journey*, 1935: 1979 edition, Mainstream

The Strathmore Arms, on the corner of North Tay Street and Overgate, Dundee 1897.

By the 1880s the consumption of alcohol was being fiercely attacked by a very active temperance movement. The Presbyterian Church, employers wanting sober workers, authorities fearing disorder on the streets, all had good reason to try to cut drinking. Some success had been achieved in 1853 with the banning of Sunday opening, but there were ways round this as hotels were still allowed to serve drink to travellers. The temperance movement was well-organised, holding meetings and marches, opening coffee houses and arranging all sorts of teetotal entertainments including concerts, outings and 'Good Templars' dances. People attending were urged to sign a 'pledge' promising never again to consume alcohol. A big effort was made to win over young people. In 1883 in Glasgow the Boys Brigade was founded to offer youngsters a disciplined and moral training. The Band of Hope offered children entertaining ways of meeting others and spending time, but as Meg Berington of Leith recalls it had another purpose:

When we were very young we used to go to the Band of Hope. We used to see magic lanterns, but they were very sad. They were nearly always about a drunken father who wasn't very nice to his wife or children. Us children used to sit and cry all night.

Leith Lives

The temperance movement pressed the government to restrict opening hours and found Lloyd George's wartime ministry ready to listen to the view that drink damaged the war effort. Opening hours were restricted and in 1921 they were confined to a total of eight hours a day with a closing time of 10.00 pm. Local districts could decide to ban the sale of alcohol altogether and 40 out of a total of 586 such authorities made this decision in 1920. Nearly all had abandoned it by the 1930s. The success of temperance movements reached a high point in 1922 when Edwin Scrymgeour, representing the Prohibitionist

Party, defeated Winston Churchill in the Parliamentary elections in Dundee. (Some historians see this as a success for the newly enfranchised women voters.) Temperance events were still popular in the twenties and the Glasgow Abstainers Union's Saturday night socials attracted as many as 3500 to its City Hall venue. Moreover there is no doubt that whisky drinking declined. By the 1930s it had fallen to .35 of a gallon per head of population. In part this was probably due to its cost as twentieth century governments began to tax spirits heavily, indeed between 1900–1920 tax levels rose more than sixfold.

Gambling, 'rough culture' and authority

The historian Callum Brown uses the phrase 'rough culture' to describe activities like drinking, gambling and betting that were popular with urban working men and suggests that in the 1880s–1930s the well-to-do and the authorities tried:

to convert plebeians from the pernicious hedonism (pleasures) of drink and urban low life and create new loyalties – to God, employer, municipality and nation.

C G Brown, *Popular Culture and the Continuing Struggle for Rational Recreation in Scotland in the Twentieth Century*

The controls applied to drinking illustrate this development, as do attempts to control gambling. Bookies taking bets in the street found themselves pursued by the police. Betting or gaming machines (which arrived in the early twentieth century) were banned. Yet gambling could not be stopped and football pools became well established in the hands of a small number of large firms during this period. By the 1930s the intense attack on gambling was fading.

However authorities had other worries too as the urban masses sought ways of bringing some kind of variety of pleasure into their lives. The Burgh Police Act of 1892 and its amendments of 1903 and 1911 gave great powers to local authorities to ban or control all sorts of leisure activities. These powers were used for example, to ban kite flying and making ice-slides in snowy weather. They enabled authorities to inspect and licence billiard halls. They allowed authorities to wage war on places that one Chief Constable called: 'dens of iniquity', namely the ice-cream parlours that became enormously popular from the 1890s and were often run by Italians. These parlours were seen as centres of disturbance and gambling, as places into which people tumbled when they left public houses. The attempt of such a parlour in Lerwick to remain open on a Sunday even brought about the creation of an anti-ice-cream political group which won elections and required closure on Sundays.

Local authorities provided alternative and 'improving' ways of spending time. During the late nineteenth century several Scottish cities and towns built art galleries and museums and laid out public parks with bandstands. The construction of public libraries, often aided with money from the millionaire Scottish emigrant Andrew Carnegie, was a marked feature of the time. The coming of compulsory education in 1872 increased popular literacy and encouraged the reading of books, newspapers like the *Daily Mail*, the *Daily Express* and the *Sunday Post* and children's comics of the inter-war years. Callum Brown suggests:

From attempts to suppress 'rough' culture on the first three decades, local and national government moved after 1935 to the encouragement of healthy national recreations in their attempt to compete with an increasingly commercialised and legitimised rough culture.

Commercial entertainment

The historian Robert Lambert maintains that:

The 1870s and 1880s saw the industrialisation of recreation in Scotland; instead of a leisure pursuit being something you did to pass the time, it became something that others were proud to do on your behalf.

R Lambert, *Leisure & Recreation* in Ed. A Cooke *Modern Scottish History* Vol 2 (1998) Tuckwell

The period 1880s–1930s saw the standard of living rising for people in work and the length of the working day tending to shrink. Concentrations of people in urban areas provided large audiences for suitable entertainment. By the 1880s a Saturday half-day free of work was common for skilled workers and within ten years unskilled workers were increasingly allowed this free time as well. In 1938 the Holidays With Pay Act made possible at least one week's paid break from work for many. This period then, saw urban dwellers having both the time and the money to afford to pay for entertainment.

Saturday afternoons focused around sport as entertainment and drew in largely male audiences, since women laboured at household chores with few labour-saving gadgets to ease their work. Greyhound racing enjoyed growing popularity, especially with the introduction in 1926 of an electric-powered hare for the dogs to chase. Horse racing had its following especially at Kelso, Ayr and Musselburgh. Golf flourished, reaching a wider audience with the building of municipal courses in the inter-war years. In Aberdeen, an inhabitant recalled the Council used unemployed men in the 1930s and:

started a scheme to build the golf course at Hazlehead … The Hazlehead course was built with sweat and tears

N Gray, *The Worst of Times*, 1985, Gower

An increase in leisure time enabled more men to take up golf.

Football was soon being efficiently organised by the Scottish Football Association and attracted such huge numbers of supporters that many clubs were able to turn professional. The income from admission charges helped fund huge new stadiums such as the one built for Celtic in the 1890s, which could hold 70 000. Rivalry between teams had, in some cases, the added tension of Catholic–Protestant differences with the result that violence sometimes broke out on a sizeable scale. Injury also resulted, in 1902, from the collapse of wooden terracing at Ibrox, killing 26 people and injuring 500. Football also provided a focus for Anglo-Scottish rivalry. In the 1937 clash between the two sides almost 150 000 spectators packed into Hampden. Football became a major leisure activity as well as a spectator sport. Even the Boys Brigade found its numbers trebled once it had established a football league.

In Borders towns rugby flourished, whilst boxing provided an escape to fame and fortune for a few determined men. But this was an age, above all, of soccer. From the creation of Queens Park in 1867 by a group associated with the YMCA, the founding of famous clubs soared and included Rangers (1872), Hearts (1874), Hibernian (1875) and Aberdeen (1903). Clubs sometimes had strong religious connections. Celtic was established in 1887 by a Catholic, Brother Walfrid, to raise money for free meals for poor Catholic children. Hibernian's constitution stated that all its players must be practising Catholics (a clause dropped in 1893) and Dundee Harps (United after 1923) was also a focus for Catholic support.

The provision of indoor entertainment flourished too with theatres and music halls providing live entertainment. Audiences could listen to classical music – the Glasgow Orpheus Choir began in 1905 – and watch serious plays. Travelling circuses and Buffalo Bill's Wild West Show turned up in towns from time to time and they, along with the 1930s Music Halls and Variety

Crowd going to Pittodrie Football Stadium, Aberdeen in the 1930s.

The cinema in the 1930s – Capitol, Aberdeen.

Theatres proved to be especially popular, for they allowed audiences to join in singing as well as watching comedians, acrobats, magicians and dancers. Glasgow Empire was regarded as an especially tough test of entertainers' ability, for audiences abused those they disliked:

If they didn't like someone they shouted 'Get off, Get away!' Sometimes they would throw orange peel and stuff like that.

5/11 a Week, Community Service Volunteers, Edinburgh

Harry Lauder and Will Fyfe both survived such experiences to become famous entertainers. Harry Lauder watched failed acts who:

were off in less than half a minute and those that didn't willingly retire of their own accord were promptly hauled off by the stage manager by the aid of a long crooked stick which he hooked round their necks.

H Lauder, *Roamin in the Gloamin*, 1928, Hamilton

Caricature of Sir Harry Lauder.

Dance halls flourished in the 1920s and 1930s (in the 1930s Glasgow had 159) introducing young people to American popular music and jazz.

Older forms of entertainment began to suffer in the 1930s from the rise of the cinema industry.

Before the construction of purpose-built cinemas, beginning with the Electric Theatre in Glasgow's Sauchiehall Street in 1910, moving images had been on show for 15 years as part of other entertainment. The purpose-built cinemas ranged from small local structures whose patrons sat on wooden benches, to huge exotically named picture palaces (Alhambras, Granadas and Odeons) whose splendour and comfort provided a refuge from urban life. By 1938 there were 104 cinemas in Glasgow alone and large sections of the population (especially the unemployed) went every week. Saturday morning children's programmes were enormously popular, showing

A MODERN BRITISH THOROUGHFARE.

The magazine *Bon-Accord*'s view of the spread of the Cinema, 1917.

serial stories to their excited audiences and charging just a penny (or a jam jar that could be exchanged for a penny). The unhygienic condition of many urban dwellers led some cinema managers to spray audiences with disinfectants. Hunched in the warmth of the cinema the urban dweller could escape into worlds created in Hollywood and, from 1927, enjoy films with soundtracks too.

For those able to afford cheap rail or steamer fare, it was possible to escape from the urban environment to the coast or country. Trips 'doon the watter' from Glasgow to Dunoon, Largs and Rothesay were especially popular whilst railway services contributed to the growth of other holiday communities. Cycling clubs had a good deal of support, walking clubs grew up and the Scottish Youth Hostel Association was established in 1931 with its first hostel in a row of cottages near Selkirk. In the 1930s especially, people

in work increasingly went away for a week's break, visiting resorts outside Scotland (especially Blackpool) as well as Scottish communities. The urbanisation of Scotland, then, produced changes in other areas that sought to provide for visitors.

Embarking at the Broomielow, Glasgow 1885.

Crowds at the beach enjoying on August Bank Holiday.

The issue of identity

How did urbanisation change Scottish cultural identity? Did it destroy or weaken a distinctively Scottish identity? Historians have differing views, Callum Brown suggests:

Many historians have argued that popular culture in the twentieth century has been replaced by mass culture, something which is little more than leisure activities.

Working class culture had its roots in the harsh work and domestic environments of congested Scottish towns and cities. The public house, the football ground and the street remained key venues in which popular culture was located.

C Brown, in *Modern Scottish History*, Ed. A Cooke

Richard Finlay observes:

New cultural institutions such as the BBC made few concessions to Scottish National Identity. The absorption and destruction of the distinctiveness of the Scottish middle class left the working class as the true heirs to authentic Scottish traditions, particularly in the field of popular culture and sport.

R T Finlay, *National Identity: From British Empire to European Union* in *Modern Scottish History*, Vol 2

A culture of radio listening, football watching and cinema going could be found across Britain. Yet distinctive Scottish activities survived, indeed shinty obtained national rules in 1879 and a ruling body in 1893, whilst Highland Games prospered, backed by Royal patronage at Braemar. The spread of tartan wearing may be a mark of an attempt to retain a distinctive identity in an age of mass culture.

> ## ➤ ACTIVITIES

1 Does the period between 1880s–1939 deserve to be remembered as 'the good old days'? What can be said for this view? What can be said against it?

2 Use the sources by Muir & Robertson and your own knowledge to answer the question:
   In what ways was Scottish urban society affected by the problem of drink?
   (Demonstrate knowledge and understanding of historical developments and events.)

3 How important was technology in shaping leisure activities 1880s–1930s?

Chapter Twelve
Religion and Education

The industrialising and urbanising of Scotland had major consequences for both the place of organised religion in Scotland and the nature and extent of education. Although these two topics are separately treated in this chapter, they have long been closely inter-linked in Scottish history. During the 1880s–1930s both were concerned with trying to calm and control the tumult of urban expansion, shaping the population into orderly and hard-working citizens. In earlier times the Presbyterian Church of Scotland tried to follow the aim of one of its key sixteenth century founders, John Knox of setting up a school in every parish. The Church's importance in founding schools had helped shape Scottish identity. Scottish universities in Glasgow, Edinburgh, St. Andrews and Aberdeen produced the ministers and schoolmasters required by Kirk and school.

The upheaval of urbanisation rendered the system that suited rural Scotland unworkable. The Church could not cope with the educational needs of rapidly growing areas and other religious groups challenged its leading role in education. Universities had to respond to the needs of industrial society and offer all sorts of new courses. Yet religion and education remained strongly inter-linked as Irish Roman Catholic immigrants poured into Scotland. The Catholic Church's determination to keep a grip on schooling led to developments that form a part of Scottish identity today.

As a result of studying the material in this chapter you should have a sound understanding of:

◆ Different religious organisations, their growth or decline as a result of urbanisation.

◆ The importance of churches in urban school life.

◆ The development of primary and secondary schooling.

◆ Changes in university education.

TASK

It is important to have clear notes on this topic and to keep in mind that you are studying the impact of urbanisation on religion and education as part of your overall thinking about the ideas of ideology, identity and authority.

1 Use the points listed above as sub-headings and make notes under each.

2 What evidence can you find for each of the key ideas of ideology, identity and authority?

Different churches

By the 1930s there were at least 40 different kinds of church in Scotland. Throughout the 1880s–1930s the Church of Scotland remained the one that Scots were most likely to attend. Unlike the Church of England, it did not have archbishops and bishops nor was the monarch the official head of the church. It was a Presbyterian organisation, very much controlled by its members and with an annual General Assembly of its ministers. In 1843 the church was much weakened by a split over whether ministers should be appointed by landowners or chosen by church members. The resulting 'Disruption' led to the setting up of the Free Church by those holding the latter view. Around 40 per cent of church goers and 37 per cent of ministers joined the new organisation. It began building its own churches and setting up its own schools. This division was still a major part of Scottish life in the 1880s even though, in 1874, Parliament had abolished landowners' rights to appoint ministers. Free Church members disliked the Church of Scotland's continuing importance in education and helped, by their pressure, to push it to one side and establish the state, instead, as the main provider of schooling.

The two Churches did not hold different religious beliefs and once further parliamentary legislation in 1921 had removed the main forms of the Church of Scotland's establishment status, they were able to re-unite in 1929. Their reunification was partly driven by the desire to be strong in the face of other competing faiths. The Episcopal Church, which had bishops, and was very similar to the Church of England, grew in strength. Congregational, Methodist and Baptist Churches had many supporters. Worries about the lives of poor people and the need to help them – and convert them to Christianity if possible – led William Booth to set up the Salvation Army in England. A Scottish section was founded in Glasgow in 1879.

But it was, above all, the Roman Catholic Church that grew in this period. In 1892 a little over a third of a million worshippers regularly attended its churches and by 1939 the figure had risen to well over 600 000. Behind this expansion lay the huge migration of Irish Catholics into Scotland, especially into the Glasgow area, but also to other urban centres such as Dundee. They

were driven to leave their homeland by desperate poverty and by the opportunities that seemed to be on offer in the Scottish economy before 1914. Other migrants to Scotland were few in number by comparison, though the period did see the arrival of several thousand followers of the Jewish faith.

The importance of religion

Isabella Morrice lived in Aberdeen in the 1890s. Her father was a shoemaker. She wrote:

We never thought of not going to church and we loved Sunday School (on Sunday afternoons). Going to Church was a family affair, we all went and all our chums went to Sunday School. We were expected to remember the text when we got home and to be able to tell what the Sunday School lesson was about.

Morrice, *Your Father & I*

William Haddow's memories of much the same time were less cheerful:

Sunday at home was a dismal ordeal for the younger generation. All newspapers and books of a secular character were carefully put out of sight . . . the whole family was marched to church. After a meal we were marched off again for afternoon service, sometimes we would read Bunyan's Pilgrim's Progress. By 9 o'clock . . . Bibles were given to each member of the family. The old man would read a chapter from the Bible. By 10 o'clock we were all bedded, some of us, I fear, thankful that this dreary day was over.

W Haddow, *My Seventy Years*, 1943

Religion played a central part in the lives of many people, indeed a number of Scots saw their Christian faith as so crucial that they devoted their lives to missionary work. In 1876 a former Dundee mill girl, Mary Slessor went to a part of Nigeria little known to white people and settled there to convert the inhabitants. She was but one of many Scots who made the conversion of

Congregation outside the Episcopal church in St Andrews, 1860.

The habit may have grown after 1900 of attending church once rather than twice on a Sunday yet regular attendance remained a strong feature of life in Scotland at this time. Even so, some historians have detected signs of the decline of religion as a result of reasons other than scientific enquiry. Professor T C Smout suggests:

At the end of the nineteenth century many blamed football, cycling, modern literature and even socialism for diverting the attention of the workers ... In all the investigations there was one hard and unattractive fact which ministers kept striking: the working class could no longer see the point of the kind of church they were faced with.

T C Smout, *A Century of the Scottish People*

others the main purpose of their lives. The British Empire at this time seemed to church leaders to be a force for good, an organisation that improved the lives of its inhabitants. But missionary work took place at home too. The crowded slums seemed to be dangerously ungodly places. Campaigns to convert the slum-dwellers were launched using American methods to rouse emotions through songs, fiery sermons and encouraging people to come forward to be 'saved'.

Religious belief faced challenges in this period, for the scientific studies of people like Charles Darwin questioned the convictions of those who saw the Bible as literally true. Biblical scholarship developed and the Bible was subjected to the kind of careful study that was used for historical documents. These developments sometimes led to fierce debate, to divisions, and to confusion that was upsetting to some. Yet the fact remained as the historian Callum Brown has shown:

Most young people were brought up in a family and social environment dominated by Sunday churchgoing and weekday religious organisations.

C Brown, *Modern Scottish History* Vol 2

The changing role of the churches

By the 1880s the Church of Scotland no longer played the key role in welfare and in education that it had occupied a century before. The historian Callum Brown comments:

Churches were becoming private clubs – very large clubs – which embodied the ideals of Victorian society.

Church representatives continued to occupy an important position on School Boards till 1919 and on County Education Authorities till 1929. Thereafter their role was not significant. The church-run teacher-training colleges were turned over to the State in 1907. The traditional role of helping the poor continued in the form of charitable work but the overwhelming burden after 1845, was born by rate and tax payers and managed by their elected representatives.

Socially, however, churches played a vital part in everyday life. Clubs, societies, sports teams, youth organisations, outings and picnics are but some of the ways in which this role was fulfilled. Boys Brigade, Scouts and Guides were based in churches, whose halls provided invaluable meeting places. The Band of Hope met there too. Many young people met their future marriage partners at church. The church stood for decent, sober and responsible behaviour; it flourished in middle-class areas and was well supported by the upper-working class. It found it less easy to reach the lower levels of society though many church members gave up a great deal of their time to voluntary work among the less fortunate. All too easily it could seem to stand for the existing state of politics and society. By the inter-war years the Church of Scotland especially seemed to represent the Union (including Ireland) of the different parts of the United Kingdom.

An early twentieth century Sunday School outing in Perthshire.

The Roman Catholic Church

The huge Irish influx altered the position of Roman Catholicism in Scotland and at times, aroused tension and even hostility from some Protestants. Irish immigrants tended to be poor and clustered together in slum areas. As a *Scotsman* newspaper journalist noted in 1850:

The Roman Catholics, living in misery, felt pride in attachment to a Church whose arms embraced the most wretched of her children.

Even in the 1930s, a Catholic priest explained the church was crucial to everyday urban life:

Religion was the only security which they had because they hadn't much of the world's goods and they found comfort and strength in their religion. Also they found security in that they could go to the local priest and he was there to assist them with writing letters, getting houses, jobs, etc. The Church afforded them an opportunity for meeting their fellow countrymen.

They developed their own schools and, in 1918 won government agreement to support their separate schooling with state money. Ulster Protestant Irish also migrated to Scotland. Their religious beliefs made it easier for them to integrate into Scottish society, but they also brought with them their suspicions of the Catholic Church. Their organisation, the Orange Order, established Scottish branches, especially around Glasgow. In the inter-war years criticism of Irish Catholics became particularly bitter, possibly because it was a time of high levels of unemployment in areas where they had settled. In both Edinburgh and Glasgow anti-Catholic Protestant political movements were set up. In Glasgow, Alexander Radcliffe's Protestant League won a third of the votes in the 1933 local elections and John Cormack's Protestant Action made an impact in Edinburgh winning 6 seats and 30 per cent of the vote in 1936. A report to the Assembly of the Church of Scotland in 1923 asserted of the Catholic Irish:

They remain a people by themselves, segregated by reason of their race, their customs and, above all, by their loyalty to their Church, gradually and inevitably dividing Scotland racially, socially and ecclesiastically.

Yet during this time Catholics were playing an increasing part in Trade Union and Labour Party activities, as well as inter-marrying with Scots and settling down as contributors to the nation's identity.

Urbanisation ended the welfare and educational importance of the Church of Scotland at a time when it was becoming but one of a number of churches. Among these other beliefs, the Roman Catholic faith loomed increasingly large, fed by Irish migrants and increasing tensions between some Presbyterians and Catholics. Church going remained a major activity and churches responded to urbanisation not only with missions to win fresh converts, but also with a wide range of activities that made them a focus for social life. But urbanisation brought alternative attractions too. It helped the growth of socialist movements, which provided a different way of using the energies of people working to better daily life, and it stimulated a whole range of attractions able to lure people away from church going. The continuing importance of Presbyterian churches, especially the Church of Scotland, meant religion contributed to a very distinctive identity for Scotland within the United Kingdom.

Schooling for all

By the 1880s urban development had already forced a major change in schooling provision, shifting the responsibility from churches and private individuals to the state. In 1872 an act of parliament required all children to go to school from the age of five to the age of thirteen. This legal compulsion was new and required attendance officers to hunt for truants and to compel parents to part with children whose earnings had hitherto helped family incomes. Schooling was managed by locally elected school boards. Not only could women who met the qualification of owning property to the value of £4 a year vote in these elections, they could stand for membership too. Thirteen were successful in the first elections.

Behind this huge change lay several causes. Churches struggled to meet the educational needs of urban areas; the better off looked to more rigorous schooling to train the urban working class in orderly and moral behaviour; many areas of employment required better educated workers; and politicians accepted that a wider franchise had educational implications too. It meant the end of the old parish schools, a distinctive Scottish system offering schooling as far as university entrance (and thus including subjects like Latin and Greek in its curriculum) for those able to afford it. Board Schools were firmly 'elementary' only. They focused on teaching reading, writing and arithmetic along with religious instruction. Though other subjects were gradually added they tended to be strictly practical, training girls in domestic skills and boys in tasks like woodwork. The historian Robert Anderson suggests that Scotland:

ended up with the same kind of mass education as every advanced country and the new urban schools had little connection with their parish predecessors. This change was accompanied by a cultural shift from an educational world which was part of Scotland's religious culture to one which was tied to the state.

R Anderson, *Education & the Scottish People*, 1995

Fees were paid by Board School pupils until their abolition in 1889 (the very poor obtained help with these from parochial boards). Children sat in rows in classes that could well number 60 pupils, were instructed by teachers and their pupil–teacher helpers and regularly checked by the inspectors of the Scotch Education Department (re-named 'Scottish' in 1918). Board Schools were prominent features of the urban environment, surrounded by playgrounds strictly split between boys and girls and with separate entrances for the sexes too.

They provided employment for a rapidly growing and largely female labour force, indeed by 1914 65 per cent of qualified staff were women. The

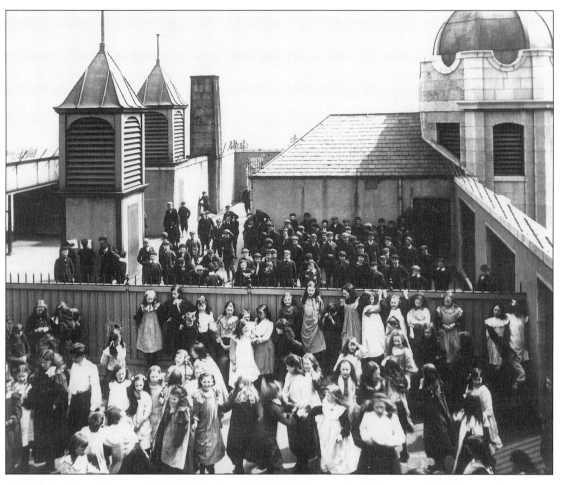

**The rooftop playground of Fredrick Street School in Aberdeen, 1907.
The area was too built up for a normal playground.**

old parish schools were dominated by male graduates whilst most Board School staff were the products of training colleges, set up by the churches, that produced certificated non-graduate staff. Headteachers, however, continued to be male and the salaries paid to female teachers remained little more than half those paid to male staff.

Over the 1880–1939 period pupil attendance requirements became more rigorous. Initially pupils able to satisfy minimum requirements in the '3 Rs' at age 11 could work half-time and attend school half-time till old enough to leave.

In 1901 the age limit was raised to 12, by then numbers working half-time as shop assistants, errand boys and in factories had fallen. In Dundee there were 4500 half-timers in 1883 but just 269 by 1914. In 1883 the general school leaving age was raised to 14, but with so many exceptions allowing children to leave earlier as to be largely ineffective. In 1901 most exemptions were swept away and 14 became the effective leaving age.

School Boards were abolished in 1918 to be replaced (till 1929) by directly elected county and city authorities, thereafter local authority education committees took over. The education offered to most pupils remained much the same with strict discipline enforced by the tawse (a leather strap for beating pupils). As Robert Anderson notes:

For the great mass of school leavers it was the field, the pit and the factory which beckoned and university and secondary schools were part of an alien world.

Professor T C Smout maintains this elementary schooling aimed:

At providing as cheaply as possible the bulk of the population with the bare minimum of elementary education combined with adequate social discipline.

T C Smout, *A Century of the Scottish People*

Schools became a focus for social care too. In 1908 they were given the task of arranging the medical inspections of pupils and the opportunity of providing free school meals.

The 1918 act that abolished School Boards also brought Roman Catholic schools within the scope of state-supported education. Hitherto their state grants did not pay for their buildings. These schools (there were 226 in 1918) retained control of their staff appointments and their religious education curriculum. They formed a very distinctive strand in Scottish schooling, with their needs met by Roman Catholic teacher-training colleges, the first of which opened in 1894 at Bearsden in Glasgow. The historian Robert Anderson suggests this arrangement:

has perpetuated a cultural separation in Scotland.

Modern Scottish History

Nothing comparable was offered in England.

Dinner hour at North Cannongate School, Edinburgh c. 1914.

Clay modelling in the Infants Class of Drummond Street School c. 1914.

Beyond the elementary stage

By the early twentieth century a number of specific subjects like History, Geography, Drawing and Physical Drill had been added to the curriculum. The latter represented the growing concern of government about the health of the inhabitants of urban environments, a worry emphasised by numbers failing fitness tests to enter the armed forces. By this time, too, alarm was growing about the rising economic strength of a number of other countries and the threat this posed to British business. Germany in particular attracted attention and encouraged the development of higher levels of educational achievement in Britain too. The later nineteenth century also saw the rise of professional qualifications and examinations to achieve entrance to professions as well as examinations as a means of entry to the Civil Service. Urbanised Scotland needed people with qualifications. University reform led to the

coming in 1889 of examination achievement as a requirement for admission. All these factors contributed to the expansion of a higher level of education, an expansion vigorously supported by Henry Craik, the powerful secretary to the Scotch Education Department until 1904.

However the provision of higher levels of education did not lead to the construction of a ladder all could climb. T C Smout notes that SED policy aimed at:

giving a small number of children of all classes, but especially of the higher classes, a more respectable academic education to qualify them for their role as a controlling élite.

T C Smout, *A Century of the Scottish People*

An SED circular of 1905 set out this strategy:

Exceptional pupils for whom instruction in secondary subjects (in languages in particular) is desired should, whenever possible, be transferred at a sufficient early stage (say before twelve years) to schools in which these subjects form the staple of the curriculum. Such transference should nearly always be possible in towns

Most pupils remained in their elementary schools. Here, it was recommended, they should be offered somewhat more demanding studies aimed at leaving elementary school for employment including:

Preparation for commercial pursuits
Preparation of manual occupations and trades
Preparation for rural life
For girls – preparation for domestic duties.

Report of the Committee of Council of Education in Scotland 1904–1905

The 1901 act left elementary schools with large numbers of 12 to 14 year olds to provide for. For those able to pass a qualifying examination, supplementary courses of two or three years were offered from 1903 that led to a Merit Certificate.

These courses were strongly vocational in character. Many pupils did not manage to achieve even this level. In 1912 in Aberdeen a third of pupils did not even begin such courses and a third failed to achieve the Merit Certificate.

Ambitious plans to alter this situation were drawn up in 1918, but came to very little. The supplementary courses were re-named 'advanced' but continued to provide a path to working class employment not a way into secondary schooling. The main new development consisted of the creation of intermediate schools where two and three year advanced courses were delivered. Entry was by examination and head teachers' report and those who failed were left to languish in their elementary schools, repeating work they had already done. For pupils in intermediate schools a Lower Leaving Certificate was developed.

Secondary schooling remained, throughout the period, a distinct educational strand available to just a minority of pupils, providing five year courses in a range of subjects, including those required for university admission. The Leaving Certificate that was introduced in 1888 for pupils to attempt at 17 years of age, was soon adopted by Scottish universities as their entrance requirement.

Distinct secondary (or 'higher class') schools came about in a number of ways. Some emerged from long-established fee-paying burgh schools (male only in Aberdeen, Glasgow and Edinburgh) that were taken over by School Boards in 1874. The 1872 act did not allow these schools' costs to be met from the rates, hence they continued to charge fees which excluded most children. A second group of fee-paying higher-class schools grew out of charity-funded schools like Robert Gordons in Aberdeen and the Merchant Company schools in Edinburgh.

Reorganisation of these schools around 1880 led to the emergence of day schools which, though they had some bursaries, depended chiefly on fees. Thirdly, School Boards developed Higher Grade schools, some of which evolved, eventually, into full secondary schools. Some of these were designed to provide girls with proper opportunities to enter secondary schooling – such as Aberdeen High School for Girls. Others were mixed schools established in response to local demand for a greater availability of a higher level of education. Harris Academy (1885) in Dundee attracted the children of mill managers, shopkeepers, clergy, for example, and Aberdeen's Central School took pupils from all over the city who had achieved a sufficiently high level of attainment in their elementary schools. Many of these schools had, by the 1890s ceased to charge fees, indeed in 1912, 171 of Scotland's 249 public secondary schools provided 'free schooling'.

By the twentieth century some sort of free secondary education was available in urban areas to those able to achieve success in an examination at 12 years and whose parents could afford to keep them at school beyond 14. The division between elementary and secondary schooling was reflected in teachers' qualifications too. Reforms in the early twentieth century ended the pupil–teacher system, allocated honours graduates to secondary schools, ordinary graduates to intermediate schools, and non-graduates to elementary schools. This secondary system was very restrictive, yet provided more places than the equivalent system in England.

Education beyond school level

Two main developments mark the education on offer to school leavers; changes in universities and the growth of technical and vocational training. Both reflect the need of urbanised industrialised Scotland for more highly trained specialists and better educated administrators. Both show the need to keep up with other countries going through similar social and economic upheavals and aware of the need to invest in education. Awareness of developments in Germany played a very strong part in these changes.

Universities

The late nineteenth century saw Scottish universities change significantly. What had been all-male institutions were opened up to women as part of the 1889 Universities (Scotland) Act. Four year honours degrees developed that allowed students to choose from specialist studies like the Sciences, English, Modern Languages, History or Classics. Three year ordinary degrees continued but students of both courses commonly began them at ages 17 or 18. The much looser and less formal system that allowed students to enter at a much earlier age and tolerated students failing to take their degrees, rapidly vanished. In 1892 entrance based on the Leaving Certificate was established, requiring an adequate performance in English, Maths, Latin or Greek, and one other subject. Numbers at Scottish universities crept up from 6000 in 1900 to 10 000 in 1938. Bursaries offered some hope to working class pupils unable to afford fees: in 1910 around 15 per cent of Aberdeen University students came from a working class background, a lower figure than achieved by Glasgow where 24 per cent of men and 18 per cent of women students were categorised as from this class. This was a much higher figure than achieved at Oxford or Cambridge but as Robert Anderson has pointed out:

We need to remember that before 1914 both secondary and university education were confined to a very small percentage of the age group – about 4 per cent completed secondary schooling and 2 per cent less carried on to university level.

R Anderson in *Modern Scottish History* Vol 2

Vocational education

Scotland's industrial–urban society needed growing numbers of technically qualified people. School Boards were given the task of providing further education for those who had left school at the earliest opportunity and rapidly developed a range of 'continuation' classes that ran in the evenings. These classes provided students with opportunities to raise their standards in the '3 Rs' and, increasingly, to develop practical skills in courses like typing, joinery and dressmaking. The SED took an interest in these courses and in 1908, allowed local authorities to make attendance at them compulsory up to the age of 17. Glasgow attempted to carry out this policy for pupils who had failed to obtain a Merit Certificate but found many practical problems, such as effective enforcement, stopped it being a complete success.

From 1898 the SED also took over management of the Technical Colleges that had begun to emerge in the 1880s. Glasgow College of Science and Art was established in 1881, formed (like Robert Gordons College four years earlier) from the reorganisation of charity endowed schools. The SED developed such colleges as central institutions, funding them from block grants, and looking to them to provide a higher level of technical education. By 1913 there were 11 such centres catering for 4800 day students and 10 900 evening students. They offered courses in areas like pharmacy, architecture, domestic science, engineering, and chemistry and helped further emphasise the importance of urban areas as centres for education.

Yet it seemed a struggle to make practical studies as attractive in Scotland as they were in Germany. The historian Robert Anderson believes:

In Scotland, Latin, university culture and a liberal education were not aristocratic but the symbols of a national democratic tradition.

Education and the Scottish People

Parents were often eager for their children to follow this route. The Principal of Heriot Watt declared, in 1908:

It is absolutely necessary if this country is to hold its industrial position, that we cease playing at technical education and living under the delusion that all that is wanted is the teaching of a smattering of science to our artisans.

Quoted R Anderson, *Education and the Scottish People*

But neither popular opinion nor SED policy makers seemed very enthusiastic about this view.

> ## ➤ ACTIVITIES
>
> 1 Compare the views of Isabella Morrice and William Haddow on Sundays in the 1980s. (Comparison of sources.)
>
> 2 Use T C Smout's comments on the reasons for church-going being under threat (Page 153) and your own knowledge to explain why church going in the 1930s was no longer quite so dominant as it had once been. (Explaining historical developments and events.)
>
> 3 In what ways did Irish migration affect Scottish identity 1880s–1930?
>
> 4 How justified is T C Smout in his view of the purpose of elementary schooling (Page 157)?

CHANGING SCOTTISH SOCIETY –
An Overview

Crowded housing, tenements, council housing, surburbs as travel improved.

Social problems of health, safety, law and order that led to more powerful local authorities, more taxes and officials.

Urban growth produced:

Leisure and Popular Culture
- Entertainments in and around the home.
- Public houses and the attempts to control and reduce drinking.
- Gambling, ice-cream parlours.
- Parks, gardens, libraries, museums.
- Mass entertainments – sports, especially football.
- Mass entertainments – theatres and cinemas.

Religion
- The Church of Scotland split and lost its grip on education and welfare.
- Irish immigration caused Roman Catholic numbers to rise.
- Church-going remained at a high level.
- Urban areas offered many alternative attractions.
- Churches played an important social role.

Education
- Primary schooling emerged from Board Schools.
- Older pupils were offered more advanced courses at 12 years, if they did well enough.
- Secondary schooling developed becoming increasingly free, but not available to all.
- Universities were reformed and expanded.
- Technical education developed in Colleges.

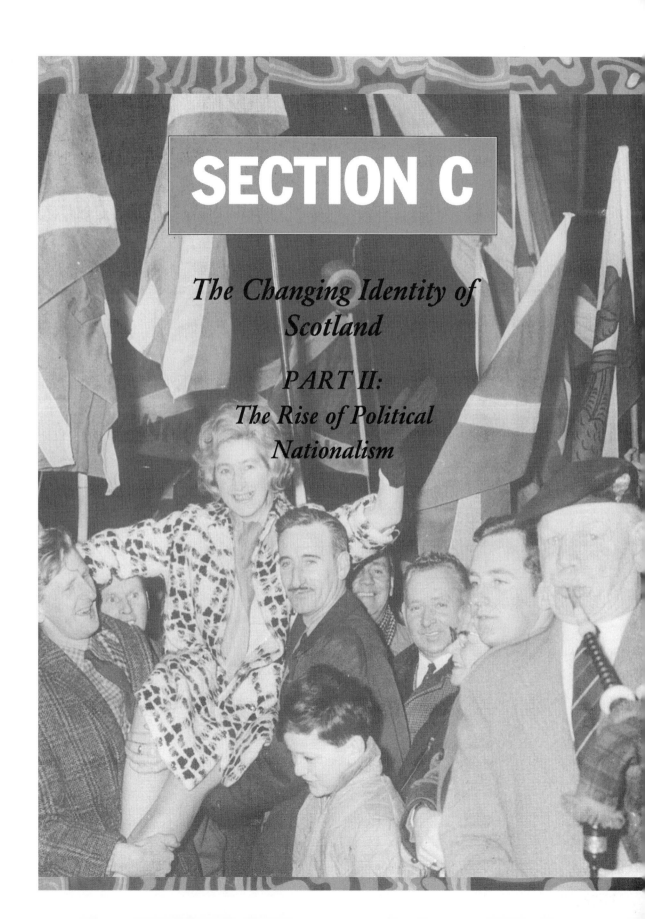

SECTION C

The Changing Identity of Scotland

PART II:
The Rise of Political Nationalism

Introduction

Throughout the period 1880s–1979 Scotland formed part of the United Kingdom, with MPs representing Scottish constituencies travelling to Westminster to take part in political decisions. Throughout the period, too, there were demands from some Scots for their country to manage some of its affairs itself through a Scottish parliament. In 1880 this desire for home rule simply took the form of unsuccessful demands, however in 1979 the people of Scotland were asked to vote on the issue in a special referendum.

Between 1880–1979, there were great changes in Scotland's political identity. In 1880 there was no serious political party to campaign for complete political independence for Scotland. By 1979 a sizeable Scottish National Party fought for this cause and had MPs at Westminster and on local councils. In 1880 there was no sizeable Scottish-based administration to deal with Scottish affairs. By 1979 a very large administration had grown up in Edinburgh, and Scotland was represented in the Cabinet by its own minister.

The material in this section deals with the aspects of Scottish political identity that are required by the Higher course i.e.:

◆ Changing attitudes to the union 1880s–1939.

◆ Issues of devolution and independence 1930–1979.

Careful study of this section will prepare you to answer such questions as:

◆ How far did Labour and Conservative Governments bring administrative devolution to Scotland 1930–1979?

◆ *'Support for Scottish nationalism has been primarily a response to economic hardship.'*
How far would you agree with reference to the period 1930–1979?

◆ Explain why the Scottish National Party did not achieve more electoral success between 1930–1979.

◆ In what ways did Scotland possess a distinct political identity, 1889–1939?

Chapter Thirteen

Changing Attitudes to the Union 1880–1939

Throughout this period Scottish affairs were managed by politicians at Westminster. None of them belonged to a party demanding Scottish independence and though some supported the idea of home rule for Scotland, this did not come about. But a Scottish administration grew in size and importance and in 1939, moved its base of operations from London to Edinburgh. Moreover, those seeking political independence became better organised, and established the Scottish National Party in 1934.

The material in this chapter deals with these developments. As a result of studying it you should have a sound grasp of:

◆ Developments that tended to integrate Scotland into the United Kingdom.

◆ Ways in which a Scottish identity was sustained and expressed.

◆ The changing circumstances that shaped attitudes to the Union.

◆ Administrative developments.

The focus therefore is on the changing political identity of Scotland, the development of administrative authority based in Scotland and the ideologies of politicians in relation to the United Kingdom and Scotland's place in it.

TASK

Gather material for an essay on:

In what ways and for what reasons did attitudes to the union change 1880–1939?

◆ Read through this chapter.

◆ Jot down key sub-headings and discuss them with others to reach an agreed list.

◆ Make notes under each subheading.

Factors challenging a distinct Scottish identity

Social and economic developments of the period tended to tie together the different parts of the United Kingdom more closely. Roads, steamer services and railways linked up hitherto remote parts of the country stimulating business, newspapers, and political parties on a UK-wide scale. People became familiar with parts of the country that previously it would have been almost impossible for them to visit. Holidays in distant parts of the kingdom became common events for the better off. As early as 1846 the pioneer of the holiday business, Thomas Cook, commented:

It was in Scotland that I first began to combine tickets for railways, steamboats, and other conveyances under one system in order that passengers travelling under our arrangements might well be able to calculate the expense and foresee the engagements they would have to enter into.

J Simmons, in *Journal of Contemporary History*, 1984, Vol 19

Increasingly people in different parts of the country wore similar clothing, ate similar food (though the Scottish affection for oats remained), and read similar books and newspapers. Addiction to the works of Charles Dickens was as strong in Scotland as in England – indeed Edinburgh had a Pickwick Club and was the first city to make the author a freeman. Letters crisscrossed the country in growing numbers rising from eight per person per year in the 1840s to 60 per person by 1900.

As the economy changed and expanded, so people moved from one part of the country to settle in another. Large numbers of Irish arrived in Liverpool and Glasgow, for example; many Welsh and Scottish people sought their fortunes in English cities. Growing businesses found their markets throughout the country, and not merely within their immediate locality. The management of the economy by the government mattered as much to Welsh coal-producers as to Lancashire cotton-workers or Scottish shipbuilders. The issue of free trade or protection affected all: Scottish farming suffered from free trade and cheap foreign imports and English farming slumped too. Lord Rosebery, a very politically active peer, felt that features of the Scottish character were inevitably fading. He wrote:

Much of that character has been taken away from us by the swift amalgamating power of railways, by the centralisation of (an) Anglicising empire, by the compassionate sneer of the higher civilisation.

Quoted in K Robbins, *Nineteenth-century Britain*

Certainly it was clear that non-English languages commonly spoken in 1800 were in retreat by the 1900s. In Scotland Gaelic-speaking declined slowly, falling from 231 595 speakers in 1881 to 220 398 by 1911. The Registrar General of 1871 had no doubt as to the need for all to speak English. He wrote:

The Gaelic language may be what it likes, both as to antiquity and beauty, but it decidedly stands in the way of the civilisation of the natives making use of it and shuts them out from the paths open to their fellow countrymen who speak the English tongue. It ought therefore to cease to be taught in all our national schools; and as we are one people we should have but one language.

J Simmons, in *Journal of Contemporary History*, 1984, Vol 19

A number of people living at the time commented on the employment opportunities offered by the United Kingdom, its law and government, its armed services and empire. Writing in mid-Victorian times in a Free Church magazine, the Scot David Masson argued:

Increased quiet, increased commerce and wealth, increased liberty, increased civilisation – these have been the consequences to Scotland of the once detested Union and since the Union Scottish talent and Scottish energy have had a wider and richer field to (expand) in than they would otherwise have possessed ... There have been Scottish Prime Ministers, Scottish Chief Justices of England, Scottish Lord Chancellors, Scottish Generals of British armies and Admirals of British fleets, Scottish Governors of India. England is full of Scottish merchants and manufacturers. London is full of Scottish literary men and Scottish editions of newspapers.

Quoted in H J Hanham, *Scottish Nationalism*, 1969

Certainly there were Scots who grasped the opportunities not only for careers in another part of the kingdom, but also for the creation of businesses with a UK-wide presence. Thomas Lipton opened his first grocery stores in Glasgow; others soon began to appear in distant parts of the kingdom. Such shops stocked the products of firms producing goods for a UK market, thus increasing the sense of the emergence of a single country. When plans to establish a separate educational department to run Scottish education were announced, an eminent Scottish scientist protested in 1884 that the proposal would:

accentuate the differences between England and Scotland for the future and tend to convert Scotland into a Province, with the narrow peculiarities of Provincial existence. No country can less afford than Scotland to narrow the ambition of its educated classes or parochialise its institutions. If it separates itself from England in administration and education it need not be surprised if in time Scotland becomes less of an outlet for Scottish enterprise.

Quoted in H J Hanham, *Scottish Nationalism*, 1969

An article in *The Times* went so far as to suggest that Scots who argued that their country was distinctive and should be treated differently were doing themselves harm:

By their exclusiveness and provincialism the Scotch have not only kept out English influence which might have done them good, but they have driven the best of their own countrymen to England; it is not merely because Parliament sits in London that England drains away the best brains from the other two kingdoms but because Englishmen have thrown away those confined notions of nationality, which still prevail in Scotland and Ireland. We, south of the Tweed, have risen to the conception of a United Kingdom … but in Edinburgh, the cry still is 'Scotland for the Scotch'. Yet the more Scotland had striven to be a nation, the more she has sunk to be a province.

Quoted in H J Hanham, *Scottish Nationalism*, 1969

Sir Henry Craik, head of the Scottish Education Department, and an MP from 1906, questioned the very notion of a Scottish nation:

What is this national entity which you are going to cut off from the whole of Southern Britain and constitute a national item by itself? Is there that intimate sympathy of race and feeling between the remote fishermen of the Hebrides and the Orkneys and Shetland, and the Lanarkshire population or that population of Glasgow constituted very largely by an influx of 1 500 000 from Ireland? Is that exactly a homogenous population? Do you think the Northern parts of Scotland will be so pleased to be ruled by the packed population of the slums of Glasgow and the mining districts of Lanark?

Quoted in H J Hanham, *Scottish Nationalism*, 1969

It was from Ireland rather than Scotland that the loudest demands came for political separation.

Factors sustaining Scottish identity

In his study of nineteenth century Scotland, the historian W Ferguson concluded:

In spite of increasing cultural assimilation, Scotland, for most of her inhabitants, retained much of her individuality, and her outstanding problems – concerning church, poor law, education or public health – differed in substance from their English counterparts. Few politicians grasped this fundamental fact.

W Ferguson, *Scotland 1689 to the Present*

Scotland has its own church, its own legal system and its own distinctive educational structure. Scots looked back to the time of independence, to victories over English forces, and to the ending of this independence by negotiation, not conquest. Indeed the later nineteenth century saw William Wallace used as a focus for Scottish identity through the building of monuments to him, notably on the outskirts of Stirling. By this time, too, the visible signs of identity represented by the wearing of tartan, and especially of kilts, were commonly adopted throughout the country.

During the later nineteenth century the coming of sporting activities that attracted mass followings further emphasised Anglo-Scottish differences. Instead of a British football league, separate Football Associations organised separate cup and league competitions in England and Scotland (1873 and 1890) following an incident in a match between Queens Park and Preston North End that led the Scottish Football Association to insist in 1886 on separation. From time to time national teams representing each country met in matches that attracted intense feelings of Scottish identity. It is a sign of developments from the 1880s, though, that several members of Scottish national sides normally turned out on Saturdays for teams in the English league. The activities of Scottish sporting heroes were duly celebrated in Scottish newspapers such as *The Aberdeen Free Press*, *The North Briton* (Edinburgh) and *The People's Journal*. Other Scottish achievements in industry and the arts – were celebrated in great exhibitions held in Glasgow in 1888, 1901, 1911 and 1938. Twelve and a half million people attended the latter event.

According to the historian Richard Finlay:

The Scottish role in the creation of the British Empire has undoubtedly been the biggest factor in the making of modern Scottish national identity. Indeed, most of the more obvious symbols of Scottish nationality owe their existence to the imperial past. In the nineteenth and early twentieth centuries the Scots prided themselves on being a race of empire builders.

Modern Scottish History, Vol 2

Scots played a major part in administering, exploiting, and defending this Empire. Scottish missionaries sought to convert its inhabitants. Glasgow prided itself on being the 'second city of the Empire'. The achievements of Scots in the Empire were celebrated as offering evidence of Scottish virtues.

Being part of the United Kingdom and accepting this situation as beneficial to Scotland did not mean a loss of a sense of Scottish identity. In fact this sense of identity was strongly evident and, as Richard Finlay notes:

Scots were excellent at self-promotion and were well-known for their clannishness in the Empire. The myth of the 'enterprising' Scot was manufactured by the Scots themselves and its success can be seen by the way in which so many believed in it, including the English.

A sense of national identity was encouraged by cultural developments. Clan societies were set up in the late nineteenth century, branches of Burns Clubs proliferated, the Scottish National Portrait Gallery opened in 1889 and the Scottish History Society was founded in 1887.

A desire for change

Before 1914

Even in the 1880s, there were demands for Scottish affairs to be taken more seriously perhaps, even, for Scotland to have her own Parliament to control purely Scottish matters. Those asking for such a change were not trying to break up the United Kingdom but were expressing their belief that Scottish issues received insufficient attention at Westminster and ran the danger of decisions being made for Scotland by MPs from other parts of the United Kingdom. Events in Ireland influenced views in Scotland too. Ireland, too, was ruled from Westminster but was the scene of economic, social, and political protests that could take violent forms. It was Irish affairs that persuaded Gladstone of the merits of home rule; hitherto he had seemed to take the massive support he received in Scotland for granted. It needed a major upheaval like the Crofters War of 1882 (in which Skye crofters resisted being cleared from their land) to jolt him. It was a source of irritation to some Scottish Liberals that in Ireland violence seemed to meet with reward in the form of a promise of home rule. The loyal and peaceful contributions of Scots did not seem to matter. The indignant crofters formed a political party of their own, though it subsided back into the Liberal Party after 1886 once crofters won acceptable rents and security of their occupation of their crofts.

Even if it owed something to the Irish situation, many Scots Liberals welcomed Gladstone's general conversion to a belief in a home rule that would give Scotland her own parliament too. In 1886 a Scottish Home Rule Association was established. In 1888 the Scottish Liberal Association resolved:

That this National Conference is of the opinion that Home Rule should be granted to Scotland so that the Scottish people could have the sole control and management of their own national affairs and suggests that the true solution of the question may be found in granting Home Rule Legislators on a federal basis to Scotland, England, Ireland and Wales.

Quoted in H J Hanham, *Scottish Nationalism*

Some Scottish Liberals were opposed to this policy and joined Liberal Unionists in campaigning against it. In the Glasgow area where Ulster influence and the Orange Order were increasingly important, Liberal Unionists did well. In 1885, 17 were voted into parliament as MPs.

Most Liberals, however, persisted in favouring Home Rule. In this late nineteenth century period it was argued that this strategy would benefit the Empire; assemblies in different parts of the Empire could concentrate on policies needed for their particular region leaving Westminster to act as an imperial parliament dealing with issues that concerned all. It was argued that this policy of 'home rule all round' would be a source of strength not a step towards disintegration. The Home Rule Association maintained

in 1890, that the Empire was created as much by Scots as by English people:

The rise of the Empire dates from the Union. Our Highland Regiments which have fought so valiantly did so to maintain the honour – not of England but of the United Kingdom. Go where you may, you will find Scotsmen occupying foremost places.

In the early twentieth century a rather different view of the value of home rule emerged, a view that reflected both the more democratic political system that had come about by this time and the great concern for social welfare issues that can be seen in the policies of the Liberal Government of 1906–1914. The chief representatives of this view were an organisation attached to the Liberal Party known as Young Scots. This movement, formed in 1900, had 50 branches and several thousand active members by 1914. It published a journal and operated very effectively at election time, focusing its efforts on key marginal seats. The historian Richard Finlay has described the impact the Young Scots made:

whereas middle-class Scotland had looked outwards to the Empire and backwards to a cosy romantic vision of Scotland past for its sense of national identity, the emergence of class-based politics increasingly focused national identity upon the inward reality of contemporary Scotland.

Modern Scottish History, Vol 2

The Young Scots and their supporters agreed with older Liberals that home rule would help the better running of the Empire. They resented the way that social reform proposals on education, temperance, land reform and housing failed to pass the Westminster Parliament when, they believed, a purely Scottish Parliament would readily have accepted them. Scottish MPs grumbled that Scotland received insufficient attention.

In 1913 the MP for East Aberdeenshire declared:

To my knowledge there has been a Scottish majority in the House in favour of temperance reform since 1885, a majority which has always been voted down by the English members. In the second place let me call attention to one urgent question – land reform . . . Scotland is being depopulated, emigration is double that from Ireland . . . a single Scottish official rules Scottish education with almost despotic sway . . . This House grudgingly allows to Scotland one day of 7 hours in each Parliamentary year for the discussion of Scottish estimates. Is it any wonder Scotland is tired and demands a Parliament of her own? That she demands her own legislation for land, for the liquor trade, for education, for housing, for fisheries, for ecclesiastical affairs?.

Quoted in H J Hanham, *Scottish Nationalism*

The home rule issue had split the Liberal Party in the late nineteenth century as, led by Joseph Chamberlain, Liberal Unionists resisted home rule and eventually tied themselves to the Conservative Party. They proved too powerful for Gladstone and thwarted his home rule bills. In 1912 Liberal Unionists and Conservatives in Scotland merged to form the Scottish Unionist Party. This party argued that the distinctive abilities of Scots best expressed themselves in a vigorous contribution to the Empire. The Young Scots had raised a different view of Scottish identity – that of Scotland as a radical society eager for major social reforms as well as a crucial component of the British Empire. They checked the loyalty to the cause of home rule of Liberal MPs and were even ready to back a Labour man when he seemed more enthusiastic for the cause than the Liberal MP for the Glasgow seat of Blackfriars. By 1914 they had reason for hope, for Sir Henry Cowans bill for Scottish home rule had passed its second parliamentary reading. The outbreak of the First World War ended these hopes.

In the years 1880–1914, then, there was general support for the union, though differences over whether Scotland needed a parliament to manage its own internal affairs. This support for union did not mean any diminution of a strong sense of identity, however. Scots were proud of their contribution to British development and, especially to Imperial development where Scots saw themselves as equal contributors with England. Any English failure to appreciate this was much resented. The Scottish Home Rule Association's journal, *The Scottish Patriot* proclaimed in 1903:

Our empire is Great Britain, our government, flag and everything concerning the empire is British. If a man belongs to Scotland he is a Scotsman, not an Englishman and if Englishmen go on persisting in abusing these terms they do so in ignorance.

Quoted D S Forsyth, 'Empire Union', *Scottish Geographical Magazine* Vol 113 No 1 1997

The historian David Forsyth concludes of this period:

There remained a quite distinct Scottish identity which coloured the view of Scotland's political classes to the imperial mission and the political system based on the treaty of union . . . Scotland as a nation had not been subsumed by England . . . there were limits to infringements of England on Scotland.

The inter-war years

By 1918 the Liberal Party was badly split. The cause of home rule, however, was picked up by the Labour Party, many of whose members, including Keir Hardie, had long supported it. The creation of a Scottish Trade Union Council in 1897 had already provided a national organisation for this key dimension of the Labour Party. Radical Clydeside Labour MPs like Jimmy Maxton saw a Scottish parliament as a means of achieving more effective social reforms than Westminster seemed to find acceptable. In 1919 the Party's Scottish Council resolved:

Now that the war is ended and an era of reconstruction begun, Scottish problems require the concentration of Scottish brains and machinery on their solution. Your committee is of opinion that a determined effort be made to secure home rule for Scotland.

The hoped for period of reconstruction rapidly faded before the impact of economic depression. Support in the Labour Party began to waver and the home rule bills that came before Parliament in 1924 and 1927 both failed. Inter-war Scotland had to cope with both more severe unemployment and poorer living conditions than England. To many Labour MPs the way to recovery lay through a concerted British effort whilst English affluence was, it was argued, necessary for funding Scottish people who were out of work. In 1931 the Labour Party split and its political representation in Parliament shrank. Home Rule within the union as a way of effecting large-scale social reform no longer seemed so attractive.

The imperial dimension to unionism began to fade too. In 1931 the dominion governments secured control of their own foreign policies, and the slump hit them as well in the 1930s. Moreover the appeal of imperialism seemed less clear as trouble flared up in India and the Middle East. The First World War had reduced the popularity of militarism, and the slump damaged Scotland's claim to be a crucial and vigorous economic element in the Empire. The whole notion of Scotland and England as partners in the great imperial adventure seemed far less convincing and attention turned to trying to revive the Scottish economy. The historian Richard Finlay observes:

Unwittingly, perhaps, Unionists established with the Labour Party an inter-war consensus that Scotland needed England for its economic survival.

Modern Scottish History Vol 2

The Unionist Party, too, was troubled by the situation, aware of the need to meet Scottish needs and alarmed by evidence of insufficient concern from some English MPs. Several Unionists voiced their fear that right-wing nationalism was in danger of emerging as a way of solving problems. This mood was fed by the denunciation of Irish Roman Catholics in Scotland pronounced by some Church of Scotland leaders who described the Irish immigrants as alien to Scottish identity. The novelist John Buchan who was also a Unionist MP spoke of his concern that nationalism:

is found among young people who are hard-headed, practical and ambitious, who are shaping for themselves careers in medicine and law and in business … They believe that something is wrong with Scotland and that it is the business of Scotsmen to put it right.

Parliamentary Papers G72, 1932

Policies that met Britain's economic problems by rationalising industries, did not seem to benefit Scotland. *The Scotsman* complained that:

continuance of the fundamentally false policy of centralising everything in London will, sooner or later, finish Scotland as a nation and reduce her to a mere province of England.

Yet businessmen and industrialists warned that any break with England would be damaging. In the words of Lord Maclay in 1931:

Anything in the way of a severance from England would almost certainly spell disaster. The setting up of a separate Scottish Parliament would certainly result in the removal to England of many Scottish industries and also many merchant traders.

Quoted R Finlay 1994, 'History' 79

On the one hand Westminster seemed unsympathetic, helping British farmers by subsidising wheat and sugar beet growing, for example, but not the major Scottish crop of oats: on the other hand Government orders, especially when rearmament began in the mid-thirties, helped Scotland and in the 1920s Baldwin's Conservative Ministry provided more generous support for new housing in Scotland than it did in England. It seemed very difficult to find a clear policy in relation to the union. It is not surprising, then, that in this period a movement emerged that was not just a pressure group or part of one of the main political parties but a quite separate movement solely concerned with Scottish matters (more fully treated in the next chapter). The outbreak of the Second World War in 1939 came amid confusion about the union and how best Scottish interests might be served within it.

A growing Scottish administration

By the 1880s there was considerable support for the view that Scottish concern about the country's place in the union might be effectively met by developing the administration that existed to manage Scottish affairs. In 1883 Gladstone unsuccessfully brought forward a bill to set up a Scottish Local Government Board to oversee health and welfare matters. In 1885 the Liberals tried again, with more success and with the additional proposal for the creation of the post of Scottish Secretary to oversee Scottish interest but not to be a member of the cabinet. Lord Salisbury's Conservatives accepted and implemented the reform: the Duke of Richmond was the first occupant of the post. In 1886 Salisbury increased the new minister's powers by giving him control over policy areas, which included law and order and local government. He also freed him from subordination to the Home Office, a step towards higher status that, by 1892, had been further enhanced by cabinet rank.

The Secretary remained London-based, however, his staff were few in number and he himself was often a peer – thus needing someone else to defend policy in the commons. Further reforms in 1919 increased the status and authority of the Scottish Office: they represented an approach that continued in subsequent years (see next chapter) without diminishing the debate about Scotland's place within the union.

➤ ACTIVITIES

1 Write the essay planned by means of the Task at the opening of this chapter.

2 Why was it so difficult in this period to develop a clear and broadly-accepted policy to shape Scotland's place in the union?

Chapter Fourteen

Issues of Devolution and Independence 1930–1979

Between the 1930s–1979 three major developments shaped Scotland's political identity. Firstly, there was a steady expansion of an administration, based in Scotland, to look after Scottish affairs, i.e. more and more power was devolved to the government's chosen Scottish ministers. Secondly, there was a growth in the demand for a Scottish parliament. By 1979 this pressure was so strong that the government organised a referendum to seek the views of the people of Scotland as to whether they wanted home rule, i.e. the devolving of power to the elected representatives of the country's inhabitants. Thirdly, the period saw the emergence of a significant political party whose purpose was to win complete independence for Scotland. This chapter deals with those themes. As a result of studying it you should have a sound grasp of:

◆ Ways in which more administrative power was devolved to Scotland.

◆ The setting up and varying fortunes of the Scottish National Party.

◆ Reasons for differing views on Scotland's place in the union and their varying popularity at different times.

TASK

1 **a)** Develop a clearly organised list of the stages in the development of a Scottish-based administration.

   b) Why did this development not end pressure for change?

2 Set out a clearly sub-divided section entitled 'The History of the SNP'.

3 Look through the whole period, 1930–1979 and divide it into sections. Explain why the importance of the issue of devolution and independence varied at different times.

The development of a Scottish administration

The Thirties

By 1930 the politician responsible for Scottish affairs had risen in status from the junior post of Scottish Secretary to the senior rank of Secretary of State. The first occupant of this enhanced post in 1926, Sir John Gilmour, thus became an important minister who was automatically entitled to a place in the cabinet. He faced a problem faced by all Scottish Secretaries of State, one well outlined by the historian Ian Levitt:

The twentieth century required not just political symbols . . . but material advancement. At a time when Government itself held greater control over social and economic investment, the Scottish Secretary had to be seen to be effective in securing jobs, houses, and social security. The real issue was how to achieve it.

Scotland 1850–1979, H A 1993

Gilmour sought to increase his authority over Scottish administration, taking a step down the road that led eventually to the creation of the modern Scottish Office. Whilst he was based in London and had control over education as part of his department, other areas of life (such as agriculture and health) were managed by Edinburgh-based boards made up of appointees over whom he did not have effective control. Gilmour proposed to abolish these boards, turning them into departments within his empire. There was some alarm in Scotland that too much power would thus move to London. Gilmour had to assure MPs that just as the SED was based in Edinburgh, so other departments would be located there too:

I have specifically inserted in the Bill a clause which declares that the Departments shall remain in Scotland ... The ambition which I have formed (is to) centralise in Edinburgh under one roof all the Departments concerned with Scottish affairs.

Hansard Vol 214, Feb 1928

In 1928 Gilmour succeeded in carrying through his reform. The episode illustrated both the determination to create a more coherent and more effective Scottish Office that was politically controlled, and also Scottish feelings that affairs should be run from Edinburgh. Yet many areas of policy were managed by London-based departments and, at a time of economic slump and high unemployment, Westminster control of the economy was especially important. Work began on developing the new Scottish departments including equipping them with appropriate expertise.

In 1934 the current Secretary (a Liberal in a Coalition Government) Sir Godfrey Collins, sought further change. He persuaded his colleagues that, under the Special Areas Act, which aimed to revive the worst areas in the troubled British economy, there should be a Commissioner for Scotland with the task of stimulating the economy of the Glasgow area in particular. Between 1935–1938 14 million pounds were spent on this work. Since the Scottish Secretary had oversight of it, some degree of influence over economic affairs was added to his department. Collins also persuaded the Prime Minister, Stanley Baldwin, to agree to an enquiry into Scottish administration with a view to concentrating it in Edinburgh. His arguments were assisted by advice that this policy would diminish demands for home rule. The outcome was the Gilmour Report, which was vigorously implemented by the able Conservative Scottish Secretary for the late 1930s, Walter Elliot. It was this final pre-war reform that produced a base for the Scottish Office – St Andrew's House in Edinburgh – and departments within it of Agriculture, Education, Health, and Home Affairs. The latter department oversaw the Special Areas Act, the Highlands and Islands, electricity and power, the Scottish Travel Association and the Scottish Development Council. Each department had its own head, and all were answerable to the Scottish Secretary who now shifted his main office to Edinburgh. More money was spent on Scottish libraries, art galleries and museums. Scottish records taken by Edward I were returned. In 1937 the Scottish Housing Association was set up to develop new building methods and improve housing provision.

After 1939

This reform was in place by the time that the Second World War began. Focusing operations in Scotland, however, still left the problem of the relationship of Scottish concerns with British policy making. The minister obtained a permanent under-secretary with an office in London to promote Scottish interests at Westminster and act as a co-ordinator between the different departments.

The Scottish Office, St Andrew's House, Edinburgh.

In 1941 Churchill installed the Labour politician Tom Johnston as Scottish Secretary. Johnston's former enthusiasm for home rule seemed to fade once in office but he proved an energetic minister keen to expand his authority. He set up committees to plan post-war reconstruction. In 1943 he took control of town and country planning from the Ministry of Planning, and the management of one of his favoured projects, the North of Scotland Hydroelectricity Board, from the Ministry of Fuel and Power. But he had to accept there had to be limits to the absorption of power by the Scottish Office, for a UK-wide strategy was needed if industries were to be directed northwards and away from the south east of England.

Post-war years saw, initially, a reinforcement of the UK-wide strategy for dealing with social and economic issues. The Attlee Government's welfare policies were especially important to Scotland given the scale of social problems in the country. Health and education were organised on a Scottish basis, national insurance and social security were not. Its programme of nationalisation for coal, railways and, eventually, the steel industry, dealt with matters of real importance to Scotland. Moreover full employment and a rising standard of living made many Scots feel that this strategy was working. In the late 1940s the Clyde built a quarter of the world's shipping tonnage, whilst the historian James Mitchell suggests:

The National Health Service helped cement the union.

Tom Johnston left his post to be succeeded first by Joe Westwood and then (1947) by Arthur Woodburn. Both tried in vain to extend their authority over economic planning. All that was conceded was for the Scottish Grand Committee to look at estimates for Scottish expenditure and consider the second reading of Scottish bills. Little changed under the Churchill Government that took office in 1951 other than the appointment of a minister of state to the Scottish Office. This freed the Secretary to spend more time in London. The Scottish Office also won control of trunk roads from the Ministry of Transport (1956) and took over the appointment of magistrates.

By the 1960s post-war full employment was collapsing. The coal market shrank and Scottish pits were especially costly to sustain. Rival shipbuilders showed up the failure of Scottish yards to re-equip and modernise. The steel industry ran into trouble. An enquiry into Scottish economic troubles produced (1961) the Toothill Report that suggested a new Scottish Office department to oversee planning and advise on economic and industrial policy. This was accepted and Government policy sought to rationalise and sustain Scotland's old industries and encourage the location in Scotland of newer industries. In 1962 the

Scottish Development Department was established, in 1965 the Highlands and Islands Development Board set up to try to regenerate that area's economy and in 1975 the Scottish Development Agency began trying to persuade businesses to locate here.

By 1979 the Scottish Office was the focus of a whole range of activities sustained by tens of thousands of civil servants. The development of a devolved administration never silenced those who sought a Scottish parliament, however, and by 1979 pressure for a political change had become significant. Nor could a devolved administration free itself from the charge that ultimately its key policies required funding from the Treasury in London. Moreover the Scottish Office Ministers might well come from a party with power at Westminster but which attracted very limited minority support in Scotland.

The Powers of the Scottish Office, 1978	
Home and Health Department:	National Health Service
	Law and order
Scottish Education Department:	Social Work
	Libraries
	Arts
	Education (except universities)
Department of Agriculture and Fisheries:	Crofting
	Forestry
	Fisheries
	Agricultural price supports
Scottish Development Department:	Local Government
	Housing
	Roads
	Transport
Scottish Economic Planning Department:	New towns
	Electricity
	Tourism
	Highland developments
	Industrial incentives
	Economic planning
Lord Advocates' Department and Crown Office:	Legal matters

J G Kellas, *Modern Scotland*, 1980

The historian James Mitchell suggests:

The post-war Scottish Office resembled a mini-Whitehall in Scotland, but the link with London remained powerful … The Scottish Office had the appearance but not the substance of autonomy. In financial matters the Treasury had the ultimate control. On the other hand discretion was greater in areas with an established Scottish tradition such as in the field of criminal law.

Scotland in the 20ᵗʰ Century, ed. T Devine, 1996

Pressures for a Scottish parliament

Background issues

Political independence for Scotland is an issue that has attracted fluctuating support and some historians suggest that its fortunes are linked to the current state of economic prosperity. It emerged in the inter-war years at a time of serious recession, though never strongly enough to seriously alarm unionist parties. It re-emerged strongly in the 1960s once post-war economic troubles became evident and developed to a degree that did concern the older political parties. Conservative, Labour and Liberal Parties all supported the union throughout this period. The latter consistently favoured Scottish home rule within the union framework, whilst support from the other two parties has varied, though the Conservatives have generally shown least sympathy for any form of political devolution.

Some historians maintain that there have been fundamental changes shaping Scottish attitudes so that, it is argued, by the 1970s:

the Scottish electorate … began to perceive themselves as Scots in terms of their political interests rather than as, for example, members of the working class.

J Brand, *The National Movement in Scotland* 1978

Both through support for Scottish sports teams and through viewing programmes offered by Scottish-based television companies, Scots have been encouraged to consider their separate identity. Jack Brand points to signs such as the unpopularity of the national anthem at sporting occasions as clues to this shift in mood. Scottish law and the Scottish Church remain as distinctive as ever, while the special shape of Scottish education has assumed great importance in a century that has put so much more stress on schooling. Although Gaelic does not have the status in Scotland that the Welsh language has in Wales, nevertheless vigorous efforts are being made to revive it.

The development of the Scottish National Party after 1945 has taken place amid wider changes that may have shaped attitudes in Scotland. A move towards increasing co-operation between Western European countries marked by the signing of the Treaty of Rome in 1957 (though excluding Britain till January 1973) suggested there might be a wider framework than Britain within which a separate Scotland could exist. The British Empire rapidly shrank to negligible size, removing the imperial dimension that the Scots had once seen as so important. British governments from the end of the 1950s seemed unable to carry out the economic regeneration that was clearly needed for prosperity in an increasingly competitive world market. As the historian James Mitchell notes:

The British State was failing to realise the post-war aspirations of the Scots.

Scotland in the 20ᵗʰ Century, ed. T Devine

The discovery of oil in the North Sea in 1965 provided supporters of independence with a powerful argument to use against the view that a weak Scottish economy required the support provided by being part of the United Kingdom.

Views in UK political parties

The rapid decline of the Liberal Party after 1922 left it with insufficient power to achieve its long-held support for political devolution. The Conservative Party under Edward Heath's leadership in the late 1960s edged towards accepting devolution. In 1968 Heath's 'Declaration of Perth' was clearly supportive of the policy, but this was an exceptional period shaped by the rise of the SNP. In general, between 1930–1979 the Conservative Party was unsympathetic to the home rule cause.

The Labour Party developed a powerful position in urban Scotland once it had recovered from its divisions in the 1930s. It held between 37 and 46 seats, 1945–1979, and was the largest party except in 1951 (when there were an equal number of Conservative MPs) and 1955 (when it lagged two behind the Conservatives). Its views were therefore very important. Its early leaders had favoured home rule but by the 1930s this support had diminished and there were some who viewed nationalism as a reactionary force that clashed with socialism. The historian William Ferguson observes:

For most Scottish Socialists, the more left they were, the less nationalist in outlook.

Scotland 1689 to the Present

Tom Johnston who had once favoured home rule, concentrated on building up the power of the Scottish Office when in power, creating a Council of State of former Scottish Secretaries to vet legislation, and using the threat of Scottish nationalism to prise concessions out of Churchill. His views were bluntly put:

What purpose would there be in our getting a Scottish parliament in Edinburgh if it has to administer an emigration system, a glorified poor law, and a graveyard?

Quoted R Finlay, in *Scotland in the 20ᵗʰ Century*

The post-war Attlee Government was pre-occupied with its huge programme of reforms, with post-war recovery and with foreign affairs at a tense time. It established UK-wide policies and organisations that greatly benefited Scotland and seemed to satisfy the test that the historian Richard Finlay suggests was commonly applied to Scotland, i.e.:

Political loyalties would be determined by the prospects for social well-being and economic prosperity and, in the circumstances, this meant looking to the British State to realise these aspirations.

Scotland in the 20ᵗʰ Century

Labour leaders had little time for home rule, arguing it would increase bureaucracy, cut Scottish MPs numbers at Westminster and reduce Scottish influence there. They officially rejected it in 1957, and persisted in showing negligible interest in the 1960s. The rise of the SNP eventually jolted this attitude for the nationalists proved capable of winning Labour-held urban seats (Hamilton in 1967 and Govan in 1973, for example). The Labour Party's slowness in responding made some of its members despair. In 1976 a group of Labour supporters of political devolution, led by Jim Sillars and John Robertson, broke away to form the quite separate Scottish Labour Party. The Callaghan-led Labour Government of the late 1970s had a very slender majority and needed the goodwill of the Scottish and Welsh nationalist MPs: this compelled a shift in attitude which took the form of a scheme for home rule in Scotland and Wales (1978) to be put to the inhabitants of those areas in a referendum in 1979. Labour proposed to set up a Scottish Assembly to be funded by a block grant to be decided by an independent board. The Assembly was not to have powers to raise revenue or to be able to seriously shape economic policy. Nevertheless these proposals probably helped a Labour revival and they held on to seats at Garscadden and Hamilton in by-elections that the SNP had hoped to win.

The emergence of the SNP

During the inter-war years a number of nationalist groups emerged which eventually joined together in 1934 to form the Scottish National Party. This development took place against a background of the cultural movement of the 'Scottish Renaissance' which included the poet C M Grieve (better known by his pen name of Hugh MacDiarmid) who was eager to see the growth of a distinctive Scottish literature. These groups included a revived Scottish Home Rule Association led by Labour men R E Muirhead and R B Cunninghame Graham, which acted as a pressure group seeking to persuade MPs to vote for a Scottish parliament. The failure of bills in 1924 and 1927, was followed by the dissolution of the Association whose members tended to join the recently formed National Party of Scotland.

Hugh McDiarmid, Trafalgar Square, anti–polaris base rally, 1961.

The National Party also brought together former members of two small pro-independence bodies, the Scots National League (1920) and the Scottish National Movement (1926). The latter was especially attractive to people in the arts for it stressed the importance of reviving Scottish arts, music, language and the study of Scottish history. The National Party of Scotland with R E Muirhead as its chairman was created in 1928 from the above groups. This occurred as a result of the efforts of John MacCormick, a Glasgow solicitor who had, a year earlier, been a key founder of yet another piece in the jigsaw of Scottish nationalism – the Glasgow University Scottish National Association. In 1930 John MacCormick was one of a group who met at Stirling to celebrate Bannockburn and to agree on a National Covenant stating 'the urgent necessity of self-government for Scotland'. The NPS grew to 5000 by 1929, a size comparable with that of the ILP in Scotland. It met with no electoral success, though one of its supporters, the writer Compton Mackenzie, was elected Lord Rector of Glasgow University in 1931.

In 1934 the NPS merged with another, more cautious, nationalist group, the Scottish Party, to form the Scottish National Party. The makeup of the Scottish Party (1932) showed the diversity of views in the nationalist camp for it attracted people from the Liberal and Conservative Parties including the Duke of Montrose, a man whose views on social policy were not designed to please the former ILP members of the National Party of Scotland. SNP members differed over whether they could also belong to another party, whether they were in favour of or against the preparations for war of the late thirties and whether John MacCormick held too much power and favoured over-moderate policies. The historian Richard Finlay notes of this time:

The SNP was riven with numerous factions. There were left-wingers and right wingers, those who wanted devolution and those who favoured independence and finally a wing which wanted to contest elections and a wing which wanted to operate through cross-party conventions. All in all the nationalist lacked the necessary coherence to operate as an effective political party.

The SNP made no serious impact on elections until April 1945. Then R D McIntyre captured Motherwell in a by-election, only to lose it in the general election that followed three months later. His brief success may well have been due to his winning protest votes from people eager to see social reform without delay. It was not to be the only time when voters used the SNP as a means of jolting the government.

The SNP after 1945

During the late 1940s and 1950s the SNP still seemed to be divided and ineffective. In 1947 the Scottish Secretary of State described the party as:

picturesque and articulate, but the support for it is negligible.

Quoted J Mitchell, *Scotland in the 20th Century*

Far more attention was given to the Scottish Convention, founded by John MacCormick as a home rule pressure group that gathered annually from 1947 to voice its hopes. MacCormick abandoned the SNP in 1945 and stood in the general election as a Liberal. The Convention's assemblies attracted people from local government and the churches, as well as politicians. In 1949 all 1200 present at it signed a Scottish Covenant asking for home rule. Nearly two million more signatures were gathered in the following years. In 1950 a group of Covenant supporters won major media attention by snatching the Stone of Destiny (on which Scottish kings had been crowned) from its resting place in Westminster Abbey. But after this episode the Covenant movement faded in importance. The Conservative Government of 1952 dealt with pressure from Scotland by setting up the Balfour Commission (1952–1954) on Scottish affairs. Minor administrative changes followed its report.

SNP fortunes improved from 1960. In 1961 Ian MacDonald, a wealthy farmer, fought a by-election at Glasgow Bridgeton and won 18.7 per cent of the votes. Encouraged by this he agreed to become the SNP's first full-time national organiser. In 1962 William Wolfe fought a by-election in West Lothian in which he managed to come second after the successful Labour candidate, Tom Dalyell. These events helped attract support to the SNP and MacDonald was able to establish a whole network of local branches supervised by a well-run central office. Vigorous fund-raising greatly improved the party's finances.

By now it was possible to deploy economic arguments too. Older industries like coal, steel and shipbuilding shrank rapidly. New industries came to Scotland but in insufficient strength. Attempts to nationalise steel-making and develop car production were not a success. It was argued that perhaps policies that focused wholly on Scottish needs might do better than those emerging from Westminster. Although North Sea oil did not begin to flow ashore till 1975, its discovery over ten years earlier made it possible to argue that this was primarily a Scottish resource that should be used to tackle Scottish needs.

In 1967 Winnie Ewing, a 38 year old Glasgow solicitor, captured Hamilton for the SNP in a by-election that gave her a majority of around 1800.

Winnie Ewing arriving at London's Kings Cross Station to take up her seat in the House of Commons, 1967.

In the local elections of the following year 30 per cent of voters chose SNP candidates giving the party a gain of 100 seats. Hamilton was lost in the 1970 general election, however, suggesting, the historian Richard Finlay argues, that some voters were drawn to the SNP for tactical reasons.

Many of their votes were protesting at government failure ... The impact of voting for a party which threatened the union was a very effective way of putting Scotland high on the British political agenda.

Scotland 1850–1979

The loss of Hamilton was offset by Donald Stewart's success in the Western Isles. In the 1970 election, the SNP won 11 400 of the vote overall. Promising by-elections were fought in the early 1970s culminating, in 1973, with the capture of the Labour seat of Govan with a majority of 571. By the February 1974 general election the SNP was ready to provide candidates in all Scottish constituencies except Orkney and Shetland. In that election Govan was lost, but the Western Isles seat was held with an increased majority, and six other seats were won: four were captured from the Conservatives, and two from Labour. SNP MPs now sat for the Western Isles, Aberdeenshire East, Argyll, Banff, Dundee East, Moray and Nairn, and Clackmannan and East Stirling. In October 1974 four more seats – all formerly Conservative – fell to the SNP. This raised its representation at Westminster to 11. 30.4 per cent of Scottish voters had chosen the SNP, and it came second in 42 other seats; it could genuinely claim to have become second only to Labour.

SNP MPs, October, 1974.

1979

Labour's reliance on nationalist votes to prop up its slender majority in parliament helped produce, in 1978, a home rule proposal to be implemented if favoured by at least 40 per cent of those entitled to vote. The referendum in March 1979 was preceded by vigorous election-eering in which a well-run campaign hostile to home rule faced 'Yes' campaigners split between home rulers and those wanting full independ-ence. 63 per cent of the electorate actually voted with 51.6 per cent of them voting 'Yes'. This meant that the requirement that at least 40 per cent of people entitled to vote had to back the measure, had not been met. The referendum failed, the Labour Party lost power, and in the 1979 election the Conservatives led by Margaret Thatcher swept into office. The SNP suffered defeats that cut its representation to just two MPs.

The new Conservative ministry set its face against devolution. Scottish affairs had to make do with the debates of the Scottish Grand Com-mittee which was where Scottish MPs gathered, together with up to 15 other MPs who attended in order to make the party balance approximate to the overall balance at Westminster. Since 1894 this body has dealt with the committee stage of non-controversial bills. After 1948 it began to consider bills at second reading stage and to debate Scottish estimates. The Grand Committee represents one of the dilemmas of devolution. It originally emerged as a device to head off the pro-home rule views of most Scottish Liberals whose party leaders had needed their Scottish MPs at Westminster if they were to stay in power. The same dilemma of risking losing control at Westminster through agreeing to home rule has faced the Labour Party in more

---

Devolution Referendum, 1 March 1979

The question voters were asked was: 'Do you want the provisions of the Scotland Act 1978 to be put into effect?'

%	Yes	%	No	%	Turnout
Borders	20 746	40.3	30 780	59.7	66.4
Central	71 296	54.7	59 105	45.3	65.9
Dumfries and Galloway	27 162	40.3	40 239	59.7	64.1
Fife	86 252	53.7	74 436	46.3	65.3
Grampian	94 944	48.3	101 485	51.6	57.2
Highland	44 973	51.0	43 274	49.0	64.7
Lothian	187 221	50.1	186 421	49.9	65.9
Strathclyde	596 519	54.0	508 599	46.0	62.5
Tayside	91 482	49.5	93 325	50.5	63.0
Orkney	2104	27.9	5439	72.1	54.1
Shetland	2020	27.0	5466	73.0	50.3
Western Isles	6281	55.8	4933	44.2	49.9
Scotland	1 230 937	51.6	1 153 502	48.4	62.9

Scottish Yearbook, 1980

recent times. Since 1957 the Grand Committee has confined its activities to second reading debates, to Scottish estimates and to a session on Scottish affairs. The committee stage of bills is dealt with by the Scottish Standing Committee made up of 16 Scottish MPs and up to 34 others. The powers of these bodies are so very limited and so easily overruled as to be no sort of substitute to satisfy supporters of devolution.

The home rule issue returned in the 1990s to achieve eventual success following a further referendum after Labour had returned to power in 1997. As Richard Finlay observes:

The shifting issue of Scottish self-government has remained a salient feature of Scottish politics throughout the twentieth century. Probably more than any other factor it has ensured that political life north of the border has remained distinctly Scottish.

Scotland 1850–1979

> **ACTIVITIES**
>
> 1 Discuss the view that 'support for home rule varied primarily, according to the state of prosperity in Scotland.'
>
> 2 Account for the varying fortunes of the SNP.

THE RISE OF POLITICAL NATIONALISM –

An Overview

1979

Referendum on Setting Up a Scottish Parliament

Since 1945

1978 proposal for Scottish Parliament.

Labour needs SNP help in Parliament.

Growing importance of European Community.

Value of union questioned.

SNP wins seats in Parliament.

Rise of SNP from 1960.

Scottish economy in increasing trouble.

Imperial decline.

Post–war Labour Government provides social reforms for all Britain.

Inter–War

Scottish Office based in Edinburgh.

Increasing power for Scottish Secretary.

Emergence of nationalist groups.

Social problems serious in Scotland.

Growing economic problems, slump, rising unemployment.

Empire becomes less secure and supportive.

Edwardian Times

Outbreak of war thwarts home rule bill.

Young Scots seek home rule to tackle social problems.

Worries about educational levels in Britain.

Growing concern about poverty.

Growing concern about health of British people.

Late Victorian Times

Scots play a crucial part in the Empire.

Scottish economy plays an important role in imperial economy.

Scottish Home Rule Association founded.

Gladstone persuaded to support home rule policy through events in Ireland.

Creation of post of Scottish Secretary.

1880

Essay writing skills are vital to success in both Intermediate 2 and Higher History.

Intermediate 2 – At Intermediate 2 a short essay is required in the examination, as well as an Extended Response that will have to be researched beforehand with a plan of up to 150 words developed. The Extended Response will then be written up in an hour. The chosen issue must come from the course.

The Extended Response will be assessed in terms of the knowledge, understanding and ability to explain historical developments and events that it provides.

Higher Level – At Higher Level Paper 1 consists of essay questions and an Extended Essay is also required. This must be on an issue from the course, be researched and a plan of up to 200 words developed. The Essay will be written up in two hours.

Both examination essays and the Extended Essay will be assessed in terms of the success achieved in applying knowledge and demonstrating historical understanding as well as evaluating historical developments, events and issues.

Topics

For both the Extended Response and the Extended Essay candidates must choose an issue for themselves. Relevant examination papers offer some guidance as to possible topics. Suitable issues are often best expressed as questions for it is important to show explaining and evaluating skills rather than simply providing a narrative or description. A title like 'The Rise of the Labour Party' is therefore not helpful. Consider, instead, a title that:

◆ Considers the importance of an individual in contributing to a change or circumstance (e.g., How far was the rise of the Labour Party due to Ramsay MacDonald?)

◆ Evaluates the reasons for events (e.g., Why did votes for women have to wait till 1918?)

◆ Discusses the relationships between political events and their context (e.g., To what extent did the First World War transform the political scene in Britain?)

◆ Evaluates the reasons, the nature and effectiveness of particular policies (e.g., How effective were Liberal reforms 1906–1914, in solving the social problems of the time?)

Tackling Extended Essays and Responses

Make sure that you:

◆ Choose an issue that interests you and that you fully understand.

◆ Select an issue that is well-resourced with suitable sources of information. At Higher Level the views of historians and of people at the time will be helpful.

◆ Make an initial plan of the various aspects of the issue that you will need to research; revise this, if necessary, as you proceed.

◆ Gather information systematically, making notes in your own words under the subheadings derived from your initial plan and gathered on a sub-divided file.

◆ Read sensibly. Very substantial books may still have invaluable introductions and conclusions. Copy short quotes of relevance showing contemporary and historians' views, noting the authors' names. It is easier to begin note making with a relatively brief book or article that broadly surveys the whole issue.

◆ Plan carefully (you will have to submit this plan to the examiners), without exceeding the word length.

Essay writing

Here you will need to:

◆ Answer the actual question, whether it be your chosen issue for an Extended answer or an examiner's question.

◆ Write clearly, grammatically, with correct spelling. (If you have time, always read through your work before handing it in.)

◆ Organise your answer logically, beginning with a brief broad introduction that surveys the whole issue, going on to develop each aspect in turn, providing evidence for your points, rounding off with a conclusion which clearly shows your views on the issue.

Bibliography

GENERAL BOOKS

Adelman P 1987 *British Politics in the 30s and 40s*

Bentley M *Politics without Democracy*

Dutton D 1991 *British Politics Since 1945*

Evans E *The Forging of the Modern State – Early Modern Britain 1783–1870*

Lloyd T 1970 *Empire to Welfare State*

Marwick A 1982 *British Society since 1945*

May T 1987 *An Economic and Social History of Britain*

Morgan K O 1990 *The People's Peace*

Pugh M 1982 *The Making of Modern British Politics*

Pugh M 1994 *State & Society*

Robbins K *The Eclipse of a Great Power, Britain 1870–1975*

Stevenson J 1984 *British Society 1914–45*

Taylor A J P *English History 1914–45*

Tiratsoo N (ed) 1997 *From Blitz to Blair*

Williams G and Ramsden J 1990 *Rule Britannia*

PARTY POLITICS AND BELIEFS

Conservatism

Blake R 1985 *The Conservative Party from Peel to Thatcher*

Coleman B 1988 *Conservatism and the Conservative Party in Nineteenth-Century Britain*

Lindsay T F and Harrington M 1974 *The Conservative Party*

O'Gorman F 1986 *British Conservatism*

Ramsden J 1978 *The Age of Balfour and Baldwin*

Liberalism

Adelman P 1981 *The Decline of the Liberal Party*

Bentley M 1987 *The Climax of Liberal Politics*

Cook C 1976 *A Short History of the Liberal Party*

Morgan K O 1979 *Consensus and Disunity*

Vincent J R 1966 *The Formation of the British Liberal Party 1857–68*

Wilson T 1968 *The Downfall of the Liberal Party*

Labour

Addison P 1975 *The Road to 1945*

Adelman P 1972 *The Rise of the Labour Party*

Brand C 1965 *The British Labour Party*

Campbell J *Nye Bevan and the Mirage of British Socialism*

Davies A J 1992 *To Build a New Jerusalem*

Laybourn K 1988 *The Rise of Labour*

McKibbin R 1977 *The Evolution of the Labour Party*

Miliband R 1961 *Parliamentary Socialism*

Morgan K O 1984 *Labour in Power*

Pelling H 1962 *A Short History of the Labour Party*

Pimlott B 1977 *Labour and The Left in the 1930s*

Ponting C *Breach of Promise, Labour in Power 1964–70*

Skidelsky R 1967 *Politicians and the Slump*

General

Ball A R 1981 *British Political Parties*

Belchem J 1990 *Class, Party and the Political System in Britain 1867–1914*

Evans E J 1985 *Political Parties 1787–1867*

Finer S E 1980 *The Changing British Party System 1945–79*

Electoral Change

Braybon G *Women Workers and the First World War*

Garner L *Stepping Stones to Women's Liberty, Feminist Ideas in the Women's Suffrage Movement*

Holton S *Feminism and Democracy, Women's Suffrage and Party Politics in Britain 1866–1914*

Jalland P *Women, Marriage and Politics 1860–1914*

Liddington J and Norris J *One Hand Tied Behind Us*

Pugh M 1978 *Electoral Reform in War and Peace*

Pugh M 1989 *The Development of the British Electoral System 1832–1987*

Pugh M 1986 *Women's Suffrage in Britain*

Walton J K 1987 *The Second Reform Act*

Wright D G 1970 *Democracy and Reform*

CLASS, CULTURE, TRADE UNIONISM

Barnett C 1986 *The Audit of War*

Barnett C 1972 *The Collapse of British Power*

Belchem J *Class, Politics, and the Political System in Britain 1867–1914*

Hindess B *The Decline of Working Class Politics*

Hington J 1983 *Labour and Socialism 1867–1914*

Houghton W E *The Victorian Frame of Mind*

Howell D 1983 *British Workers and the ILP*

Joyce P *War, Society and Politics*

Marsden G (ed) 1990 *Victorian Values*

Martin D 1979 *Ideology and the Labour Movement*

McKibbin R *The Ideologies of Class 1880–1950*

Meacham S 1977 *A Life Apart*

Moorehead C 1987 *Troublesome People: Enemies of War 1916–86*

Neale R S 1973 *Class and Ideology in the 19th century*

Pelling H *A History of British Trade Unionism*

Pimlott B *Trade Unions in British Politics*

Sigsworth E M *In Search of Victorian Values*

Sked A 1987 *Britain's Decline*

Wald K D *Crosses on the Ballot*

SCOTLAND

Brand J 1978 *The National Movement in Scotland*

Checkland S 1984 *Industry and Ethos, Scotland 1832–1914*

Cooke A, Donnachie I (ed) 1998 *Modern Scottish History (2)*

Devine T and Finlay R J 1996 *Scotland in the 20th Century*

Hanham H J 1969 *Scottish Nationalism*

Harvie C 1981 *No Gods and Precious Few Heroes, 1914–80*

Harvie C 1977 *Scotland and Nationalism*

Hutchinson I *A Political History of Scotland 1832–1924*

Kellas J 1980 *Modern Scotland – the Nation since 1870*

Kellas J 1988 *The Scottish Political System*

Kemp A 1993 *The Hollow Drum*

Lee C H 1995 *Scotland & the United Kingdom*

Lynch M (ed) 1993 *Scotland 1850–1979*

Robbins K 1988 *Nineteenth-Century Britain: Integration and diversity*

Smout T C 1987 *A Century of the Scottish People*

Webb K *The Growth of Nationalism in Scotland*

THE WELFARE ISSUE

Birch R C 1974 *The Shaping of the Welfare State*

Bruce M 1961 *The Coming of the Welfare State*

Constantine S 1980 *Unemployment in Britain between the Wars*

Cook C and Stevenson J 1977 *The Slump*

Fraser D 1973 *The Evolution of the Welfare State*

Hay J R 1978 *The Development of the Welfare State*

Hay J R 1975 *The Origins of the Welfare State*

POLITICIANS

Adelman P 1989 *Gladstone, Disraeli and Later Victorian Politics*

Feuchtwanger E J 1968 *Disraeli, Democracy, and the Tory Party*

Feuchtwanger E J 1975 *Gladstone*

James R R 1973 *Churchill, A Study in Failure*

Marquand D 1977 Ramsay MacDonald

Middlemass K and Barnes J 1969 *Baldwin*

Montgomery Hyde H 1973 *Baldwin*

Montgomery Hyde H 1973 *Neville Chamberlain*

Morgan K 1971 *Lloyd George*

Morgan K 1971 *The Age of Lloyd George*

Pelling H 1974 *W A Churchill*

Willis M 1989 *Gladstone and Disraeli: Principles and Politics*

Young K 1976 *Baldwin*